SWORDS AND
PLOUGHSHARES

SWORDS AND PLOUGHSHARES

War and Agriculture in Western Canada

EDITED BY R.C. MACLEOD

The University of Alberta Press

First published by
The University of Alberta Press
Athabasca Hall
Edmonton, Alberta
Canada T6G 2E8

Copyright © The University of Alberta Press 1993

ISBN 0-88864-218-0 paper

CANADIAN CATALOGUING IN PUBLICATION DATA

Main entry under title:

Swords and ploughshares

   Includes bibliographical references.
   ISBN 0-88864-218-0

   1. Canada, Western—History. 2. Agriculture—
Canada, Western—History. 3. Métis—Canada,
Western—History. I. Macleod, R.C., 1940–
FC3217.S96 1993   971.2'02   C93–091301–9
F1060.9.S96 1993

Printed on acid-free paper.
Printed by University of Alberta Printing Services,
Edmonton, Alberta, Canada

Contents

Contributors

MAURICE F.V. DOLL is Curator of Government History, Provincial Museum of Alberta.

GERHARD ENS is Assistant Professor of History at Brandon University.

JOHN GILPIN is Lecturer in History at the University of Lethbridge.

ROTA HERZBERG LISTER is Professor of Drama at the University of Western Ontario.

R.C. MACLEOD is Professor of History at the University of Alberta.

J.E. REA is Professor of History at the University of Manitoba.

PATRICIA ROY is Professor of History at the University of Victoria.

DAVID E. SMITH is Professor of Political Science at the University of Saskatchewan.

DONALD B. SMITH is Professor History at the University of Calgary.

GEORGE F.G. STANLEY is Professor Emeritus of History at Mount Allison University and former Lieutenant Governor of New Brunswick.

E. BRIAN TITLEY is Professor of Education at the University of Lethbridge.

JUDITH P. WIESINGER is a planner with the Association of Universities and Colleges of Canada in Ottawa.

Acknowledgements

THE FINANCIAL SUPPORT of the Social Sciences and Humanities Research Council of Canada for the conferences and for the publication of this volume is gratefully acknowledged. The University of Alberta Press also acknowledges the financial support of the Alberta Foundation for the Arts, a beneficiary of the Lottery Fund of the Government of Alberta.

 The Alberta Foundation for the Arts

Providing a foundation for the arts

Introduction

THE BIBLICAL EXHORTATION TO BEAT our swords into ploughshares makes agriculture a metaphor for peace. The farmer in his fields producing food to nurture life seems the polar opposite of the soldier bent on death and destruction. In fact, the two activities are more closely related than one might think. Anthropologists have noted that with the advent of agriculture, warfare becomes an altogether bloodier and more terrible business.[1] Pre-agricultural peoples were not rootless wanderers; they occupied quite well-defined territories, but conflicts did not impose the imperative of defending that territory to the death. The alternative of moving to a new hunting area was almost always available.[2] The farmer by contrast has everything invested in his land. It is not merely his livelihood but his inheritance from the past and his hope for the future of his descendants. Farmers since the beginning of recorded history have been more than willing to drop their ploughs and pick up their swords if it seemed necessary to defend their lands or, sadly, when there was a reasonable prospect of acquiring someone else's land. It is hardly a coincidence that natives and fur traders lived together in western Canada for a century without war and that armed conflict followed the beginnings of agricultural settlement within a few years.

Nor does the connection between the two kinds of human behaviour end with the defeat of the indigenous forces at Batoche in the spring of 1885. That little war signalled the entry of western Canada into the world-wide capitalist economy. Henceforth events on the other side of the globe would affect the daily lives of prairie farmers. Some of the most drastic and far-reaching changes were the result of wars. The First World War directly affected western Canadian farmers by drawing thousands off to Europe to fight. Indirectly it created the final great surge of the wheat boom, tempting established farmers into borrowing for expansion and pushing homesteaders onto marginal lands.[3] Inept handling of the war's massive costs brought economic chaos in Europe, falling grain prices and rural depopulation in southern Alberta and Saskatchewan in the 1920s, all of which was just a warm-up for the catastrophe of the depression in the following decade.[4] The Second World War did not reproduce the 1914–18 boom in grain farming because Canada's traditional markets were swallowed up by Hitler's lightning conquest of western Europe. Instead it forced massive changes in the kinds of agricultural commodities produced on western farms. War and agriculture were intimately connected in the Canadian West at least until the middle of the twentieth century.

The First World War brought to fruition the idea of direct political action by farmers. The sudden appearance and almost equally rapid decline of the Progressive movement after the war has traditionally been interpreted as a triumph of ideology over political reality. Ed Rea's discussion of the leadership dilemmas faced by T.A. Crerar after the 1921 election shows that this is an oversimplification. Many of Crerar's crucial decisions grew out of practical problems rather than abstract theoretical concerns. Most of those issues, in turn, were direct consequences of the war. The Chanak crisis which drew the Progressives to the support of the Liberal government was one example. The abrupt decline in wheat prices in 1920 with its impact on the fortunes of United Grain Growers of which Crerar was president was another.

The second great conflict of the twentieth century produced a much different political response on the part of the agricultural community. The leadership of the redoubtable Jimmy Gardiner, as David Smith's analysis reveals, provided western farmers with a highly effective united front. This time there were no radical political theories or new parties put forward to solve agrarian problems. Gardiner believed third party experiments were a recipe for disaster. After the Progressive adventures of the 1920s, farmers were ready to follow his lead. He used their support to deliver a series of federal government programs to counter the effects of drought, depression and war. The kind of sympathetic attention Ottawa devoted to western farmers under Gardiner's tutelage was in many respects the goal that the rebels had sought in 1885. Gardiner's tenure as Minister of Agriculture marked the culmination of an era in western Canada that began with the introduction of capitalist agriculture.

That era began with the Métis who were both the forerunners of agricultural settlement on the prairies and at the same time among the first farmers in the region. The nature of their economic activities during the fur trade period are well documented and have received attention from many historians over the years.[5] What the Métis did during the transition to an economy dominated by agriculture is much less well known and, perhaps for that reason, more controversial. Once out of the orbit of the Hudson's Bay Company clerks, the Métis generated few records. In some cases their activities can only be inferred from archaeological evidence. It is now becoming apparent that one of the most important transitional activities was buffalo hunting for the American market in buffalo robes rather than the old hunt to supply pemmican for the fur trade. Maurice Doll's paper on the preliminary surveys and excavations of the Buffalo Lake site reveal a surprisingly large community there in the 1870s. This is part of an ongoing multi-disciplinary research project funded by Alberta Culture which, when published, should clarify a rather shadowy period in our history.

Gerhard Ens's intensive study of the Parish of St. François Xavier underlines the importance of understanding this period. Most early historians of the west, echoing the prejudices of the European settlers in the Red River Colony, saw the Métis turn to the hunt as a reversion to primitivism.[6] A recent variation has the Métis driven from their lands at Red River by unscrupulous speculators abetted by Ottawa.[7] Ens, by examining the nature of agricultural practices in the period

1835–70, suggests a very different hypothesis. Agriculture as practised at Red River in that period was stagnant and unproductive, rarely able to achieve self-sufficiency. The buffalo robe trade represented a more, rather than a less, modern kind of economic activity. The Métis were opting out of agriculture years before the Canadian takeover because it was an economically rational choice for them; a choice that was not open to the English-speaking population who had not been involved in the hunt.

The process by which the Canadian West passed from an economy dominated by hunting and trapping to capitalist agriculture was enormously complex. As I have argued elsewhere, it created very different strains in different parts of the region.[8] At the eastern end it led to a three-cornered territorial dispute involving the federal government and the provinces of Ontario and Manitoba. The complexities of the Ontario boundary question would be even more obscure than they are, had not the legal case which resolved the issue also had to deal with the question of aboriginal title. *St. Catharine's Milling and Lumber Company v. The Queen* established Canadian legal doctrine on native title to land and in spite of numerous recent challenges, that doctrine remains in effect. Legal scholars, to the extent they have concerned themselves with the history of the case at all, have assumed that the courts dealt with aboriginal title as a side issue. Since the Judicial Committee of the Privy Council issued the final judgement, it has also been characterized as an alien imposition by British judges ignorant of Canadian conditions.

Don Smith's fascinating study of the circumstances surrounding the case and the judge who made the original decision modify both these conclusions. Chancellor John Boyd confronted the question of the nature of aboriginal title directly and at length. He was one of the best educated and well-informed lawyers of his day. Boyd had to be acutely aware of native issues since his son was with the Canadian militia in the Spring of 1885 helping to suppress the rebellion. The higher courts, including the Judicial Committee of the Privy Council, found his judgement admirable and made only minor changes. For better or worse, our law on the most fundamental aspect of aboriginal rights was made in Canada, by Canadians in response to Canadian issues.

Conflict between the aboriginal population and the incoming settlers was inevitable in the period after 1870. With a lot of luck and
skilful management that conflict might have been held below the level
of war. One of the important reasons why the shooting started in 1885
was the hostility generated by Hayter Reed's methods of administering the native peoples of the prairies. Brian Titley's article reveals
Reed as a highly effective bureaucrat who was, within the narrow
limits of his conception of his duties, working for the betterment of
those under his charge. The tragedy was that his considerable political and administrative skills were not balanced by any understanding
of native culture or sympathy for the difficulties they faced in adapting to change. Instead of interpreting the attitudes of the native population and acting as a mediating force between them and Ottawa he
reflected back the bureaucratic values of his superiors. As a recipe for
personal success this was highly effective but it led directly to the
blunders that brought on the rebellion.

The point that conflict need not blossom into full-scale war is well
illustrated by the situation in British Columbia in the 1880s. Conflicts
between the native population and settlers or miners abounded, especially in the northern interior. Patricia Roy examines the disputes that
produced worrisome unrest and the occasional killing. The geography of British Columbia, however, made it next to impossible for anything like a concerted native resistance to arise. This freed British
Columbians to indulge themselves in the pleasures of jurisdictional
disputes with Ottawa. The rebellion on the prairies was echoed only
by empty speculations in eastern newspapers and indignant denials
in British Columbia papers intent on preserving the province's peaceful image.

Thomas Flanagan has argued that the federal government in 1885
did all that could reasonably be expected of a government in dealing
with the survey and land title problems of the Métis in the months
leading to the rebellion.[9] The situation at Batoche no doubt appeared
to Ottawa no more threatening than any of the numerous local disputes in British Columbia. John Gilpin's article on the Edmonton land
situation in the early 1880s adds support to this view. Here the land
situation involved river lot surveys, Métis and white settlers, and ran-
corous disputes over land. Here, too, there were long and irritating

delays produced by government inaction and apparent indifference. Unlike the situation farther east, no fighting resulted. No doubt there were subtle differences between the circumstances at Edmonton and Batoche but those differences were too small to be visible from Ottawa.

Settlers on the homesteads and in the emerging urban centres of the prairies felt lonely and vulnerable. Hence their somewhat ambivalent behaviour in 1885. They could side with the Métis in protesting federal government policies but when fighting broke out they flocked to join the government forces. The underlying reality was that they were part of an immensely powerful international economic development. As Judith Wiesinger demonstrates, the process of urban growth tied into an international network of trade and communication was rapid and irreversible in this period. The rebellion caused scarcely a pause in this process.

Not surprisingly, war has inspired more playwrights who have attempted to interpret this period, than has agriculture. While the novel seems to be the literary vehicle of choice for the agrarian experience of western Canada, a large number of dramatists have been attracted by the rebellion. As Rota Herzberg Lister notes, apart from the very first play about the rebellion which was written by one of the militiamen who participated, most authors have concentrated on the rebel side. This is as true of those writing in English as in French. From Elzéar Paquin in 1886 to John Coulter and Claude Dorge in this century, the charismatic and tragic figure of Riel has drawn the attention of all except George Woodcock.

Much of English Canada's understanding of the formative events of the Canadian West comes from George Stanley's remarkable work, *The Birth of Western Canada*. Considering that it was one of the earliest works by an academically trained historian in this country, it has stood the test of time remarkably well. No other work of Canadian history published before the Second World War is as regularly read by historians, students and the general public. Dr. Stanley's autobiographical essay provides unique insights into the genesis of this seminal work and its rediscovery in the 1950s. In 1992 it was reissued once again and is reported to be selling briskly. George Stanley wrote many other distinguished works of history during his long career, but he returned to Louis Riel and the rebellion on several occasions. The last, but certainly not the least significant, was his editorship of *The Collected Writings of Louis Riel*.[10] Anyone with even the slightest interest in western Canadian history will be fascinated at how his upbringing and education brought him to the subject that will always be identified with his name.

NOTES

1. H.H. Turney-High, *Primitive War: Its Practice and Concepts* (Columbia: University of South Carolina Press, 1971).
2. John S. Milloy, *The Plains Cree: Trade, Diplomacy and War, 1790 to 1870* (Winnipeg: University of Manitoba Press, 1988).
3. John H. Thompson, *The Harvests of War: The Prairie West 1914–1918* (Toronto: McClelland and Stewart, 1978); Paul Voisey, *Vulcan: The Making of a Prairie Community* (Toronto: University of Toronto Press, 1988).
4. David C. Jones, *Empire of Dust: Settling and Abandoning the Prairie Dry Belt* (Edmonton: University of Alberta Press, 1987).
5. Marcel Giraud, John Foster and Gerald Friesen are among the most prominent.
6. Marcel Giraud, *The Métis in the Canadian West*, translated by George Woodcock, 2 volumes (Edmonton: University of Alberta Press, 1986); G.F.G. Stanley, *The Birth of Western Canada* (London: 1936).
7. D.N. Sprague, *Canada and the Métis, 1869–1885* (Waterloo: Wilfrid Laurier University Press, 1988).
8. R.C. Macleod, "Law and Order in the Canadian West," in John McLaren, Hamar Foster, and Chet Orloff, eds., *Law for the Elephant, Law for the Beaver: Essays in the Legal History of the Northern American West* (Pasadena, California: Ninth Judicial Historical Society, 1992).
9. Thomas Flanagan, *Riel and the Rebellion: 1885 Reconsidered* (Saskatoon: Western Producer Prairie Books, 1983).
10. George F.G. Stanley, ed., *The Collected Writings of Louis Riel*, 5 Volumes (Edmonton: University of Alberta Press, 1985).

I WESTERN CANADA IN THE ERA OF THE REBELLION

GEORGE F.G. STANLEY

1 The Making of an Historian
An Autobiographical Essay

WHILE CHILDREN INHERIT certain physical quali-
ties from their parents, their colouring, their physique, their muscular
and mental dexterity, it is their environment, the surroundings in
which they are raised, the talk they hear, the everyday things they see
about them, that shape the pattern of life they will eventually follow—at least within the limitations imposed on them by their innate
or inherited mental and physical abilities. Or in other words, one does
not inherit an interest in history, even if one may inherit the qualities
that lead a person into making history. There is a difference here
between writing and making history; although they are not mutually
exclusive.

I did not become a historian because it was in my blood, or more
correctly, in my genes. I became a historian because I was brought up
in surroundings that stimulated an interest in history during my formative years. The dominating figures in these years were my mother
and father. My mother, Della Lillywhite, was of English-French-
Dutch mixture. Her grandfather came to Canada in the mid-nineteenth century and settled in Western Ontario. My father, John Henry
Stanley, was of English-Scottish descent. His great-grandfather came
to Canada in 1790 as a British soldier who, in 1802, at the time of the
Peace of Amiens, settled on the banks of the St. Lawrence River in
Stormont County in Ontario. He served in the War of 1812 against the

3

Americans. Following the War he moved north to Lanark county, near Ottawa. The Stanleys were not farmers. They were lumbermen, and part-time soldiers, milling timber for the growing settlements of Upper Canada, and turning out with the militia when required. They did not remain fixed in one community. Instead they moved each generation, first from Stormont to Lanark and then from Lanark to Bruce county. It seems to have been a continuation of my great-great-grandfather's military experience, moving from station to station in Upper Canada and Nova Scotia.[1]

From Bruce my father travelled in the early 1890s to the Pacific coast, where he went to sea. After several voyages he became purser's mate on RMS *Empress of Japan*, the first Canadian Pacific vessel to cross the ocean from Vancouver to Yokohama.[2] Early in 1898 he yielded to the sensuous appeal of gold, becoming one of that outlandish crew who made their way to the Dyea River in Alaska, and from the base at Sheep Camp, staggered up the slippery Golden Stairs to the top of the Chilkoot Pass.[3] But there was no City of Gold for my father! With his memories filled with stories of the North, and his pockets empty, he abandoned hope of finding the end of the rainbow in the Yukon and moved to southern Alberta. In Lethbridge, he found employment as a clerk in Harry Bentley's store. Here, in southern Alberta, he met Della Lillywhite, and on 19 September 1900 they were married at Fort Macleod. A few years later (1903), they moved to Calgary. And it was in Calgary I arrived to join my parents. The year of my birth? It was in the summer following the coldest winter on record; one year before the Calgary Natural Gas Company, under Archibald Dingman, drilled a successful gas well on the Colonel James Walker Estate in east Calgary; and one year before the town of Fernie, in the Crow's Nest Pass, was destroyed by fire. I mention this last detail, because, at that time, my mother and I were visiting a small village not far from Fernie.[4] It was here, at Baynes Lake, that I learned to walk.

How important are these family details? I admit that environment is not the total causation in culture-shaping, but I believe it is the most conspicuous single factor. As a child, I listened with avid interest, and so too did some of my schoolboy companions, to the tales my father passed on to me from his grandfather, whose life spanned almost a century between 1805 and 1901. These were stories about early days in Upper Canada, about the War of 1812, when father's grandfather carried water to soldiers wounded at the Battle of Crysler's Farm in 1813; stories about his service with the Perth Volunteer Artillery at the time of William Lyon Mackenzie's futile rebellion. My mother, too, had her stories. Sporting stories of John Lillywhite's legendary exploits as a cricketer in England and about the visit of Fred Lillywhite's cricket team to Canada in 1859.[5]

But most exciting of all were my father's stories of his own life: his high school days in Wiarton, Bruce county, Ontario (to which he was sent because there was no high school in Chesley where he was born); his experiences in the Orient as a seaman; his exciting and harrowing days when he thought to make himself rich but almost ended his life at the time of the famous Chilkoot avalanche in April 1898,[6] his early days in Lethbridge, and Fort Macleod, and his friendships with members of the North West Mounted Police; and of the time, in 1902, when the Lethbridge Lacrosse Club, of which he was president, won the Levasseur trophy as champions of the North West Territories.[7] Frequently, as a boy, when we visited Lethbridge, I would listen intently to the stories exchanged between my father and his friend, Sheriff Malcolm Young, and old Mrs. Jonathan Rose (whom we always called "Granny Rose") who had gone through "the siege of Battleford" in 1885 and remembered Poundmaker's Crees as vividly as if they were familiar neighbours in Lethbridge. And in Calgary I was reduced to wondering silence when I met Colonel James Walker, who had made the march across the prairies in 1874 with the Mounted Police, and Robert Armstrong, to whom Riel had surrendered in May 1885, and William Cameron, who had survived the slaughter of the whites at Frog Lake in 1885, and perhaps most of all, when I met that famous Oblate, the Reverend Father Albert Lacombe, who had been born in 1827, in Lower Canada, and who had accompanied the Hudson's Bay Company brigade to Edmonton in 1852, to convert the Indians to Christianity.[8] And I can still see the Anglican Bishop Cyprian Pinkham, he of the thick white beard, who projected the image of an Old Testament prophet, as he stood in the pulpit of the Cathedral Church of the Redeemer in Calgary.

The storms and stresses of the "Heroic Age" were to me the essence of the Western Canadian epic. How exciting they seemed to be; how tame the present. Then came the First World War. Even today I feel a lump in my throat when I listen to a military band playing "Colonel Bogey." My father was offered a commission as Captain-Quartermaster of the 137th Battalion C.E.F., recruited in Calgary in 1916.[9] But a wobbly heart, his legacy from the Yukon, led to his rejection for active service. I can still see him in the living room, silently reading the casualty lists as they appeared each night in the Calgary *Herald*. When the troops—or some of them—came home, I watched them as they marched down Eighth Avenue towards the Mewata Armouries. I joined in the shouts; but even at that age I was able to detect a note of sadness underlying the cheers. I do not think I quite understood its meaning then. Certainly I never realized how quickly my own world would disintegrate and how soon another world war would be upon us.

Because of my father's tales of the War of 1812, and my recollections of World War I, I was interested in soldiering. Was it the uniform and the martial music? I confess that I loved to watch the Mounted Police in their red tunics, their lances and bouncing horses, and the Strathconas with their brass helmets and plumes. I frequently visited Sarcee Camp with my parents both before and during World War I, and dreamed of being a soldier, a cavalry-man by preference, an infantry-man only as a last resort. I was never a proficient cadet, but I did my cadet training in good spirit, both in Public and High School every year from Grades Five to Eleven.[10] With great interest I read the illustrated volumes in my father's library dealing with the South African War and World War I. I resolved to go to the Royal Military College in Kingston, Ontario, with one of my High School contemporaries, Gerald Talbot, when I graduate from High School. But my parents were less enthusiastic, particularly my mother, after my father suffered a severe heart attack in 1925 and was forced to retire. And so I went, instead, to the University of Alberta, hopefully, in my mother's mind, to become a lawyer. Not until some years later, after I had completed my university education, did I receive a commission in the Militia. That was in 1 January 1938. But here I am running ahead of my story.

It was not just oral history, the vocal echoes of the past to which I was exposed—and let me assure you, I do not underestimate their importance—that set me on the road to writing history. Both of my parents were great readers of books. The walls of the living room in our house in Calgary were filled with books. There were sets of Fenimore Cooper, Charles Lever, Robert Louis Stevenson, Benjamin Disraeli, Honoré de Balzac, and Francis Parkman. There were novels by Bulwer Lytton, Walter Scott, James Oliver Curwood, Gilbert Parker, Ralph Connor, and Robert Stead and poems by Robert Service. My mother's taste ran to Charles Dickens, William Thackeray and Jane Austin. There were other books, many of them novels, some of them philosophy, belles-lettres, and history. My own inclinations were always in the direction of historical novels. Had our library contained books by Henty, I would probably have dug as deeply into them as Charles Stacey did in his boyhood. As it was, I devoured Cooper, Parker, and the western Canadian writers, Connor and Stead.[11] But what was important was not so much the content of the books I read, as it was the fact that I adopted the parental pattern of spending hours reading, and enjoyed doing so. I suspect that my special interest in the Leatherstocking tales was stimulated by the fact that Indians were a familiar sight in Calgary. We lived on Seventh Street S.W., along a route normally followed by the Sarcee Indians who drove into town in their democrats followed by the usual clutter of dogs. It was, therefore, much easier for me to relate to the farmers, cowboys, adventurers, and clergymen in Connor, Stead, and Robert Service, than to the knights in *Ivanhoe,* or the crusaders in *The Talisman.* Why I did not delve into the volumes of Francis Parkman, at that time, I do not recall. When I did start on Parkman, during my University days, I wondered why anybody else would even bother to write about that period in our history. I questioned if anybody could do better than Parkman!

I cannot honestly say that my Public or High School teachers did much to stimulate my interest in History. I remember hardly anything about the History taught in Connaught Public School. I suppose I must have heard something about Canada's past, for I have vague recollections of teachers talking about Jacques Cartier, and about Wolfe and Montcalm. And also equally dim recollections of one of my Public School teachers disagreeing with the way I pronounced "Cartier." The teacher called it "Carteer." My father, whose sister had married a French-Canadian, Henri Routier, insisted that I pronounce the name "Cartshay." In High School, Canadian History was taught in Grade Ten from a dull, little book, Duncan's *Story of the Canadian People*. The pages were copiously illustrated with portraits, to which I carefully added mustachios, side-burns, whiskers, horn-rim spectacles, cigars, pipes, or curly locks of hair, as might seem fitting or unfitting. More interesting, was a little book my mother had use at school in Ingersoll, Ontario, during the 1880s; the maps in it showed Canada as it was in the mid-nineteenth century with some of the rivers in the North West indicated in dotted lines and marked "unexplored." Unexplored! That was exciting; it stimulated the imagination; it suggested new regions to be seen for the first time; it hinted at the possibilities of individual initiative rather than group action. And I always preferred historical individuals to historical peoples. A book by the brothers Botsford, our text in Grades Eleven and Twelve, compact, dull, factual, was about the Egyptians, the Assyrians, the Greeks, the Romans. That much only I remember. I used to ask myself, why not more about Alexander, Leonidas, Hannibal, Fabius, Antony and Cleopatra? The Botsford book aroused no curiosity, stimulated no interest whatsoever. At that stage of my life, I wanted something that would make me aware of individual personalities, particularly in my own country; books about the sailors who sailed the Pacific Ocean like my father; about explorers like La Vérendrye and Franklin, or about individual miners like my grandmother's father, who went to British Columbia in 1859 in search of gold and who was drowned in Shuswap Lake in 1863. More interesting history than that to be found in school texts, I could find in the faded photographs I sometimes discovered in cabinet drawers, when looking for something else. And so I continued to listen to my father, who was an active member of the Bruce County Old Boys Association, the Caledonian Club of Calgary, and the local Historical Society. Much of what I learned from talk and unguided reading, was only "parish pump" history, and some of it was undoubtedly inaccurate; but a builder must bake his bricks before he can construct his house, and he must also have some knowledge of the strength of his materials.

After High School I spent a year at the Calgary Normal School and then went to the University of Alberta in 1925. The career my parents had determined upon for me was the law. I believe it was because I was inclined to be argumentative! However, I liked history, literature, and languages. And so at the University of Alberta I planned a program that, while including some law, was basically devoted to the subjects I liked.

My first professor of history at Edmonton, was A.L. Burt, one of the two members of the History Department of the University.[12] He was an excellent lecturer, lively and interested in what he was teaching. His enthusiasm for teaching, his vitality, made his subject come alive. The books to which Burt directed my attention were vastly different from the High School texts I had previously encountered. They were written by knowledgeable historians, written for mature readers, and well written, most of them at least. Before my first year at University came to an end, I determined to abandon a law career and devote myself to the study of history. This decision was confirmed a year later when I enroled for Burt's class in Canadian History. I was impressed that Burt was actively engaged in writing as well as teaching history. He was, at that time, working on his study of Guy Carleton[13] and his lectures were filled with quotations from contemporary sources. I loved the intimacy of it. This was history seen through the eyes of those who made it: Canadian history dull and uninteresting? Here, at last, was the blood and life of Canada; here was my country, courageous, brash, sincere, controversial, at times even abrasive, cocking a snoot at the aggressive Americans. Explorers, soldiers, *coureurs du bois*, politicians, the brass of the Canadian band with an occasional sexual *obligato* in the background. That settled it. Canadian history would be my future. Burt's Canadian history course was the only Canadian course I ever followed at University but, because of it, Canadian history became my career.

My other interest was French. My father had always found languages easy to come by. He had picked up some Chinese and Japanese while at sea, as well as Chinook Jargon, acquired in British Columbia. Interested in Canadian politics, although never active in the political arena, he insisted that I study French at school. I recall his admonition: "if you, son, ever think of going into politics in this country, you had better have a good knowledge of French." He was much more long-sighted than many of his contemporaries, or even many of my own. When I dropped French in Grade Twelve while at Central High School[14] because I did not consider the teacher qualified to teach the subject, he sent me to a private tutor in Calgary, a Belgian woman, who gave me the start in oral French I so urgently needed. At the University I continued to study French literature under the drill sergeant methods of Edouard Sonet and the patient approach of Auguste-Paul Pelluet. When I graduated in 1929 with an honours degree in history, I had a pretty good reading knowledge of French and a functional proficiency in speaking that language. This latter received polish from a summer session at the Université de Grenoble, in 1929, before I went on to Oxford University.

———————

The "grey-walled academic paradise of Oxford" was a new experience for me and a powerful influence upon me. It was impossible for me to walk through the narrow streets of that old city without being aware, at each step, of the presence of the past. It was everywhere, in the colleges, in the layout of the streets, in the architecture, in the names I read: the very atmosphere recalled people and events of days as far back as Alfred the Great. All Souls College, erected to commemorate the soldiers who died on the field of Agincourt in 1415; Duke Humphrey's library, recalling that reckless and foolish son of Henry IV; Balliol College, recalling the days when John de Balliol thought he might become King of Scotland; Christ Church, that grand monument to Cardinal Wolsey who lost his head because he would not and could not swing a divorce for Henry VIII; Corpus Christi, whose dons were canny enough to bury their silver plate so that it could not be melted down to replenish Charles I's diminishing treasury during the

Great Civil War; Oriel, the college attended by Cecil Rhodes whose benefactions made my presence at Oxford possible. My own college, Keble, was comparatively new; but even it was associated with the religious controversies that rocked the Church of England in the mid-nineteenth century.[15] And I had once thought Athabasca Hall, at the University of Alberta, was old, because someone had carved initials and the date 1911 on the window sill of my third floor room!

At Oxford I read for honours in History. The substitution of the tutorial system for the lecture system, and the contact with historians who were, like A.L. Burt, writers of history, was what I needed; and the two years drill of writing weekly essays improved my skill, modest though it may still be, in writing English prose. For my tutors spent as much time in telling me how to write historical prose as in directing my thinking along historical lines.

I completed my honours baccalaureate in two years at Oxford and then started on a program for the degree of B.Litt.[16] I wanted to make use of my knowledge of French and suggested as a topic of research, the career of François Bigot in New France. This suggestion received short shrift. There were few documents; certainly no first hand sources in England on François Bigot. At that point Vincent Harlow, Rhodes House Librarian, who had tutored me in my "special subject" (British Colonial Policy) during my B.A. program, remarked that he had been collecting materials on a certain "Louis Riel." Would Riel interest me? There would undoubtedly be plenty of source materials to consult in the Public Record Office, in the Colonial Office Library in London, and of course, in the *Canadian Sessional Papers*.

Riel! As a thesis subject, Riel held far greater interest for me than the venal Bigot. Riel's career was the kind of thing I used to daydream of writing, while sitting in the family pew in the Cathedral Church of the Redeemer, in Calgary, reading the memorial plaques, instead of devoting my mind to the sermon. How well I recall the plaque to Corporal W.H.T. Lowry, "E" Division of North West Mounted Police, who died of wounds at Cut Knife Creek, 3 May 1885. So I leaped at the chance of doing research and preparing a thesis on Riel. My B.Litt. thesis, which dealt with Riel in Red River was accepted, and these being the years of the Great Depression when jobs were few and far between I remained at Oxford continuing my work on Riel. This time for a doctoral degree.

Once again, the unforeseen came to my assistance. It was the custom, in those years when the headquarters of the Hudson's Bay Company were still located in London, for the Company to entertain Canadian Rhodes Scholars at a luncheon at the Savoy Hotel. At one of these luncheons I was seated beside Sir Archibald Murray, then Deputy Governor of the Company. To make conversation, he inquired about the nature of my studies. I told him I was working on the early history of western Canada. He was interested. He suggested that the Company Archives might provide some useful information. Of course they would! Then he continued by telling me that the Company was giving thought to making their archives available to serious historians, and promised to take up with the Governor, Ashley Cooper, the possibility of my receiving permission to dig into the Company's records. He was as good as his word, and before long I found myself in the basement room of Beaver House in London, looking at papers I had scarcely ever hoped to see. There was another scholar working there at the same time. He was A.S. Morton of the University of Saskatchewan, then preparing his monumental *History of the Canadian West*. Morton was no selfish individualist. He was a true teacher who provided me with guidance and useful suggestions. Towards him and the Hudson's Bay Company Archivist, R.H.G. Leveson-Gower, I continue to feel a deep sense of gratitude.

My initial good luck—and what is luck but a happy coincidence of events that seem, in retrospect, to form a pattern—was followed by the award of another scholarship. This time it was the Beit Senior Research Scholarship in Colonial History. The scholarship fortunately included a substantial travel grant. Thus, with the aid of more South African money—Cecil Rhodes had supplied the first—I returned to Canada in March 1933, to continue my research in the Public Archives. In Ottawa I found a fruitful source of historical information—virtually untapped at that time—the files of the Department of Indian Affairs. The Deputy Superintendent-General of Indian Affairs, Dr. McGill, was a former Calgarian and friend of my father. He not only gave me access to these files but put me in the care of two of his archivists, Messrs. Matheson and St. Louis, both of whom were friendly and helpful. Regrettably for historians, some of the files I consulted were destroyed by fire not long afterwards. Old files were only an embarrassment in a building where space was needed for more recent, and therefore more relevant, data. After a session at the State Department, I returned to England in November to continue my research in the Public Record Office and in the archives of the Hudson's Bay Company.

Finally, in 1935, my thesis was completed, submitted for examination, studied, criticized, accepted by the examiners, and recommended for publication. Publication was virtually a *sine qua non* for a doctoral thesis in those days. My B.Litt. (M.Litt.) and D.Phil. theses were combined in a single volume, and, with financial assistance from the University and from the Rhodes Trustees, the book was published by Longmans Green, in London, in the spring of 1936. The title was *The Birth of Western Canada*.

Did my book add anything to the Riel-Métis story? In the way of factual data? Yes. Subsequent historians have, however, gone beyond the point I reached. In the way of interpretation? Also, yes. For fifty years after Riel's death, most Canadians saw Riel and his supporters in western Canada only through the eyes of men and women obsessed with the idea that the dominant factor in Canadian history was the long-standing Anglo-French, Protestant-Catholic rivalry, Anglo-Canadian Protestants saw Riel as a threat to the new Confederation; French Canadian Catholics saw him as a defender of the French fact and Roman Catholic rights in a region that had originally been explored and exploited by French Canadian fur traders. French versus English. *Ipse dixit.*

To my mind, this thesis was unilluminatingly dogmatic, deterministic. I saw the Riel-led western movement as the reaction of men, whose livelihood had been based upon the fur trade, to the threat imposed by a new economic and social order based upon private ownership, agriculture, and money. This idea did not spring Athena-like from my head: It was suggested to me by Dr. Harlow, and in particular by Dr. E.P. Morell, a New Zealander, then teaching at Oxford, who wondered aloud if the Indian and Métis resistance to English settlement did not follow the path of Maori resistance to white settlement in his own country?[17] This thesis of cultural conflict, which I elaborated in *The Birth of Western Canada*, was subsequently adopted by other historians, including Marcel Giraud. After all, there is no copyright on ideas. Nor should there be. Today, however, the Riel story has taken on new shapes and colours. Riel now appears in the role of defender of western political and economic rights; some writers see him as the precursor of western separatism; and some would, so it seems to me, picture him as a kind of Métis Lenin.

Was *The Birth of Western Canada* welcomed by the public in 1936? Did it enjoy a wide circulation and give a new impetus to Western Canadian Studies? As Eliza Doolittle remarked in Bernard Shaw's *Pygmalion* "not bloody likely." The book enjoyed only a short flight in the 1930s, landing with a faint, dull thud. It prompted a few modest reviews in Canadian historical periodicals, including a favorable one by Professor A.L. Burt, by this time at the University of Minnesota;[18] and a less than enthusiastic and slightly patronizing one by R.O. Mac-Farlane of the University of Manitoba. *The Birth of Western Canada* sold a couple of hundred copies in Canada, even fewer in the United States. Then it went into a long Rip Van Winkle-like slumber for a quarter of a century. Actually the book did rather better in England. Reviews were good, including a "Book of the Week" distinction by Edward Shanks in *John O'London's Weekly*.[19] Hopefully those who bought my book, read it. But sales were depressingly slow, and in the end, the bulk of the copies printed remained quietly gathering dust on the shelves of the Longmans Green warehouse in Paternoster Row in London, until they were burned by Hitler's *Luftwaffe* during the London blitz of 1940. Twenty years later the copyright was acquired by the University of Toronto Press; *The Birth of Western Canada* enjoyed a rebirth. Since that time the book has appeared, off and on, in paperback, a useful reference for students in Canadian universities, specializing in western Canadian history.

If I were disappointed at the indifference with which the Canadian book-buying public greeted my first effort, I was shocked when a firm of lawyers in Alberta applied for an injunction blocking any sale of the book on the public market on the grounds that I had infringed copyright of title. It was, I discovered, a bluff, and had no sound basis in law; if only because no book with that title had ever appeared in print! The late R.B. Bennett, to whom I appealed for advice, told me to put *The Birth of Western Canada* back on sale, even to take a counter-action to recover moneys lost because of the temporary withdrawal of the book from the market. But as a young lecturer, who had just landed a job at Mount Allison University in New Brunswick, I had no stomach for getting involved in an expensive law suit. My conclusion was that little in the way of money was to be made by writing nonfiction history.

The Birth of Western Canada did well after 1960; but I imagine that its role as a university text will be a diminishing one. There are still history students in our universities, but sociology and political science have become the prestige subjects of higher education; professors of history are considered relevant, but only in so far as they play the role of social scientists. There seem to be few places left in the world in which humane historians can do their own thing. Statistics, diagnoses, tabulations, computers, all designed to back up foregone conclusions, represent the new patterns of academic order, in the Arts as well as the Sciences. Perhaps these things appeal to the young, who are always more attracted by the certainties of knowledge. Middle and old age bring a realization of how uncertain the rational process really is, as well as an appreciation of the virtues of creative inertia.

But I was still young enough in the 1930s, while disappointed, not to be discouraged. I had the strength and the determination to keep writing, if not books, at least articles. Then World War II intervened. And after seven years military service, I accepted an appointment at the Royal Military College of Canada. At this point I shifted the emphasis of my writing from western Canadian history to military history. Hence, *Canada's Soldiers*, *The Invasion of Canada 1775–6*, *The War of 1812*,[20] and various articles on military matters. But my first love never died. And, from time to time, I paid court to her, writing a biography, *Louis Riel*,[21] and acting as general editor of the Riel Project, the five volumes of which were officially launched 7 November 1985.[22] And, I add, to write articles on various aspects of native history, ranging from the first Indian reserves in French Canada to the reception of the Sioux refugees in Manitoba and Saskatchewan in the nineteenth century.[23]

Do I regret having chosen history as my life's work? Not at all. After a lifetime, I know the limitations of my discipline. I know that it does not reveal the whole meaning of life. All it does, is to let loose a few fire-fly flares of illumination, provide a few vague answers to the eternal "why." But that is better than utter darkness. Cynics have called written history at its best "a distillation of rumour" and at its worst "a caricature of the surveyor's chart."[24] Fragmentary as our vision of the past and the passing scene may be, that vision is better than no vision at all. History is the record of man's life on this planet; as such I believe that it holds the secret, not perhaps of man's soul, but surely of his humanity. Can the meaning of man's existence be found outside history? History and man exist together. When history shall stand still in time, then, and only then, will there be an end to man and history.

Shall I cease to write history even though I no longer teach it; cease to study history, though I have contributed very little to the making of it? Shall I cease to respond to the stimulus of my past or of my present environment? Some concerned friends say, "why not rest now upon your oars?" To tell me to suspend activity is to tell me to accept, without challenge, the distasteful idea that age is the nemesis of creativity. Were I to yield to such advice, I would, I fear, alienate myself from my fellows and from my discipline. To forfeit the fun and mental excitement of a lifetime is a sure way to loneliness. And that kind of loneliness is not for me. Would I not do better, instead, to follow the injunction of Sir Andrew Barton (modified somewhat to fit this occasion):[25]

A little weary am I now, but yett still sane;
Ile but lye down and reade a while,
And then Ile rise and write againe.

NOTES

1. My second and third names, Francis Gilman, commemorate those of Captain Francis Gilman, Quartermaster of the Royal Nova Scotia Regiment of Fencible Infantry, raised in 1793. According to family lore, Captain Gilman saved my great-great-grandfather from drowning and was told that his name would be borne by great-great-grandfather's son. This has been done for four generations.

2. For an account of the *Empress of Japan*, see R.D. Turner, *The Pacific Empress* (Victoria, 1981).

3. For illustrations of the region in 1898 see Pierre Burton, *Klondike Quest: A Photographic Essay, 1897–1899* (Toronto, 1983).

4. Two cousins of my father's, Frederick William and Frank Adolph, operated a small lumber mill, the Adolph Lumber Company, at Baynes Lake, B.C. The mill ceased to function in the early 1920s.

5. F. Lillywhite, *The English Cricketers' Trip to Canada and the United States* (London, 1860).

6. Pierre Berton, *Klondike: The Last Great Gold Rush 1896–1898* (Toronto, 1979), pp. 236–47; pp. 256–60.

7. The team included Dr. Mewburn (Honorary President), John H. Stanley (President), Dr. McClure (Vice President), A. Scott (Team Captain), S.G. Davies, E.J. Fraser, F.W. Gow, F. Kenney, E.G. Myers, Alvin Ripley, A. Ritchie, A.B. Stafford, Alex Scott, Dr. Stewart, F.S. Wallace and C.W. Van Horne.

8. For Lacombe's biography see, Une Soeur de la Providence, *Le Père Lacombe* (Montréal, 1916); Josephine Phelan, *The Bold Heart: The Story of Father Lacombe* (Toronto, 1956).

9. The 137th Battalion C.E.F. was commanded by Lt. Col. Morfitt. The second-in-command was my father's friend, Major H.J. Robie. The Battalion was disbanded in the U.K. and its members became part of the general reinforcement pool serving the Canadian Corps in France. For a note on H.J. Robie see A.O. MacRae, *History of the Province of Alberta* (Calgary, 1912), Volume II, pp. 807–8.

10. Cadet training was a compulsory part of the school system. The cadet training officer was Captain Alex Ferguson.

11. I could add the name of the Reverend Hiram Alfred Cody. I used to wonder if Cody were a westerner. Not until years later did I discover that he was born and raised in New Brunswick.

12. The other member of the History Department was Morden H. Long. Long's work and preparation were thorough; his presentation somewhat uninspiring. Professor Cecil Burgess of the Architecture Department lectured on the history of art and architecture through the Renaissance; his knowledge was great but his skills as a teacher of history were negligible.

13. A.L. Burt, *The Old Province of Quebec* (Toronto, 1933).
14. My first French teachers at Central High School included Mr. McKim and Miss MacPhail. The latter was a good and successful teacher. So successful indeed, that she was lured away to teach in Toronto. Her successor, Mill Kaulbach, was considerably less skilful both in her knowledge of her subject and in her teaching, at least as far as I was concerned.
15. Keble College was erected in 1870 as a memorial to John Keble, who, along with John (later Cardinal) Newman, Hurrell Froude, and Edward Pusey, were the moving spirits behind the Oxford Movement (Tractarian Movement) of the 1830s.
16. Because the Oxford M.A. signified full membership in the University, the research degree, B.Litt., was often referred to as a "fancy baccalaureate." Finally, in the 1970s, the University changed the degree to M.Litt. Those holding the B.Litt. were given the option of accepting the new form or retaining the old designation. I chose to accept the M.Litt., if only to avoid the innumerable explanations I had been obliged to give to the *non cognoscente*.
17. I think this thesis warrants a thorough examination by some scholars familiar with both the Canadian and New Zealand scenes.
18. Professor Burt had previously warned me of the dangers of hurrying into print. His enthusiasm for my book was therefore gratifying to me.
19. *John O'London's Weekly*, 1 August 1936.
20. G.F.G. Stanley, *Canada's Soldiers: The Military History of an Unmilitary People* (Toronto, 1954); revised editions 1960 and 1974. A French edition, *Nos soldats: l'histoire militaire du Canada de 1604 à nos jours*, appeared in 1974 published by Les Editions de L'Homme, Montréal; *The Invasion of Canada* (Toronto, 1973); *The War of 1812: Land Operations* (Toronto, 1983). The French edition is *La guerre de 1812: les operations terrestes* (Montréal, 1984).
21. *Louis Riel* (Toronto, 1963). Recently reprinted in paperback by McGraw-Hill Ryerson (Toronto, 1985).
22. *The Collected Writings of Louis Riel/ Les écrits complets de Louis Riel* (Edmonton, 1985).
23. *Revue d'histoire de l'Amérique francaise*, vol. IV, no. 2, Septembre 1950 "The First Indian Reserves in Canada" pp. 178–210. See also "Displaced Redmen: The Sioux in Canada" in Ian Getty and D.B. Smith, *One Century Later, Western Canadian Reserve Indians since Treaty Seven* (Vancouver, 1978).
24. These phrases remain in my mind, although I have forgotten the names of the men or women who wrote them. I suspect Thomas Carlyle may have been responsible for the first. The second completely escapes me.
25. With apologies to J.R. Colombo, *Colombo's Canadian Quotations* (Edmon-

ton, 1974), pp. 153–54. The original, attributed to Sir Andrew Barton in *Percy's Reliques* (1765), reads

A little Ime hurt, but yett not slain;
Il e but lye downe and bleede a while,
and then Ile rise and fight againe.

DONALD B. SMITH

2 Aboriginal Rights in 1885
A Study of the St. Catharine's Milling or Indian Title Case

THE CONSERVATIVE SPEAKER had just explained to the House of Commons the federal government's new Franchise Bill. Among its provisions the Bill proposed extending the federal franchise to all adult male Indians, living on or off their reserves who had an income of $300 a year or more. Never before had the vote in federal elections been given to status Indians. On that day, 30 April 1885, David Mills, the former Minister of the Interior under the Liberals, continued with his interrogation. Point-blank he asked the Conservative:

MILLS: "This will include Indians in Manitoba and British Columbia?"
CONSERVATIVE: "Yes"
MILLS: "Poundmaker and Big Bear?"
CONSERVATIVE: "Yes"
MILLS: "So they can go from a scalping party to the polls..."[1]

The context should be noted. The ruling Conservatives had first introduced the Bill on 19 March.[2] Only one week later the Métis under Louis Riel had clashed with a group of about one hundred Mounties and volunteers in the South Saskatchewan River valley. At Duck Lake, the Métis had won, killing twelve Canadians, including

21

Skef Elliot, a Prince Albert Lawyer and first cousin of Edward Blake, the leader of the federal Liberal Party.[3] The North West Rebellion had begun. Within days the federal government rushed 3,000 eastern militia men westward to Qu'Appelle, and later to Swift Current and Calgary. More distressing news followed. The Cree Indians of Poundmaker's band had surrounded the town of Battleford. Then, on 2 April, the Crees in Big Bear's band rose, killing nine whites at the tiny settlement of Frog Lake, a hundred miles northwest of Battleford. On 24 April the Métis had held the Canadians on their way to Batoche, the Métis headquarters, to a draw at Fish Creek. In the House of Commons on 30 April 1885, feelings against giving the Indian the vote ran high.

On 4 May the same Conservative speaker who had defended the Franchise Bill on 30 April again took the floor. Just two days earlier the Canadians had suffered another major reversal. Poundmaker on 2 May had defeated Colonel Otter and his column at Cut Knife Hill west of Battleford, the Canadians losing eight men and being forced to retreat. Now the Conservatives as well yielded some ground, this time to the Liberals. The western Indians would not obtain the federal franchise immediately, instead, in the beginning only those Indians in the eastern provinces who met the property qualification on the same terms as the white population, would obtain it. Not satisfied by this partial retreat the Liberals kept up their attack.

The Conservative member's stand, in hindsight, was courageous in the face of continual jibes and taunts from the opposition. The Conservative speaker, whose own son marched in the column against Batoche,[4] had as much reason as any other federal politician for seeing the Métis and Indian resistance crushed. Yet, as he said in his remarks on 4 May, justice demanded that the Indians receive the franchise:

> ...here are Indians, aboriginal Indians, formerly lords of the soil, formerly owning the whole of this country. Here they are, in their own land, prevented from either sitting in this house, or voting for men to come here and represent their interests.[5]

The Conservative speaker's call to give the federal vote to the Indian becomes all the more remarkable when his identity is revealed. In the spring of 1885 this distinguished politician, a veteran of over forty years in Canadian politics, filled two portfolios. He served as the Superintendent General of Indian Affairs,[6] and also as Prime Minister of Canada. John A. Macdonald would later term the enactment on 4 July 1885, of the Electoral Franchise Bill "the greatest triumph of my life."[7] It would, in his opinion, help undo the injustice done to the Indians, who in his words, "have been great sufferers by the discovery of America, and the transfer to it of a large white population."[8]

Other surprises follow if one closely examines the Prime Minister's involvement with other Indian matters in 1885. Through D'Alton McCarthy, a prominent Ontario lawyer whom he had tried (unsuccessfully) to entice into his cabinet as his new Minister of Justice in 1884,[9] the Prime Minister endorsed a theory of Indian land title that seems most unusual for a man frequently remembered today as the murderer of Louis Riel and the supreme oppressor in 1885 of the Plains Cree and Métis. D'Alton McCarthy and the Prime Minister championed an interpretation of Indian rights, which, if recognized today, would give the Dene in the North West Territories, and all other Indian groups living on unsurrendered lands, considerable control over their homelands.

As late as a century ago Canada had no legal statement on the nature of Indian aboriginal land rights. One of the first legal definitions was arrived at in the St. Catharine's Milling, or Indian Title Case, which first reached the courts in the year of the North West troubles of 1885. The case arose from the long-standing dispute between Ontario and the federal government over the proper location of the province's northwestern boundary. Article 6 of the British North America Act had assigned the province the same territorial limits as the former Upper Canada, or Canada West, but it did not specify what these boundaries were. Before Confederation the Government of the

Canadas had contested the claims of the Hudson's Bay Company to possess all the lands drained by the rivers flowing into Hudson Bay and Hudson Strait. The Canadians had argued in the late 1850s that the Canadas had inherited the western claims of the French Crown, those based on the discoveries of French explorers like La Vérendrye. When the new Dominion of Canada purchased the Hudson's Bay Company's lands in 1869, and created in 1870 the province of Manitoba, then only the small area around the Red River Settlement, the boundary between the old territories of the Hudson's Bay Company and the new province of Ontario still lay undefined. The boundary negotiations which began in 1871 between the federal government and Ontario quickly broke down the following year.[10]

Upon becoming the new Liberal Premier of Ontario in 1872, Oliver Mowat found the provincial government seriously involved in this western boundary dispute. It appeared to Mowat, as it had to Edward Blake, his Liberal predecessor as Premier, that the federal government wanted to pare down the size and influence of Ontario, denying it ownership of territory that rightly belonged to it, and which would increase its power and influence in the new Dominion. At the very least, Mowat argued, Ontario's boundary should run due north from the source of the Mississippi, slightly west of Lake of the Woods. Until its electoral defeat in 1874 the Macdonald government had held that the boundary should be drawn near Port Arthur, on Lake Superior. A board of arbitration, however, set up in 1874 by Alexander Mackenzie, the new Liberal Prime Minister, accepted in 1878 almost all Mowat's claims: the western boundary should run due north from the northwest angle of the Lake of the Woods to the English River, then along the Albany river to the shore of Hudson Bay, and then follow the shore to a point north of the head of Lake Temiskaming. Ontario appeared to have doubled its area, winning 110,000 square miles of territory, but the last word belonged to John A. Macdonald. The general election of October 1878 returned Macdonald and the Conservatives to power, and they refused to ratify the award.

In 1881 Macdonald took the offensive. Mowat's fears proved justified. The Prime Minister wanted to keep Ontario subordinate, and incapable of ever posing a serious challenge to the federal government. The Prime Minister awarded the disputed territory to Manitoba, thereby introducing that province into the controversy. Since the Dominion continued to control the natural resources of Manitoba this arrangement allowed the federal government to retain the land and mineral rights to the disputed territory, from the Lake of the Woods to Thunder Bay. Despite Ontario's protests the Prime Minister began to grant land and timber rights within the disputed area. Finally in 1883, after two years of legal chaos in the area, both Manitoba and Ontario agreed to submit the issue to the Judicial Committee of the Privy Council in London, the supreme legal authority in the British Empire. Mowat personally pleaded Ontario's case for the vast territories west of Port Arthur, against D'Alton McCarthy, and he won. The Judicial Committee in July 1884 upheld the award of the arbitrators in 1878, fixing the western limits of Ontario at the northwest angle of the Lake of the Woods.

Mowat had won, yet the wily Sir John A. Macdonald refused to yield. Until ratified by legislation the decision was not binding, and despite Ontario's formal request the Dominion delayed implementing the Judicial Committee's advisory decision. The Prime Minister continued to assert the federal government's claim to the natural resources of the territory awarded Ontario. As he had once stated: "Even if all the territory Mr. Mowat asks for were awarded to Ontario, there is not one stick of timber, one acre of land or one lump of lead, iron or gold that does not belong to the Dominion or to the people who have purchased from the Dominion government."[11] The Prime Minister based his claim on Treaty 3 made in 1873 between the federal government, and the Ojibwa Indians of the area.

In return for (listing only the most important financial considerations): a present to each Indian ($12.00), an annuity to each ($5.00), an extra salary for chiefs and headmen ($25.00 and $15.00 per annum), $1,500.00 annually for twine (for fishnets) and ammunition, the gift of tools and supplies, and the promise of schools, the Ojibwa, apart from small areas to be held as Indian reserves to be set up on the basis of 640 acres for a family of five, surrendered 55,000 square miles of their homeland.[12] The federal position, even after the Privy Council's advisory decision of 1884, remained that the Indians' rights to the natural resources of the Treaty 3 area had passed to the Dominion immediately after the treaty's signing.

Ontario refused to accept this federal claim over what it regarded as its own resources. It launched a suit against the St. Catharine's Milling Company which in 1883 had been issued a federal timber licence for a tract some twenty miles southeast of present-day Dryden. The Dominion received $4,152.52 for the licence, under which the company had cut two million feet of timber.[13] In late 1884 suit was filed in Chancery for ejectment of the St. Catharine's Milling company and for all damages incurred by its trespass. The Dominion openly assisted the St. Catharine's Milling Company to defend its claims.[14] D'Alton McCarthy represented the company's position, and Oliver Mowat that of Ontario. McCarthy and Mowat appeared before John Alexander Boyd, the Chancellor of Ontario, the man who perhaps more than any other judge in Canada had the best background to adjudicate on this important historical case.

Born in 1837 and raised in Toronto, John Boyd had received his early schooling at the Bay Street Academy, where his father, a former student at Glasgow University, was the principal. Later his father farmed north of Toronto and taught in a small school in the village of Eglinton. At the age of eleven John entered Upper Canada College, walking a good five miles each day down Yonge Street to the school, and then back that evening to the family farm at Eglinton. At the age of fourteen he temporarily ended his studies and worked for two years in Toronto and Quebec City. His months in the historic city no doubt deepened his love of the French language, and of Canadian history. Deciding against a career in commerce he returned to Upper Canada College in 1853, graduating in 1856. The gifted student won a scholarship in modern languages to the University of Toronto, where he studied English, French, German, and history.[15]

John Boyd did extremely well, winning in his first year the University prize for history, the prize book being, *The Historical and Other Works of William Robertson*, duly signed by John McCaul, President of the University, and Daniel Wilson, John's Professor (who in 1862 published his anthropological study, *Prehistoric Man: Researches into the Origin of Civilization in the Old and New World*). In 1858 the young man, then in his second year, obtained prizes for English, French and

German literature. Strangely, the university awarded history books to its top student in modern languages: a set of the works of William Prescott: *Ferdinand and Isabella, Phillip the Second, the Conquest of Mexico* and *The Conquest of Peru*.[16] John Alexander Boyd graduated as the gold medalist in modern languages in 1860, and received his M.A. in 1861.

The choice of prize books reveals much about current perceptions and images of North American Indians. William Robertson, who wrote his *History of America* in 1777, believed that the North American Indian had little or no sense of property or of wealth. He was a roamer, a savage living in a savage society, and in a savage environment.[17] Similarly Prescott in discussing the Aztec civilization in Mexico, cited their cannibalism as evidence of a barbarism, which not only explained European conquest but also justified it. (Prescott gave no consideration to the significance of the act in the cultural setting in which it was performed.)[18]

Just after graduation John Alexander completed *A Summary of Canadian History: From the Time of Cartier's Discovery to the Present Day*, for use in the schools. Like many others before and since, he began his text with the arrival of the French, and regarded our past as beginning only with the European's arrival. The approach taken is strictly chronological with questions adapted to each paragraph. The Indians appear only in relationship with the Europeans, and are not mentioned at all after the War of 1812.[19]

After graduation John Boyd chose law as his future profession and articled with David B. Read, a former mayor of Toronto, and later an historian who wrote lives of both John Graves Simcoe (1890) and Isaac Brock (1894).[20] Once called to the Bar in 1863, John became the junior member of Read and Boyd, a partnership with his former employer. The young lawyer married that same year Elizabeth Buchan, a daughter of David Buchan, Bursar of the University of Toronto, and began his large family, which would eventually number nine boys and three girls. In 1869 he became a partner in Edward Blake's firm, which now became Blake, Kerr and Boyd. He stayed with this partnership until his appointment by Prime Minister Macdonald as Chancellor of Ontario in 1881. The *Canada Law Journal* welcomed the choice: "The new Chancellor is known to all as a courteous

gentleman and a favorite in the profession, a scholar of high attain-
ments, an accomplished lawyer, gifted with an eminently judicial cast
of mind..." Similarly the *Canadian Law Times* praised the appointment
as "at once the most popular and best deserved that could have been
made," and described Boyd as "a sound lawyer, of extensive practice
and experience."[21]

Chancellor Boyd had served for four years as President of the
Chancery Division of the High Court of Ontario at the time the Indian
Title Case reached him. It raised a number of questions: What was the
legal scope of the Indians' title? In what ways might native title properly be extinguished? And what was the effect of treaties that ceded
lands to the Crown?

The Chancellor, at least if his *Summary of Canadian History* is taken
as the sum total of his pre-existing knowledge, did not have a great
knowledge of Indian matters before the Indian Title Case began. In
Toronto (population nearly 200,000) he would hardly, if ever, have
encountered Indians. A band of 200 Mississauga Indians had lived on
a reserve bordering Toronto until 1847, but in that year Chief Peter
Jones and his people had moved from the Credit River to the Grand
River about 100 miles to the west.[22] The nearest reserves after 1847
were on Lake Simcoe roughly fifty miles to the north, and Lake Scu-
gog, approximately the same distance to the east.

John Boyd certainly, though, had met Indians, not in Toronto but
on Georgian Bay near Parry Sound. In 1881 the Chancellor had purchased several islands from the Crown, just west of the Indian reserve
at Parry Island. When he and his family went north each summer
during the judicial recess, they must frequently have encountered the
Parry Islanders out fishing or berry-picking.[23] Yet, even if he recognized, say James Pegamagabow, Charles Senebah, or Dan
Tabobadong by sight, it is unlikely that he knew any of the Parry
Island Ojibwa and Pottawatomi Indians well.[24] As the *Canadian Law
Times* wrote in its obituary of the Chancellor in 1916: "It could not be
said that he encouraged intimacy, indeed he was somewhat reserved
in manner..." Or to quote the Toronto *Star*: "Sir John, while courteous, considerate, and held in general regard, was not known as a
'mixer'."[25]

Suddenly in the spring of 1885 the Chancellor found himself facing two Indian issues simultaneously, publicly the Indian Title Case, and privately, the North West uprising. As soon as news of the Métis' victory at Duck Lake reached Toronto his eldest son, Alex, had volunteered for duty.[26] He left on 30 March, travelling with his brother, Len, who was so anxious to fight Riel that, according to one account,[27] he had hidden under a railway car seat until the volunteers were well out of Toronto, just to make sure he was taken along. On 2 May Alex fought at Cut Knife Hill, and fortunately escaped injury in the skirmish, which cost the Canadians eight killed and fourteen wounded. In one piece Alex rejoined Leonard on garrison duty at Battleford. Although Batoche fell on 12 May, and Riel surrendered himself on 15 May, Poundmaker and Big Bear still remained at large when the St. Catharine's Milling case began.

On 18 May Oliver Mowat and Walter Cassels (for the province), and D'Alton McCarthy and A.L. Creelman (for the St. Catharine's Milling and Lumber Company) appeared before the Chancellor. All present, on a general human level, shared one concern: that the North West Rebellion, now that Riel had been captured, would reach a speedy conclusion. Over the course of the previous month the firm of McCarthy, Osler, Hoskin and Creelman had contributed $25.00 to the Volunteer Supply Fund. Walter Cassels, whose nephew fought at Cut Knife Hill, himself gave $20.00; and Oliver Mowat and Chancellor Boyd, $25.00 each[28] (to give a comparison, the value of $20.00 to $25.00 in 1885 was roughly the equivalent of two weeks' wages for a railway labourer).[29]

The court called only one witness: Alexander Morris, the former Lieutenant Governor of the North West Territories, and Chairman of the Commission that had made Treaty 3 in 1873. Morris, currently the deputy leader of the Conservative opposition in the Ontario legislature, recalled for the court the circumstances of the treaty. The government had made two previous attempts to secure it, and on this third occasion, "it was fourteen days before I was able to complete this treaty three."[30] Morris's book, *The Treaties of Canada with the Indians* (1880) was submitted as evidence.[31]

Oliver Mowat, a short, stocky, near-sighted man appeared for the plaintiffs.[32] Many, to their cost, had underestimated the man who had already served for thirteen years as the Premier of Ontario, and but one year earlier, had successfully presented Ontario's case in the Boundary dispute before the Privy Council in London. Mowat began: "We say that there is no Indian title at law or in equity. The claim of the Indians is simply moral and no more."[33] The Indians, in short, had no legal title to their lands. As for the Royal Proclamation of 1763, often cited as evidence of the British recognition of their title, Mowat termed it merely, "a provisional arrangement...expressly repealed by the Quebec Act of 1774."[34] The Indians had no transferable title, and, he added, after Treaty 3 the Crown in right of Ontario owned all the land.

In reply D'Alton McCarthy spoke for the defendants. Physically the Barrie lawyer stood in marked contrast to Mowat: lean, athletic-looking, with a strong jaw, and piercing eyes.[35] He also spoke for the Prime Minister. As early as February 1885 Walter Cassels had deduced that McCarthy and Macdonald were collaborating closely together, and they had indeed met in January.[36] On 17 February Cassels had written Mowat that the "defendants deny the title of the Province to the lands in question...I notice by this morning's paper that Sir John intends to claim the lands for the Dominion and I presume this defence is set up in pursuance of an arrangement with the government."[37]

In court McCarthy, with some assistance from A.R. Creelman, argued that Treaty 3 had transferred to the Dominion all the Indians' rights in the land. According to McCarthy and Creelman the Royal Proclamation of 1763 remained very much in force. The Proclamation had reserved the Indians' hunting grounds for themselves, and had recognized the Indians' perpetual right to the area's lands, timber, and minerals, until they were surrendered. According to the Proclamation, the Indians could only sell their land to the federal government. Such a sale, once completed, transferred all Indian rights to the federal Crown.[38]

Chancellor Boyd now had three weeks to consider the respective arguments of both sides. In the interval he still had many court duties to perform, appearing almost every day at Osgoode Hall.[39] At home he also had great family responsibilities, for although his two oldest sons were away, eight other children remained. One is amazed that he had the time to write a judgement, sections of which have received much praise and endorsation by other judges and legal authorities from 1886 to the present day.[40] By the date of his judgement on 10 June, the North West Rebellion now neared its end, Poundmaker had surrendered, and only Big Bear was at large.

In his judgement Chancellor Boyd began by citing the benevolence of the British Crown. His readings on the early history of Indian-white relations led him to these conclusions. (As he wrote these lines I wonder if any of the faces of the Parry Islanders flashed through his mind?)

> The Colonial policy of Great Britain as it regards the claims and treatment of the aboriginal populations in America, has been from the first uniform and well-defined. Indian peoples were found scattered wide-cast over the continent, having, as a characteristic no fixed abodes, but moving as the exigencies of living demanded. As heathens and barbarians it was not thought that they had any proprietary title to the soil, nor any such claim thereto as to interfere with the plantations, and the general prosecution of colonization. They were treated "justly and graciously," as Lord Bacon advised, but no legal ownership of the land was ever attributed to them.[41]

Chancellor Boyd resolved the case by holding that Treaty 3 Indians had no rights and therefore could not convey anything to the federal government. As the Dominion had no authority to grant the federal licence to the St. Catharine's Milling Company, it was invalid. In legal terms, he continued, the treaty was meaningless, so much so that a refusal by the Indians to adhere to it would not have stopped the country's expansion.

> While in the nomadic state they may or may not choose to treat with the Crown for the extinction of their primitive right of occu-

pancy. If they refuse the government is not hampered, but has perfect liberty to proceed with the settlement or development of the
country, and so, sooner or later, to displace them.[42]

The defendants had argued that the Royal Proclamation of 1763
best explained the nature of the Indians' land right. The Chancellor
recognized the key passage in the document, that "such Indians with
whom we are connected, and who live under our protection should
not be molested or disturbed in the possession of such parts of our
dominions and territories, as not having been ceded to or purchased
by us, are reserved for them or any of them, as their hunting-
grounds." He recognized as well that, in his words, "this proclamation has frequently been referred to, and by the Indians themselves, as
the charter of their rights." But, he added, accepting Mowat's and
Cassels's arguments, the Proclamation "was superceded by the Quebec Act." The document, he concluded, since 1774, "must be regarded
as obsolete."[43]

The defendants immediately appealed the Chancellor's decision to
the Ontario Court of Appeal. McCarthy and Creelman again
appeared for the appellants. Mowat and Cassels were now joined by
David Mills, the vociferous opponent of the extension of the franchise
to Indians (which went into effect on 4 July 1885).[44] The rebellion tri-
als, with D'Alton McCarthy's partner B.B. Osler serving as one of the
government's three-man prosecution team, had all ended.[45] Louis
Riel had been hanged one month before the appeal was heard in mid-
December in Toronto.

After listening to both sides make their presentations, the Ontario
Court of Appeal unanimously upheld Chancellor Boyd's judgement.
Chief Justice Hagarty praised it as having been "mapped out with
much care and perspicacity."[46] The Appeal Court agreed that the
Crown's obligations to treat for Indian land title were strictly politi-
cal, not legal.[47]

With John A. Macdonald's backing D'Alton McCarthy now
appealed to the Supreme Court of Canada for redress.[48] In their presentation McCarthy and Creelman again argued that: "In Canada,
from the earliest times, it has been recognized that the title to the soil

was in the Indians, and the title from them has been acquired, not by conquest, but by purchase." Until the Crown bought their territory: "The Indians had a right to occupy the land, to cut the timber and to claim the mines and minerals found on the land, and the land descended to their children..."[49] The Supreme Court heard McCarthy and Creelman for the appellants, and Cassels and Mills for the respondents, in mid-November 1886, passing judgement on 20 June 1887.

A century later certain points in McCarthy and Creelman's brief puzzle the historical observer. Apparently they never considered, at any stage, to request that an Indian witness from the Treaty 3 area appear, or even to use quotations from Alexander Morris's book, to stand as evidence of the Ojibwa's own conception of their land rights (the following chief's statement would have more than sufficed: "we have a rich country, it is the Great Spirit who gave us this; where we stand upon is the Indians' property, and belongs to them").[50] The omission, in hindsight, seems extraordinary, but in view of the predominant racial beliefs of the day, so negative against native peoples, perhaps not surprising.[51]

One cannot help criticizing McCarthy and Creelman for their poor presentation of their side of the case. They did indeed contest the province's statement that the Quebec Act of 1774 annulled the Proclamation of 1763, but then spent little time proving their assertion with Upper Canadian examples. They could have done so by examining all the surviving documentation on Indian policy from 1763 to 1827. By his own admission Chancellor Boyd had relied heavily on the Report of the Commissioners appointed to examine Indian Affairs in the Province of Canada (the Bagot Commission), published in 1845 and 1847.[52] In their report the commissioners state that they had not examined any documents before 1827.[53]

Today one has to make only the most cursory investigation to confirm McCarthy's and Creelman's assertion that the Proclamation remained in effect in Upper Canada after the Quebec Act.[54] To select but three examples: first, the statement of Lieutenant Governor John Graves Simcoe to the Western Indians at Navy Hall, Niagara, in 1793:

These authentic Papers will prove that no King of Great Britain ever claimed absolute power or Sovereignty over any of your Lands or Territories that were not fairly sold or bestowed by your ancestors at Public Treaties. They will prove that your natural Independency has ever been preserved by your Predecessors, and will establish that the Rights resulting from such Independency have been reciprocally and constantly acknowledged in the Treaties between the Kings of France formerly possessors of parts of this continent, and the Crown of Great Britain.[55]

Peter Russell, the Administrator of Upper Canada, wrote to the same effect to Lieutenant Governor Robert Prescott in Quebec in 1798: "I likewise desired them [the Mississauga] to be Assured that the King would never Accept (of) an Acre of their Lands before he had fully satisfied them for it, by paying them as usual a Valuable consideration and that they would never be forced to part with them contrary to their intentions."[56] Similarly in 1811 William Claus, Deputy Superintendent-General of Indian Affairs, told the Ojibwa Indians of Matchedash Bay and Lake Simcoe: "The King your Great White Father never has nor never will take a foot of land from any of his Indian Children without their free consent..."[57] Moreover, in 1794, the procedures for the purchase of Indian lands in Upper Canada had been fully elaborated.[58] Why did McCarthy and Creelman not search diligently through the surviving state papers that could be located between 1885 and 1887?

At all stages of their appeal McCarthy and Creelman overlooked a number of arguments which would have weakened their opponent's position. They accepted, for instance, Chancellor Boyd's description of the Indians as being in the "nomadic state," and having "as a characteristic, no fixed abodes, but moving as the exigencies of living demanded."[59] The Indians of Treaty 3 were Ojibwa, a tribe which in the late nineteenth century extended from the north shore of Lake Ontario to the Canadian prairies. On the north shore of Lake Ontario the Ojibwa were known as Mississauga. McCarthy and Creelman, if they had consulted only two printed sources, could have obtained strong support for the argument that the Mississauga were not nomadic, but operated within circumscribed areas. In Peter Jones posthumously published work, *History of the Ojebway Indians* (1861) the Mississauga Chief (1802–1856) mentioned:

> Each tribe or body of Indians has its own range of country, and sometimes each family has its own hunting grounds, marked out by certain natural divisions, such as rivers, lakes, mountains, or ridges; and all the game within these bounds is considered their property as much as the cattle and fowl owned by a farmer on his own land. It is at the peril of an intruder to trespass on the hunting grounds of another.[60]

Another Mississauga, George Copway (1818–1869) from Rice Lake, wrote in his *Life, History and Travels* (1847): "The hunting grounds of the Indians were secured by right, a law and custom among themselves. No one was allowed to hunt on another's land, without invitation or permission."[61]

The point that the Indians did not wander aimlessly around would have led to a higher appreciation of their use of the land. It certainly would have helped to dispose of Cassels's and Mills's statement to the Supreme Court that the Indians "have no government and organization, and cannot be regarded as a nation capable of holding lands."[62]

McCarthy and Creelman's position was again rejected. The majority of the Supreme Court of Canada, four judges out of six, essentially agreed with the judgement of Chancellor Boyd. Many of the particulars of the hasty judgement made over the course of three weeks, between court sittings, and amidst the general background of an armed uprising, had been upheld. All that remained was the final court of appeal, the Judicial Committee of the Privy Council, the highest court of law in the British Empire. Once again D'Alton McCarthy faced Oliver Mowat, assisted on this occasion by Edward Blake, who had just resigned as the federal Liberal leader.

The ruling of the Privy Council in July 1888 denied once again the Dominion's contention that the Indians had been the absolute owners of the territory (owners in fee simple), and that they had relinquished that ownership to Canada by Treaty 3. The Privy Council found instead that the title to the soil rested with the Crown even before the Treaty: "The Crown has all along had a present proprietary estate in the land, upon which the Indian title was a mere burden."[63] (As a contemporary Indian lawyer has written: "The result of the *St. Catharine's Milling and Lumber Company* case is that the British, by simply setting foot on North America and planting a rag attached to a pole on the shores, acquired the title to Indian lands.")[64]

Yet the Privy Council deviated significantly from the Chancellor's judgement in one major respect. Lord Watson, unlike Chancellor Boyd, did recognize that the Indians had had a property right in their lands prior to the signing of Treaty 3, though admittedly only one of a low order (much less than a fee simple interest). It was a right of occupancy "a personal and usufructuary right, dependant upon the good will of the Sovereign."[65] The treaty had ended the right, which gave the province full ownership of the land. Contrary to Chancellor Boyd the Privy Council held that this usufructuary right originated in the Royal Proclamation of 1763. Apart, though, from this one alteration the Chancellor's contention that the province of Ontario had full proprietary rights, including the right to all natural resources had gained acceptance in three courts of law. John A. Macdonald, influenced as well by the alliance of the provinces at the inter-provincial conference of 1887, at this point conceded. The representatives of five of the seven provinces had met in Quebec in 1887, and had demanded that the northern and western boundaries of Ontario, as determined by the Privy Council, should be enacted into law by the British Parliament.[66] In 1889, the federal government confirmed Ontario's new boundaries and its full rights to the natural resources within them.

In the years to follow Chancellor Boyd's decision has had a long life. It has been incorporated in numerous judgements, and endorsed once again as recently as December 1984. In his Supreme Court of Ontario decision on the Temagami Land Claim case Judge Steele stated, "I agree with Arnup J.A.'s assessment of the judgement of Chancellor Boyd." Judge Steele cited Judge Arnup's comments in *Isaac et al. v. Davey et al.* (1974) in full:

The nature of Indian title in Ontario and the policy of the British Crown in relation to Indians and their rights has been authoritatively determined in a series of cases, in which much of the historical background is recounted, particularly in those cases decided when the events of the last 15 years of the 18th century were still present in the minds of living persons in the middle of the 19th century, and were recorded in documents available to the Judges of that time. As Osler, J., did, *I find the judgement at trial of Chancellor Boyd, a most learned, accurate and respected Judge, in R. v. St. Catharine's Milling and Lumber Company, to be of great assistance.* It is reported in (1885), 10 O.R. 196. The history of public lands is dealt with at pp. 203–6, and the colonial policy of Great Britain concerning the aboriginal populations in America is dealt with at great length commencing at p. 206. The judgement was affirmed, 13 O.A.R. 148, 13 S.C.R. 577, and by the Privy Council, 14 App. Cas. 46. [emphasis added][67]

As for the Prime Minister he won his next election in 1891. He had the satisfaction of knowing that Indians in Eastern Canada could vote (once back in office the Liberals, in 1898, denied Indians the federal franchise).[68] He won but the election was his last; he died three months later. Oliver Mowat remained Premier of Ontario until 1896, when he entered Wilfrid Laurier's new federal cabinet as Minister of Justice. He died in 1903. Chancellor Boyd was knighted in 1899 and continued as President of the Ontario High Court of Justice until his death at age 79 in 1916.

Despite all the litigation about their homeland the Indians of the Treaty 3 area fared very badly. The Dominion and Ontario governments could not agree on the promised selection, location and extent of their reserves. Some bands in the mid-1980s still had not received their reserves.[69]

One suspects that despite John A. Macdonald's genuine concern to see the federal franchise given to Canada's Indians, he was only interested in their land rights in the St. Catharine's Milling case to further the ends of the federal government. D'Alton McCarthy, his loyal lieutenant, certainly had no long-term commitment to the cause. Shortly after the conclusion of St. Catharine's Milling he embarked on a crusade much dearer to his heart. In 1889 McCarthy began his campaign to make Canada a unilingual English-speaking country, and to eliminate the French language wherever possible, particularly in Manitoba and the North West.

ACKNOWLEDGEMENTS

Many thanks to Kay Boyd, granddaughter of John Alexander Boyd, for her help in the preparation of the section on Chancellor Boyd. I am grateful to Harold Averill, University of Toronto Archives, for clippings about Chancellor Boyd. The late Robert M. Brown of Blake, Cassels and Graydon also provided useful references to John Alexander Boyd, once a member of the firm. Andrew Johnson of the Judges' Staff, Supreme Court of Ontario, Osgoode Hall, kindly supplied me with a photostat copy of Chancellor Boyd's bench book for April and May 1885. Dr. Jim Miller of the University of Saskatchewan forwarded me background material on D'Alton McCarthy. John Bell, Archivist, Prime Ministers' Archives, National Archives of Canada, sent photostats of D'Alton McCarthy's letters to the Prime Minister about the case. I am grateful to William Henderson and Leo Waisberg for suggesting source materials on "St. Catharine's Milling." Donna Bloomfield assisted in locating references to Chancellor Boyd in the Toronto *Mail* and *World*, from April to June 1885.

I have profited greatly from conversations with Jim Morrison, Dr. Brian Slattery, Bruce Clark and Dr. Tony Hall over the issues involved in the case. John Goodwin, Lou Knafla, and Peter Sibenik also assisted me in gaining an appreciation of the legal issues. Lou Demerais, Director of Media/Public Relations, Assembly of First Nations, Ottawa, provided the background on the current constitutional status of the Royal Proclamation of 1763. Any errors or misunderstandings of the legal issues involved are, of course, my responsibility.

NOTES

1. Canada, House of Commons, Debates, 30 April 1885, p. 1484. The Liberal speaker was David Mills, the Minister of the Interior in the administration of Alexander Mackenzie, 1876–1878.

2. Two studies of the bill have been made, Malcolm Montgomery, "The Six Nations Indians and the Macdonald Franchise," *Ontario History*, No. 57 (1967): 13–25; and Gordon Stewart, "John A. Macdonald's Greatest Triumph," *Canadian Historical Review*, No. 63 (1982): 3–33. The Montgomery article is the more useful of the two for details on the Indian franchise.

3. Bob Beal and Rod Macleod, *Prairie Fire: The 1885 North West Rebellion* (Edmonton: Hurtig, 1984), p. 159. Beal and Macleod state that Skeffington Elliot was Blake's nephew; actually he was his first cousin. Skef Elliot's and Edward Blake's mothers were sisters, hence they were first cousins. See: Gwendoline Davis, "Diary of Judge William Elliot," London *Free Press*, 15 July 1950, in London Library Scrapbook, Volume 35. My thanks to Glen Curnoe, London Room librarian, London, Ontario, for this reference.

4. Keith Wilson, *Hugh John Macdonald* (Winnipeg, 1980), pp. 22–26.

5. Canada, House of Commons, Debates, 4 May 1885, p. 1575.

6. Frank Pedley, Deputy Minister, Department of Indian Affairs. "Department of Indian Affairs," in *Handbook of Indians of Canada* (Geographic Board, Canada, 1912; Ottawa, King's Printer, 1913; New York: Kraus Reprint, 1969), p. 233.

7. Donald Creighton, *John A. Macdonald: The Old Chieftain* (Toronto, 1955), p. 427.

7. Canada, House of Commons, *Debates*, 5 May 1880, p. 1991.

8. Creighton, *Macdonald*, pp 389–90.

9. Two excellent treatments of this complicated issue are: Morris Zaslow's "The Ontario Boundary Question," in *Profiles of a Province*, ed., Ontario Historical Society (Toronto, 1967), pp. 107–17; and Christopher Armstrong, "Chapter 1, Remoulding the Constitution," *The Politics of Federalism: Ontario's Relations with the Federal Government, 1867–1942* (Toronto, 1981), pp. 8–32. A short popular summary appears in Joseph Schull's *Ontario Since 1867* (Toronto, 1978), pp. 95–101.

10. Quoted in Zaslow, "Ontario Boundary Question," p. 114.

11. "The North-West Angle Treaty, Number Three," in Alexander Morris, *The Treaties of Canada with the Indians of Manitoba and the North-West Territories* (Toronto, 1880), pp. 320–29.

12. *Regina v. The St. Catharine's Milling and Lumber Company*, Ontario Reports, No. 10, (1885), pp. 197–98.

13. J.C. Morrison, "Oliver Mowat and the Development of Provincial Rights in Ontario: A Study in Dominion-Provincial Relations, 1867–1896," in *Three History Theses* (Toronto, 1961), p. 170. See also the letters from D'Alton McCarthy to John A. Macdonald in the Macdonald Papers, National Archives of Canada, 5 January 1885 (pp. 98291–94) and 15 January 1887 (pp. 26762–64). My thanks to John Bell, Archivist, Prime Ministers' Archives, for these references.

14. W.H.C. Boyd's "The Last Chancellor," Law Society of Upper Canada, *Gazette*, Vol. 15, No. 4 (December 1981), pp. 356–67, provides the most complete view of Chancellor Boyd's life.

15. William Robertson, *The Historical and Other Works of William Robertson, D.D., Comprising the History of Charles V; Disquisition on Ancient India; The History of America; The History of Scotland; etc. etc.* (Edinburgh, 1847).

    William H. Prescott, *History of the Reign of Ferdinand and Isabella*, 2 Volumes (London, 1854). Awarded for "Literas Anglicanas."

    William H. Prescott, *History of the Reign of Phillip the Second, King of Spain*, 2 Volumes (London, 1857). Awarded for "Literas Anglicanas."

    William H. Prescott, *History of the Conquest of Mexico, With a Preliminary View of the Ancient Mexican Civilization*, 2 Volumes (London, 1857). Awarded for "Literas Gallicus."

    William H. Prescott, *History of the Conquest of Peru: With a Preliminary View of the Civilization of the Incas*, 2 Volumes (London, 1858). Awarded for "Literas Germanicus."

    My thanks to Kay Boyd, of Toronto, granddaughter of Chancellor Boyd for these titles.

16. Roy Harvey Pearce, *Savagism and Civilization: A Study of the Indian and the American Mind* (Baltimore, 1953; revised edition, 1965), pp. 87–88.

17. "Ethnohistory: 'History in the Round'," *Ethnohistory*, No. 8 (1961), p. 34.

18. J.A. Boyd, *A Summary of Canadian History from the Time of Cartier's Discovery to the Present Day, With Questions Adapted to Each Paragraph. For the Use of Schools in British North America* (Toronto, 1869). The first edition appeared in 1860.

19. W. Stewart Wallace, "David Breakenridge Read (1832–1904)," *The Macmillan Dictionary of Canadian Biography* (Toronto, 1963), p. 621.

20. *Canadian Law Journal* (1881) 17 Can. L.J. 200; *Canadian Law Times* (1881) 1 C.L.T. 353. Both are cited in Boyd, "Chancellor," pp. 360–61.

21. Peter Jones, "Removal of the Credit River Indians," *Christian Guardian*, 12 January 1848.

22. Boyd, "Chancellor," pp. 360–61.

23. I have taken these three names from the list of Parry Island band councillors for 1885, see: E.S. Rogers and Flora Tobobondung, "Parry Island Farmers: A Period of Change in the Way of Life of the Algonkians of

Southern Ontario," in *Contributions to Canadian Ethnology*, ed., David Brez
Carlisle (Ottawa, 1975), p. 292. This study (pp. 247–359) and that by Dia-
mond Jenness, *The Ojibwa Indians of Parry Island: Their Social and Religious
Life* (Ottawa, 1935), contain a wealth of information on the Parry
Islanders.

24. Anon., "The Last Chancellor of Ontario," *Canadian Law Times*, Vol. 36,
No. 12 (December 1916), p. 912. The full quote is: "It could not be said
that he encouraged intimacy, indeed he was somewhat reserved in manner, but he was simple and democratic in his ways, quite approachable at
proper times, and certainly kind-hearted." "Chancellor John Boyd is
Dead after Short Illness," Toronto *Star*, 23 November 1916.

25. "Alexander James Boyd," *Commemorative Biographical Record of the County
of York, Ontario* (Toronto, 1907), p. 544.

26. "Northwest Veteran John L. Boyd Passes," Toronto *Star*, 31 May 1935
[clipping in the file of John Leonard Boyd, University of Toronto
Archives]. The anecdote about "a young son of Judge Boyd, presumably
Leonard, the younger of the two sons who volunteered, was told by
George Exton Lloyd (later Bishop Lloyd), a fellow University of Toronto
North West Rebellion veteran, in a talk in 1909 in Saskatoon. See: "Rebel-
lion of 1885 is recalled. Rev. Principal Lloyd at St. George's Gives an
Interesting Lecture on his Personal Experience in the Stirring Days of the
Riel Rebellion," Saskatoon *Daily Phoenix*, 9 October 1909.

27. "For the Volunteers," Toronto *World*, 27 April 1885, p. 1. "For Those at
the Front," Toronto *World*, 28 April 1885, p. 1. "Nearing Two Thousand,"
Toronto *World*, 2 May 1885, p. 1.
    Richard Scougall Cassels, nephew of Walter Cassels, wrote the excel-
lent diary, edited by R.C. Macleod, "The Diary of Lieutenant R.S. Cassels,
Northwest Field Force, March 30th to July 23d, 1885," in *Reminiscences of
a Bungle*, ed., R.C. Macleod (Edmonton, 1983), pp. 103–240. Robert Cassels, Richard Scougall Cassels's father, was an older brother of Walter
Cassels; see the sketches of the two brothers in Wallace, *Macmillan Dictionary*, p. 123. the name of Richard Scougall Cassels's father is listed in his
obituary, "R.S. Cassels, K.C., Dies in 76th Year," Toronto *Mail*, 18 July
1935.

28. Pierre Berton, *The Last Spike: The Great Railway, 1881–1885* (Toronto,
1971), p. 197.

29. Alexander Morris quoted in evidence taken at the trial which was held at
Toronto before the honorable Chancellor Boyd, 18 May 1885, *In the Court
of Appeal, Appeal Book* (Toronto, 1885), p. 12. Copy in the Ontario
Archives, Irving Papers, MU 1479, Box 41, Package 41, Item 1.

30. Alexander Morris, *The Treaties of Canada with the Indians* (Toronto, 1880;
facsimile edition, 1971). Jean Friesen provides a full sketch of Morris's

life in her biography of him in the *Dictionary of Canadian Biography*, volume 11 (1881–1890), pp. 608–15.

31. A. Margaret Evans, "The Mowat Era, 1872–1906: Stability and Progress," in *Profiles*, ed., Ontario Historical Society, p. 97.

32. *Regina v. The St. Catharine's Milling and Lumber Company, The Ontario Reports, No.* 10 (1885), p. 199.

33. Ibid., p. 201.

34. J.R. Miller, "'As a Politician He is a Great Enigma': the Social and Political Ideas of D'Alton McCarthy," *Canadian Historical Review*, Vol. 58 (1977), p. 401.

35. D'Alton McCarthy to John A. Macdonald, 5 January 1885, Macdonald Papers, pp. 98291–94, National Archives of Canada.

36. Walter Cassels to Oliver Mowat, 17 February 1885, Irving Papers, MU 1480, Box 42, Package 41, Item 8 (1), Ontario Archives.

37. *Regina v. The St. Catharine's Milling and Lumber Company, The Ontario Reports, No.* 10 (1885), pp. 201–3. See also "An Important Suit: *The Queen v. The St. Catharine's Milling and Lumber Company*," Toronto *Mail*, 19 May 1885.

38. See the column: "The Law Courts: Chancery Division," in the Toronto *Daily Mail* for Chancellor Boyd's appearances: 20, 21, 22, 23, 27, 29, 30 May; 2, 3, 9, 10, 11 June.

39. Chief Justice Hagarty in *Regina v. The St. Catharine's Milling and Lumber Company, Ontario Practice Reports*, Vol. 13 (1886), p. 148 [The Ontario Court of Appeal, 1886]; to Justice Steele in *Attorney-General for Ontario v. the Bear Island Foundation et. al.; Potts et. al. v. Attorney-General for Ontario, The Ontario Reports*, second series, Vol. 49, Part 7 (1985), pp. 380–83.

40. *Regina v. The St. Catharine's Milling and Lumber Company, The Ontario Reports*, Vol. 10 (1885), p. 206.

41. Ibid., pp. 229–30. A very useful summary of the case is contained in Douglas Sanders, "The Nishga Case," *B.C. Studies*, No. 19 (1973), pp. 6–9.

  William B. Henderson's several pages on the case, in his *Canada's Indian Reserves: The Usufruct in Our Constitution* (Ottawa, 1980), pp. 4–12, should also be examined. These are the only two secondary studies that I located that discuss, in any length, the Indian title aspect of this important case.

42. *Regina v. The St. Catharine's Milling and Lumber Company, The Ontario Reports, No.* 19 (1885), pp. 225–27. The first citation in this paragraph is from the Royal Proclamation of 1763.

43. Montgomery, "Franchise," p. 14.

44. Beal and Macleod, *Prairie Fire*, p. 292.

45. *Regina v. St. Catharine's Milling and Lumber Company, Ontario Practice Reports*, No. 13, p. 148.

46. Geoffrey S. Lester, *Inuit Territorial Rights in the Canadian Northwest Territories* (Ottawa, 1984), p. 49.

47. D'Alton McCarthy to Sir John A. Macdonald, 15 January 1887, Macdonald Papers, pp. 26763–65, National Archives of Canada. "Mowat," p. 170.

48. "The St. Catharine's Milling and Lumber Company and the Queen, on the Information of the Attorney General for the Province of Ontario," *Supreme Court Reports*, No. 13, pp. 580, 589.

49. A chief from the Treaty 3 area quoted in Morris, *Treaties*, p. 62. D'Alton McCarthy might also have asked Charles Nolin (1837–1907), Riel's first cousin, to appear; Nolin witnessed the signing of Treaty 3 in 1873, see Morris, *Treaties*, p. 325.

50. For a general review of racial attitudes in nineteenth century Canada, see Thomas F. Gossett, *Race: The History of an Idea in North America* (Dallas, 1963) and for the Canadian experience, Bruce G. Trigger, *Natives and Newcomers* (Kingston, Ontario, 1985), pp. 3–49.

51. Boyd called the Report, "an admirable *resumé* of what has been done in the earlier history of Canada." Boyd in *Regina v. St. Catharine's Milling and Lumber Company, The Ontario Reports*, No. 10 (1885), p. 211. My thanks to Jim Morrison for this insight.

52. "Report on the Affairs of the Indians in Canada, laid before the Legislative Assembly, 20th March 1845," Canada, Legislative Assembly, Journals, Session 1844–5, Volume 4, Appendix EEE, p. 5. "The Commissioners have not had an opportunity, and they did not consider it necessary, to examine the official correspondence prior to the year 1827."

53. I confess the difficulties of locating documents (before the establishment of well-organized Canadian archives) would have been horrendous. Gilbert C. Paterson, "Land Settlement in Upper Canada, 1738–1840," in *16th Report of the Department of Archives for the Province of Ontario* (Toronto, 1921), p. 219, points out some of the difficulties.

54. Speech of Colonel Simcoe to the Western Indians, Navy Hall, 22 June 1793, published in *The Correspondence of John Graves Simcoe*, ed. E.A. Cruikshank, 5 volumes (Toronto, 1923–31), Vol. 1, p. 364.

55. Peter Russell to Robert Prescott, 3 July 1798, published in *The Correspondence of the Honourable Peter Russell* ed. E.A. Cruikshank, 3 volumes (Toronto, 1932–36), Volume 2, p. 199.

56. Proceedings of a Meeting with the Chippewa Indians of Matchedash and Lake Simcoe at Gwillembury, 8–9 June 1811, C.O. 42, 351, p. 132 (mfm. Ontario Archives).

57. Paterson, "Land Settlement," p. 220. See also *the Correspondence of Lieutenant-Governor John Graves Simcoe*, ed. Cruikshank, Vol. 3, pp. 240–42.

58. *Regina v. St. Catharine's Milling and Lumber Company, The Ontario Reports*, Vol. 10, pp. 239, 206.

59. Peter Jones, *History of the Ojebway Indians* (London, 1861), p. 71.

60. George Copway, *The Life, History and Travels of Ka-ge-ga-gah-bowh (George Copway)* (Albany, 1847), pp. 19–20.

61. "The St. Catharine's Milling and Lumber Company and the Queen, on the Information of the Attorney General for the Province of Ontario," *Supreme Court Reports*, Vol. 13, p. 596.

62. Lord Watson in St. Catharine's Milling and Lumber Company and the Queen, on the Information of the Attorney-General for Ontario," *A.C. [Appeal Court]*, Vol. 10, pp. 31–32. Morris Zaslow provides a short, useful summary of the Privy Council decision in *The Opening of the Canadian North, 1870–1914* (Toronto, 1971), p. 150.

63. Leroy Little Bear, "A Concept of Native Title," Canadian Association in Support of Native Peoples, *Bulletin*, Vol. 17, No. 3 (December 1976), p. 30.

64. "St. Catharine's Milling and Lumber Company and the Queen, on the Information of the Attorney-General for Ontario," *A.C. [Appeal Court]*, Vol. 10, p. 25.

65. Jim Miller to the author, 6 December 1985. Armstrong, *Politics*, pp. 29–30.

66. Cited in *Attorney-General for Ontario v. Bear Island Foundation et al.; Potts et al. v. Attorney-General for Ontario, The Ontario Reports*, second series, Vol. 49, Part 7 (1985), p. 382.

67. Montgomery, "Franchise," p. 25.

68. David T. McNabb, "The Administration of Treaty 3: The Location of the Boundaries of Treaty 3 Indian Reserves in Ontario, 1873–1915," in *As Long as the Sun Shines and Water Flows*, eds., Ian A.L. Getty and Antoine S. Lussier (Vancouver, 1983), pp. 145–57.

69. Leo Waisberg, Ethnohistorian, TARR Grand Council Treaty #3, Kenora, Ontario to the author, 17 December 1985.

MAURICE F.V. DOLL

3 The Archaeology of the Buffalo Lake Métis Settlement, Approximately 1872 to 1878

THE PROVINCIAL MUSEUM of Alberta began research in historical archaeology in 1965. In conjunction with the Historic Sites program at the Museum, the focus was on the early fur trade. As outlined by Kidd (1985: 14), attention was directed towards various objectives, initially two:

(1) The positive identification, by date and company, of various fur trade sites.

(2) The recovery in context of a representative collection of early fur trade artifacts, also facilitating the first objective.

With respect to an individual historic site, archaeological methods were used to emphasize the following:

(1) The delineation and identification of structural features within the site.

(2) The identification of construction methods used.

(3) The establishment of the relationship of features within the site.

(4) The reconstruction of the past environment and subsistence base through the recovery of faunal remains and other organic material.

(5) The qualitative conformation or delineation of human behaviours within the site.

With the establishment of a data base and in conjunction with inter-site comparisons and archival data, Provincial Museums researchers attempted to achieve the following results:

FIGURE 3.1.   Present extent of Aspen Parkland and the location of the
Buffalo Lake Métis site, Alberta

(1) The construction of a regional chronology of fur trade artifacts with reference to form and manufacture, and perhaps of architectural types in the late eighteenth and early nineteenth centuries.
(2) The formulation of a set of criteria to distinguish the major trading companies, in particular the North West and Hudson's Bay companies, prior to 1821.
(3) The production of a more sophisticated analysis of faunal materials and of the environmental base of the fur trade, using studies of butchering methods, quantitative analysis, etc.
(4) The development of a demographic analysis delineating the fur trade post population and its composition, with some reference to the use of impinging environments and the interaction with satellite populations such a Métis hunter's camps, temporary Indian encampments, etc.

It was with these same objectives that archaeological research was begun in 1970 at Métis buffalo-hunter's camp on Buffalo Lake believed to have been occupied between 1872 and 1878.

THE AREA

The Buffalo Lake region of south-central Alberta (Figure 3.1) is characterized by a glaciated landscape with numerous moraine and outwash features. The Buffalo Lake moraine system, in which the Buffalo Lake Métis site is found, covers the entire eastern part of the Central Highland physiographic division and extends beyond it to the north and east (Stalker 1960: 8–9). Four other adjacent Métis sites are also located in wooded areas of similar topographic relief: Salois' Crossing or Duhamel, Tail Creek, Dried Meat Hill and Todd's Crossing, near Ponoka.

The Aspen Parkland that characterizes the Buffalo Lake area contains two major ecosystems, woodland and grassland. These tend to form a patchwork of aspen stands and irregular open grassy areas. Scattered throughout are several bodies of water dominated by Buffalo, Boss and Lynn Lakes, and including numerous smaller permanent and temporary sloughs. One would expect to find great diversity

FIGURE 3.2.   Map of Buffalo Lake Métis site, showing locations of excavated and
unexcavated cabins

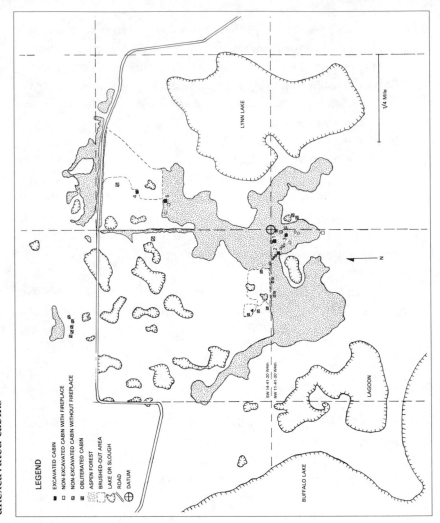

LEGEND

■ EXCAVATED CABIN
□ NON-EXCAVATED CABIN WITH FIREPLACE
▨ NON-EXCAVATED CABIN WITHOUT FIREPLACE
▨ OBLITERATED CABIN
     ASPEN FOREST
     LAKE OR SLOUGH
     ROAD
⊕ DATUM

LYNN LAKE

BUFFALO LAKE

LAGOON

N

1/4 Mile

SW 14-41-20 W4th
NW 11-41-20 W4th

in the floral assemblage, a diversity and richness that is also reflected in the faunal assemblage of the area (Doll 1982: 16).

The remaining visible portion of the Buffalo Lake Métis site is situated on a rise of land strategically located between Buffalo and Lynn Lakes (Figure 3.2). During periods of high lake levels, this rise forms a peninsula with very limited access by land. According to local residents this "peninsula" contained the only major source of logs for the construction of houses after the turn of the twentieth century. The forest growing in the area subsequent to the abandonment of the site by the Métis Hivernants (Winterers) grew uninhibited, being protected by the surrounding lakes and sloughs, until destroyed by a major fire in 1910, which also destroyed what remained of any superstructures of the Métis cabins. The peninsula, except for areas under cultivation, has become reforested since the end of the Second World War.

A general ecological framework was used as a guide to research strategy, since the location of plant and animal resources, in very large measure, determined the location and distribution of past human settlements.

Marcel Giraud, a noted ethno-historian, realized in the 1930s the ecological importance of the Parkland to the Métis buffalo hunters, a theme which is constant throughout the archaeological research at Buffalo Lake:

> Everywhere, winter-rovers [Hivernants] were attracted by these wooded, undulating lands which dominated the horizons of the Prairies (like Touchwood Hills and Boss Hill) because of the resources which they offered and in spite of the uncertainty created by the vagaries of the climate (Giraud 1954: 13).

PREVIOUS RESEARCH

In 1959, Dr. Richard G. Forbis, then of the Glenbow Foundation, initially recorded the Buffalo Lake Métis Site, assigning to it the Borden designation FdPe1. The existence and location of the site, however, had been well known among the local farming community for at least sixty years prior to its "official" recording, notably among the Hereonomous, Rider and Hays families (Doll 1983: 2).

Although portions of the site had been plundered by unscrupulous "pothunters," and there has been some inevitable loss to agriculture, it is to the very great credit of the present land owners, the Rider family, that a good portion of the main site still exists. Portions have been protected by the Hays family as well.

It was not until 1970 that professional archaeologists began scientific investigation of the site. Initiated by Robert S. Kidd, Curator of Archaeology at the Provincial Museum of Alberta, preliminary excavations were conducted with David Crone in 1970 and Kendal Arnold in 1971 on two of the more badly disturbed cabin localities. The writer, under the supervision of Robert S. Kidd, took responsibility for the field operations of the Buffalo Lake Project between 1973 and 1982, with the mapping of approximately 88 Métis cabin locations grouped in small clusters, the partial excavation of three Métis cabins (Cabins 3, 4 and 5), and the excavation of two major prehistoric sites (Boss Hill Locality 1 and 2).

RESULTS

For the region as a whole, research has documented continuous, though seasonal, human occupation of the northeast shore of Buffalo Lake for approximately 8,000 years (Doll 1982). At the Métis site, the partial documentation of architectural features has been accomplished (see Doll 1977, 1979, 1982, 1983; Doll and Kidd 1976), although this represents a sample of only about 3 per cent of the site. The dimensions of the five excavated cabins are as follows:

1. 30 x 13 feet
2. 14.5 x 13 feet (with some suggestion that the length may have been as much as 30 feet)
3. 24 x 15 feet
4. 24 x 24 feet
5. 26 x 24 feet (approximately).

Wood preservation was especially poor, and the wood is bound to deteriorate even further through natural decomposition. In addition, Cabin 5, with the best preserved features, was only superficially excavated because of a lack of time, insufficient manpower, and problems in obtaining an archaeological research permit.

The location, apparent type of construction, artifact sample, and faunal remains from the excavated cabins have demonstrated cultural and chronological contemporaneity. More specifically, the cultural features excavated in Cabins 4 and 5 exhibit similar characteristics to those excavated in Cabins 1, 2 and 3. Most depressions, regardless of whether they were located in the cabin interior or exterior, appear to have served as borrow pits for clay used in fireplace construction and for wall plaster or chinking. Subsequently, these features were used as storage pits, notably those located in the interior of the cabins. Many of the depressions were ultimately used as refuse pits. The notable exception to this sequence was a feature associated with Cabin 4. This was the only cribbed and bark-lined depression found. Its only function appears to have been that of "clean" storage, perhaps for fresh meat. There was no evidence to suggest that it was initially excavated to exploit a natural clay lens for mud plaster, or ultimately used as a refuse pit.

Interior depressions (storage pits) were covered by a log or plank trap door lid, as attested by the rotted wood remains with nails and the hinge found associated with these features. There is no evidence for anything other than packed clay for flooring in the remainder of the cabin structures, despite the numerous historical references to wooden floors in Métis cabins at other sites such as Tail Creek, St. Albert, Cypress Hills, and Batoche.

All cabin structures were heated by a single fireplace located in the centre of either the north, west, or south wall. The fireplace bases were generally constructed using granitic cobbles from the nearby lake shores (Boss Lake, Lynn Lake, or Buffalo Lake). Chimneys do not usually survive in the archeological record, but archival resources and local informants report a wattle-and-daub superstructure.

The existence of associated adjacent structures such as barns, sheds, toilets, icehouses, or smokehouses is not demonstrated. Upon examination of the surface features of Cabin 5, it is obvious that there is a much more complex architectural association than was observed in previously excavated cabins. The other cultural information derived from the investigation of such associations might be expected to reflect this complexity. It is, therefore, critical to the overall inter-site and intra-site interpretations that field investigations at Cabin 5 be resumed and completed.

The artifact sample from the Métis cabins is generally homogeneous, suggesting cultural contemporaneity, and it is comparable to assemblages from other historic sites which date from the mid-1870s. The cabins provide evidence for the use by their occupants of a variety of firearms, including flint and percussion-lock muzzle-loading arms as well as rim-fire and centre-fire breechloading arms.

Of architectural importance is the general paucity of iron nails, other than a few associated with interior storage pits. This certainly suggests that construction techniques were adopted which minimized the use of, and dependence upon, nails.

The artifact sample from the Buffalo Lake Métis site also reflects the commercial intercourse with traders who had access to both British and American sources of supply.

The intra-site distribution of certain ceramic patterns, faunal remains, and lithic tools may be important with respect to establishing population distinctions between the many different Métis core groups wintering at Buffalo Lake. Kinship patterns are beginning to emerge through the use of archival records; however, much of this data it still undergoing analysis.

In conclusion, the Buffalo Lake Métis Site, FdPe1, offers a unique opportunity in which archaeological, ecological ethno-historic, and socio-political data can be combined to produce a holistic anthropological study. The data derived from this study upon its completion will not only serve the academic community but the public as well. The latter concern can best be addressed through the creative use of the scientific data in continued field research, and eventually, a site development program in conjunction with a travelling and permanent museum exhibit. We have only scratched the surface, so to speak; much more field research must be done.

REFERENCES

Doll, Maurice F.V. 1977. *Report on Project 76–15, Field Season 1976; The Boss Hill Site (FdPe4) Locality 2; The Boss Hill Site (FdPe) Locality 1; The Buffalo Lake Métis Site (FdPe1)*. Alberta Culture, Provincial Museum of Alberta, Human History Section, Archaeology Program, Edmonton. Report on file at the Archaeological Survey of Alberta, Edmonton.

————. 1979. *Report on Project 78–36, Field Season 1978: The Boss Hill Site(FdPe4) Locality 2; The Boss Hill Site (FdPe) Locality 1; The Buffalo Lake Métis Site (FdPe1)*. Alberta Culture, Provincial Museum of Alberta, Human History Section, Archaeology Program, Edmonton. Report on file at the Archaeological Survey of Alberta, Edmonton.

————. 1982. *The Boss Hill Site (FdPe4) Locality 2: Pre-Archaic Manifestations In the Parkland of Central Alberta, Canada*. Provincial Museum of Alberta, Human History Occasional Paper No. 2, Alberta Culture, Historical Resources Division.

————. 1983. *Report on Project 82–27, Field Season 1982; The Buffalo Lake Métis Site (FdPe1)*. Alberta Culture, Provincial Museum of Alberta, Human History Section, Archaeology Program, Edmonton. Report on file at the Archaeological Survey of Alberta, Edmonton.

Doll, Maurice F.V. and Robert S. Kidd. 1976. *Report on Project 75–26, Field Season 1975; The Buffalo Lake Métis Site (FdPe1)*. Alberta Culture, Provincial Museum of Alberta, Human History Section, Archaeology Program, Edmonton. Report on file at the Archaeological Survey of Alberta, Edmonton.

Giraud, Marcel. 1954. "Métis Settlement in the Northwest Territories." *Saskatchewan History* 7, no. 1, pp. 1–16.

Kidd, Robert S. 1985. *Archaeological Tests at the Probable Site of the First Fort Edmonton or Augustus, 1975 to early 1980s*. Provincial Museum of Alberta, Human History, Occasional Paper No. 3, Alberta Culture, Historical Resources Division.

Stalker, A.M. 1960. "Surficial Geology of the Red Deer-Stettler Map Area Alberta." *Geological Survey of Alberta*, Memoir 306, Department of Mines and Technical Surveys Canada, Queen's Printer, Ottawa.

PATRICIA ROY

4 Law and Order in British Columbia in the 1880s
Images and Realities

IN MAY 1885 as General Middleton's forces closed in
on Louis Riel, residents of Victoria gathered at a public meeting
chaired by Mayor R.P. Rithet to consider the "defenceless condition"
of the city and to plan the organization of a volunteer defence service.
A few days later, some patriotic ladies discussed how they might care
for the war wounded. Throughout the spring, British Columbia newspapers carried frequent reports on the military situation and rued the
vulnerability of the province. "Our present artillery armament consists of one gun and a half, which might be useful to frighten the
crows," mused the *Mainland Guardian* of New Westminster. "The simple truth," explained the Victoria *Daily Standard*, "is that the whole
coast of British Columbia is undefended." "Remote as this 'Victoria of
ours' is from the centre of government and the seat of trouble,"
observed the *British Colonist*, "the people are prepared to move with a
common impulse in defence of the honor of the motherland." The
more Canadian-minded Victoria *Times* suggested that

> if Canada is so loyal to the Empire that she is prepared to send reg-
> iments to the Soudan...she surely is not lacking in a loyalty to her-
> self that will prompt her to defend her own territory...The danger
> of Fenian or other piratical expeditions against our city, or of
> Indian disturbances, will be increased with a prolonged and gen-
> eral European war...[1]

The enemy that British Columbians feared was not Riel but the Russians. Indeed, most British Columbia newspaper readers in the spring of 1885 were as well informed about the threat of war between Britain and Russia in Afghanistan as they were about the events on the South Saskatchewan.

Because war with Russia would be a British war, the Imperial Navy at its Esquimalt base would have a major role in protecting the province. Though additions to the Imperial fleet at Esquimalt were reassuring,[2] British Columbians were also pleased when Canada's Minister of Militia and Defence, Sir Adolphe Caron, and General Middleton arrived in the fall to ascertain local defence requirements. The needs were great. The only fortifications were four earthen and timber batteries constructed at Dominion expense in 1878 but now out of repair and 202 militia officers and men in Victoria. Increasing the strength of this force was almost impossible because of the high wages civilians could earn and "the paucity of the inhabitants."[3] Militia officials were not unduly concerned; in case of emergency they could bring in reinforcements via the Canadian Pacific Railway.

The strategists who sat at editorial desks had ambivalent views of the defensive role of the CPR. They agreed it could transport reinforcements; they feared its role in commerce and imperial defence would make it an attractive target for Russian invaders. As well, some argued that British Columbia was a likely target because of her "inexhaustible coal supply."[4] Nevertheless, debates on whether defences should be concentrated at Esquimalt or dispersed to such vulnerable points as Nanaimo, Burrard Inlet and New Westminster reflected real estate rivalries as much as military considerations. Indeed, some editors were more enthusiastic about the business opportunities an influx of soldiers would create than they were fearful of war.[5]

Despite the local excitement, British Columbians closely followed the North West Rebellion though some got their news via New York and Montreal.[6] British Columbia editors quickly judged Riel. Indeed, in August 1884, on receiving news of his return from the United States, the *Times* proclaimed that "the cruel, cold-blooded murder of poor Scott...calls for revenge." While they might attack the Dominion government's administration of Indian affairs and blame Sir John A. Macdonald for the Rebellion, all agreed that if Riel, as ring leader, got "his just desserts he will dangle from the end of a rope." As racial conflict rose, the British Columbia press had no sympathy for those who opposed his execution. British Columbians also sought to turn the Rebellion to their advantage. As it ended, the *Colonist* noted that a "feeling of insecurity" would persist in the North West while "the perfect security which British Columbia has to offer immigrants ought to be and is an important factor in promoting the settlement of the country."[7]

Because they were anxious to have immigrants and investors, British Columbians were keen to promote their province as a place where law and order prevailed. Local newspapers noted "the reverence for the law, which is a marked characteristic of this community, and the best proof of their advanced social condition and fitness for self-government..."[8] In particular, British Columbians contrasted their experience favorably with that of the United States. Immigration propaganda clearly expressed these images; the reality, as shall be seen in several case studies, suggests that British Columbia's hold on law and order was often tenuous.

A wide variety of promotional literature praised the province's law-abiding characteristics. A standing advertisement of the provincial Immigration Bureau in the booster magazine, *Resources of British Columbia*, proclaimed "law and order prevail in a high degree and justice is firmly and fairly administered." A catechism about British Columbia for use in British schools included the question: "Are the people orderly and Loyal? Yes; the same as in Great Britain and in Canada." Despite this apparent uncertainty about British Columbia's place in Canada, the federal government, in a pamphlet designed to attract settlers to the Pacific coast province stated:

Administration de la Justice. Elle toujours été satisfaisante. La vie et la propriété sont protégé par des lois juste *et bien exécutées*. La grande affluence de travailleurs pour les chemins de fer de toute nationalités, a dû nécessiter l'emploi de quelques constables additionels. Le "Bulletin de San-Francisco" (Californie), dit: "Il est bon que nos concitoyens remarquent que nos voisins de la Colombie Britannique ne sont pas aussi indulgents pour les meurtriers que nous les sommes de ce côte-ci de la ligne.

Such a statement cannot be dismissed as Canadian chauvinism. In his *History of British Columbia, 1792-1887*, the American historian Hubert H. Bancroft reported, "the law has been brought to everyman's door. Of late years it has been a matter for congratulation that notwithstanding the variety of race and diversity of interests, peace and order have been maintained without resorting to any unusual expedients." Such claims continued. An immigration pamphlet published in 1890 pronounced: "Public order in most exemplary. In very few respects does British Columbia partake of the character of the 'Wild West.' While legislation is not puritanically restrictive, there is at the same time little disorder and less crime."[9]

There was some puritanism. A young man in Victoria, charged with swimming in the nude, was let off with a warning to himself and others that "boys and young men cannot any longer be permitted to expose their persons as they have been doing in the past." In New Westminster, a similar case caused a great sensation since charges were laid by some of the city's most prominent ladies after several skinny-dipping boys, including future premier Richard McBride, disturbed their picnic.[10] That such breaches of morality led to court suggests that the two major cities of the province were more Victorian than a part of the "Wild West." Yet a CPR guidebook reported that in Victoria there was:

> ...a little disproportion in some callings. For instance there are ten breweries and wholesale liquor establishments and forty-five retail bars, besides twenty-two groceries where liquor can be sold but there are only two bookstores. The plenitude of liquor, however, speaks well for the climate, for in spite of these establishments and of four stores especially devoted to the sale of fire arms, there are only two undertakers.[11]

Despite the lack of bookstores, Victorians were interested in culture. They talked about founding a university to attract those who might wish, "their children to enjoy benefits of a thorough British education without exposing them to the extremes of climate in the eastern provinces." They also persuaded the provincial government to establish a museum, not only for the practical benefit of studying the province's minerals and natural history but also to retain and display Indian antiquities which were yearly being, "taken away in great numbers to the enrichment of other museums and private collections."[12]

The Indians were more than just creators of curios. They were, in fact, the majority of the population. The 1881 census recorded that slightly more than half the population consisted of Indians and that in every part of the province, except immediately around the settlements of New Westminster, Hope, Yale, Nanaimo, Victoria, and Quesnelmouth (where Chinese dominated), Indians formed an overwhelming majority of the population.[13] British Columbia wanted more white immigrants.

As part of the campaign to encourage immigration and investment, both the federal and provincial governments advertised that the Indians of British Columbia were peaceful and law-abiding. An 1883 federal immigration pamphlet declared:

> The Indians of British Columbia are remarkable for their peacable and law abiding character. They are largely employed in the salmon fisheries and in seal hunting etc. Some of them are farmers and raise cattle, others are miners, and altogether they contribute largely to the trade and industries of the province.

Similarly, a special British Columbia issue of the Portland-based *West Shore* magazine promised that, "the intending settler may depend upon finding the Indians peacable, intelligent, eager to learn and industrious to a degree unknown elsewhere among the aborigines of America."[14]

For local consumption, however, there were notes of foreboding. In New Westminster, for example, controversy developed over the, "presence of half civilized gangs" who camped in vacant places. Some residents claimed the Indians provided trade for city merchants; others contended that the Indians were a "nuisance" and a "blot" on the city. While admitting there were a, "number of most respectable Indians in the city," the *British Columbian* argued that

Indians should, "be put upon their own reserves" where they would, "be under the control of the responsible agent and free from many corrupting influences which are now leading them to ruin." In a paternalistic but honest editorial, the *Mainland Guardian* advised its readers: "The Indians are our wards, and we should look after and protect them, not only from themselves, but from the avaricious and vicious habits of the disreputable whites... We are indebted to them for the lands we have appropriated in this country." Similarly, the *Colonist* contended: "The Indians of the province have claim to the land which a due regard for the public safety should deter the government, the house and the people from ignoring."[15] In the more settled parts of the province, the Indians could do little to protest against the creation of reserves and the opening of the remaining lands for white settlement, but in the remote parts of the province, major confrontations made British Columbians aware that native peoples would not quietly surrender their lands or accept the government's rule. Some long-simmering conflicts in the north west illustrate this point and two other themes: a perennial conflict between the Dominion and provincial governments over their respective responsibilities for the administration of Indian affairs and the determination of the provincial government to maintain law and order and protect life and property even in the remotest parts of the province "at whatever cost."[16]

The first conflict to attract attention in the 1880s occurred at the "model" Indian community of Metlakatla on the Skeena River. This well-known story is complicated by rival claims of the Nishgas and Tsimshians to fishing rights on the Nass River,[17] by conflicts over the ownership of land, and by theological and personal quarrels between William Duncan, the evangelical lay preacher of the Church Missionary Society, and his fellow Anglican, Bishop William Ridley. No one doubted that the disputes between the rival missionaries were "inimical to the peace and harmony of the village" as well as to the spreading of the gospel in surrounding territories.[18]

Late in 1882 a dispute over the ownership of two acres of land known as Mission Point and the buildings thereon threatened violence between Duncan's numerous followers and the handful who supported Ridley. The provincial government deemed the "emergency...sufficiently serious" to send officials to investigate.[19] Unfortunately, no suitable British vessel was available. Thus, Premier Robert Beaven accepted the offer of the captain of an American revenue cutter, the *Oliver Wolcott*, to take provincial officials to Metlakatla to investigate and restore the peace. Dependence on a foreign vessel offended the local press. The *Columbian*, for example, complained "it would have been bad enough to have sent one of our own war ships to settle a personal squabble between two Christian missionaries: but we all know how ready the Americans are to shoot Indians."[20] Even when Americans were trying to be helpful, British Columbians could not resist the chance to advertise the alleged superiority of their law and order!

The peace was a temporary one. During the summer of 1883 both the federal government and the British Admiralty urged the provincial government to intervene to end the "unhappy variances" between Ridley and Duncan.[21] By the fall of 1883 the dispute had taken on new and more ominous overtones as two of Ridley's supporters started to build a dwelling on the disputed land. A justice of the peace from nearby Port Simpson warned of bloodshed.[22] Premier William Smithe, who was anxious to pass responsibility for maintaining law and order among the Indians to the federal government, believed the disturbance threatened "most serious consequences to the settlement...and will probably involve the whole Indian population of the North West Coast."[23] He persuaded the federal government to appoint an Indian Agent but Duncan's adherents refused to accept his authority, in part because they denied the right of the government to survey land which they claimed through aboriginal title.[24]

Fears of "lawlessness among the natives on the coast" continued. Increasingly, it was apparent that the quarrel was not a theological one but reflected the Metlakatlans' beliefs that the federal Indian Act was unsuitable for them, that giving them an agent "would be like trying to put a small pair of shoes on feet too big for them," and that they owned the whole of Metlakatla.[25] Premier Smithe was not impressed. Such resistance, he argued, was "fraught with danger to the persons and welfare of the entire Indian population of the north west coast of British Columbia and indeed to the whole community in that vicinity of white traders and settlers also."[26] Eventually, the federal government agreed to contribute to the salary of A.C. Elliott, a former premier, as Stipendiary Magistrate at Metlakatla but Elliott did not take up his post immediately.

Meanwhile, the Metlakatlans refused to allow a government surveyor to survey the Mission Point lands. More significantly, the dispute was becoming part of a greater conflict that threatened white settlers, including some miners, throughout the Skeena Valley. An Indian in the employ of A.C. Yeomans had drowned in the course of his work. In revenge, Aht-ah, the drowned man's father, stabbed Yeomans. The Skeena River Indians threatened to murder all the whites in the area and take possession of their property if Aht-ah were found guilty and executed.[27] No one, at least in Victoria, wanted mercy for Aht-ah. The *Standard* argued that his execution would "impress the natives forcibly with the terribly serious consequences which attended the taking of life," that the Indians "must be taught that they have to obey the law as strictly as the white man." When the government did commute the death sentence, miners, who were wintering in Victoria, passed a resolution warning that a commutation would be "the means of inciting and encouraging the Indians to commit more murders and depredations." They called on the government to protect their lives and property.[28]

Nevertheless, Metlakatla remained the focus of the provincial government's attention. As Attorney-General A.E.B. Davie explained to the federal Minister of Justice:

Two ideas dominate Indian minds, first, all lands belong to them—second, Government powerless to enforce law. They talk Majuba Hill & refer recent abortive visit gunboat with Powell and McKay [the Dominion Indian Agent]. The white community that region generally accuses Duncan of disloyal teaching and being cause disaffection, which has already spread amongst neighbouring Indians of North West Coast and continues. Have now direct evidence of Duncan's recent seditious utterances and would have proceeded for treason felony but for time limit Dominion Act. We intend however arresting and prosecuting him at Common Law for high misdemeanour of seditious speaking...[and have asked for] instructions to Naval Authorities to aid civil power.[29]

Rumours circulated in Victoria that HMS *Mutine* was under orders to sail for Metlakatla but the order was withdrawn pending the appointment of a Commission of Inquiry.[30] Despite some recognition that the Indians had a "fundamental grievance in the question of land," the press was not prepared to concede that the Indians had a claim to all lands outside the reservations. In any event, several editors called for "decisive action" to let the Indians know that "they have to obey the law as strictly as the white man."[31]

Reluctantly, for it was hesitant to spend the money,[32] the provincial government had appointed a Commission of Inquiry. The commissioners, who recognized the importance of the ownership of the two acres at Mission Point, were also concerned that the Indian Council at Metlakatla, a body without any legal status, was making laws itself "irrespective and in disregard of the laws of the land" and thus setting "an evil example to neighbouring Indians." The Commission's preferred solution to the main problem was "To assert—and if necessary, by force of arms—the right of the province to the two acres, by the survey of it as Government land."[33]

The Legislature, agreeing with the warning of M.W.T. Drake, a Victoria City M.L.A., that "the government would either have to rule the country as white men or give it up to the Indians," called on the Dominion government to compel obedience to the law. It also instructed the provincial government to survey the lands at Mission Point as government lands and "take measures to protect the white settlers from the encroachment of Indians." Some editors applauded the decision as demonstrating to the Indians that the authorities were "in earnest in their endeavors to stamp out the high-handed and lawless proceedings that have taken place on the Northwest corner." If the government did not survey the land, the *Post* suggested, the Indians would regard it as a sign of weakness. The *Colonist*, however, feared that armed force might be necessary to complete the survey.[34] In the end, it was.

When provincial surveyors, accompanied by Superintendent Roycraft of the Provincial Police, arrived at Mission Point, the residents presented only a written protest.[35] Eighteen months later, when the surveyor returned to complete his work, the Metlakatlans seized his instruments and prevented his party from landing in the village.[36] Certain Metlakatlans also invaded Bishop Ridley's premises. Ordinarily, explained Premier Smithe, this was a matter for the courts, not the provincial executive. However, in view of the strain and complicated conditions of things generally at Metlakatla, the absence of competent judicial authority on the spot and the danger that "breaches of the peace...might result in possible bloodshed and involve the entire Indian population of the coast," Smithe sent a stipendiary magistrate, a posse of policemen, and a warship to destroy the building on the land held in trust for the Church Missionary Society. He stressed he was only acting to prevent bloodshed.[37] The commander of the warship, who believed the law must be "enforced at once,"[38] positioned his ship so he could use force if required. Fortunately, the civilian authorities had little difficulty in establishing order, completing the survey, and bringing eight of Duncan's supporters to trial.[39] In response to continued Indian concerns over land, the provincial and Dominion governments appointed a joint commission to examine this problem. The Commission discovered many roots for these worries but did not accede to the Indians' request for a treaty.[40] By that time Duncan and his followers were on their way to Alaska.

Duncan's departure meant the end of Metlakatla as a centre of unrest; it did not ensure peace on the north west coast. The inland settlement of Hazelton soon became the scene of conflict. In March, 1888, Alfred E. Green, a Methodist missionary, reported that only a promise that the government "would see that the man who did the murder would be punished" had persuaded friends of the late Chief Neatsgu from murdering Kit-wan-cool Jim, the alleged killer of the chief. Green warned that some Indians on the Upper Skeena were constantly making trouble and "the life of a white man is not safe in that part of the country." The Attorney-General's office immediately ordered the constable at Port Simpson to arrest Kit-wan-cool Jim.[41]

Administering justice from a distance was never easy; when the men on the spot did not co-operate with one another, it was very difficult. When Constable Anderson refused to act until he had more information and the weather improved, Magistrate S.Y Wooton accused him of being "insulting," "discourteous," and "as obnoxious as he can possibly can." The tension mounted. A Hudson's Bay Company official reported the Indians would not allow the company or anyone else to take a pack train on the portage, that miners were no longer willing to winter at Hazelton, that he was advising the Company to build a stockade around its store at Hazelton since "the existing state of affairs at that place is deplorable and the law is to all intents and purposes a dead letter," and that Kit-wan-cool Jim was still "at large and openly defies arrest."[42]

By the time Constable Anderson had laid an information against Kit-wan-cool Jim, he had requested help to check any resistance. Specifically, he wanted five men "armed each with a revolver and a Winchester carbine." The provincial government sent the five constables but, as Kit-wan-cool Jim, who held a pistol, tried to escape, one of the constables shot him. Another constable reported, "Excitement ran high and it became threatening, I though it best to be gone before too late, most on account to prevent bloodshed." Concerned about the safety of the white settlers and the police, he asked that "without delay," fifteen to twenty men be sent along with Superintendent Roycraft of anyone with "high authority" as he had pacified the chiefs by promising they would soon be able to present their grievances to such a person.[43] The fact that the promise of a "high authority" calmed the chiefs suggests the unrest was not as great as it seemed.

Meanwhile, another provincial policeman, Captain Napoleon Fitzstubbs, set off alone from Port Simpson to visit Hazelton and other points where he hoped to restore peace by counselling the Indians. Despite problems in thinking "composedly under the attacks of mosquitoes and gnats," the general feeling of hostility among the river Indians, and their complaints that "the whites had interfered with the operation of their own laws and had taken the life of one of their own race," Fitzstubbs tried to get the various chiefs to co-operate "in the maintenance of order and peace." Telling them that "the law was like the Skeena, it must run its course and not be diverted," he warned that "the law of the whites was supreme and would have to be obeyed to the extinction of their own." Fitzstubbs ascertained that most of the Indians' ill-feelings resulted from a deadly measles epidemic, their continuing fear that whites would seize lands, the lack of checks on previous misconduct, and familiarity with the few whites in the district who had tended to destroy or "lessen the respect and fear in which our race was once held by them." Fitzstubbs admitted that none of the Indians favoured "the supremacy of any law but their own," but believed there was no reason to be alarmed.[44]

To the handful of white settlers who were barricaded in the Hudson's Bay building, the situation was much more alarming. The called the government's attention "to the unsettled state of affairs" around Hazelton and "the fact that our lives and property are in great, and we fear immediate danger." A Mr. Borland, a nonresident packer, who claimed that he had been allowed to leave only because he was a stranger and had promised not to return with policemen, carried the petition to Victoria.[45] Within a day of the news reaching the capital, the provincial cabinet asked that Battery "C" of the Active Militia be sent to Hazelton with a naval vessel.[46]

The federal government refused to accept any responsibility or pay any costs. It even advised Dr. I.W. Powell, its Superintendent of Indian Affairs in British Columbia, that the matter was "a purely Provincial one," that if he wished to accompany the provincial expedition, he must not commit the Dominion government to any expense. Nevertheless, it was "as Canadians" that the *Colonist* expressed pride in "our brave defenders as they marched through our streets." Excitement was high in Victoria and crowds gathered to see "the very unusual scene of a body of armed men marching along to uphold the supremacy of British law."[47]

The provincial government had been so alarmed by "the threatened Indian rising," compounded by rumours that a provincial constable and a Hudson's Bay Company official had been killed, that it alone authorized the despatch of the militia. The militia carried instructions that their chief goal was "to conciliate the Indians and win their confidence." Yet they were also told to disabuse the Indians of any notions "that the Queen has no authority, that the Dominion & Provincial Governments are foes instead of friends and that the Indians must keep out the white people and lawful authority." To avoid further conflict, the Attorney-General advised that in several cases involving homicide among the Indians themselves, the matters were "best let alone in a country in which hitherto only the tribal laws of the Indians have prevailed." He also ordered the militia to fire only "in the case of last resort," and informed the white residents of Hazelton that the government did not plan to keep an armed force in the area and they should move to the coast if they felt insecure.[48] The provincial government was determined to maintain law and order but not at all costs.

For almost two weeks, people in the southern part of the province, who had read such headlines as "The Indians in Arms," and "The Massacre Begins," knew nothing of what was happening on the Skeena. The press variously assessed blame for the uprising on the lenient treatment of Yeomans's murderer, the incompetence of the Department of Indian Affairs special agents, and the inadequacies of provincial special constables. It debated the efficiency with which the force had been organized and expressed the hope that the "Indian scare" would encourage Dominion authorities to put the local militia in order.[49]

The only interior newspaper, the Kamloops *Inland Sentinel*, had warned "a great deal of injury is done to the whole community by the publication of untruthful reports of an Indian rising and threatened massacres." Indeed, while waiting for news from the Skeena, British Columbians could read sensational reports in the eastern press. The Ottawa *Free Press* had a headline, "3,000 British Columbia Redskins on the Warpath"; a Montreal journal reported that Gabriel Dumont had warned the government that the British Columbia Indians were "dangerous"; and General Middleton was quoted as saying that he could have 5,000 men en route to British Columbia in twenty-four hours. Such "blood-curdling narratives," complained the *Colonist,* could "cause serious damage to the Province's future, more especially in the matter of immigration" as intending settlers, ignorant of provincial geography, would probably think Skeena was "very close to Victoria." A comment in the Montreal *Gazette* suggesting that order was being speedily restored was more welcome but a suggestion of the Toronto *Mail* and other Liberal journals that the dispute really arose from a conflict over land was summarily dismissed with the note that the issue "was consistent merely upon the killing of a fugitive from justice." Yet a few days later, in an editorial rejoicing in the fact that "'The Indian War,' as eastern papers have gratuitously termed the little difficulty on the Skeena, is at an end," the *Colonist* recalled: "We must never forget that the Indians have rights which should not be unduly interfered with. They were the original occupiers of the land."[50]

Finally the "cheering news" arrived; the affair was less serious than reported; the killing of white people was only a rumour; the militia had to do nothing more than set up their camp; the police had no trouble with the few Indians on the river; and the white residents of Hazelton were "at liberty."[51]

General satisfaction prevailed that the "show of force" would "have a good and lasting effect upon the Indians." As Superintendent Roycraft explained to the Attorney-General, the Skeena Indians "seem now to perfectly understand our power. They have promised to keep the law and their Chiefs will bring all offenders to justice." Six weeks later, one of his officers on the Skeena confirmed that because of the visit of the militia,

> the Indians even to the remotest interior...have now learned that the few scattered whites in the distant parts of the Province are neither forgotten, nor uncared for and many are the stories (exaggerated) of the vast numbers and power and appliances of the military encamped at the mount of the Skeena.

Yet he warned that there were still "some restless spirits" and he could not recommend discontinuing the service of one of his constables. The following spring, the provincial government was asking the

Dominion government to appoint an Indian agent at Hazelton because of "a growing feeling of distrust and discontent among the Indian population" as a result of the influence of certain native missionaries.[52] Law and order had been established but the government's hold on it was not very secure.

The Metkatla and Skeena incidents demonstrate how fears of Indian uprisings led to the possibility of armed intervention. Similarly, exaggerated fears led the provincial government in 1887 to request the Dominion government to send the North West Mounted Police to quell an apprehended Indian uprising in the East Kootenay.[53] Yet, incidents involving Indians were not the only cases illustrating the difficulty of maintaining law and order in an isolated setting and the potential for conflict over the administration of the law between Dominion and provincial authorities. Indeed, one of the liveliest examples of the lack of law and order concerned only white men—and officers of the law at that! These incidents, which make the convoluted plots of Gilbert and Sullivan seem simple and dull, occurred at Farwell (now Revelstoke), a major divisional point on the Canadian Pacific Railway which was then under construction.

Whereas in other provinces conflict over the regulation of the liquor trade led to the Judicial Committee of the Privy Council, in British Columbia such conflict threatened "civil war." In order to enforce prohibition and to assist in the maintenance of law and order, the federal government in 1869 passed the "Peace Preservation on Public Works Act" forbidding the sale of liquor within ten miles of railway construction. Because of the difficulties in enforcing the law and the lightness of its penalties, a number of British Columbia entrepreneurs engaged in the liquor trade and sometimes took out provincial licences. According to a CPR construction manager, "at all the available places near our Store Depots and large construction camps, we have numerous tents erected as stores, hotels, billiard saloons and the like, where liquor is freely sold." Not only were "drunkenness and crime...prevalent and increasing" but it was difficult to eject squatters whose tents often stood on the land the railway planned to use as right of way. In seeking to have the jurisdiction of the North West Mounted Police extended west to Kamloops, William Van Horne, the vice-president of the CPR stressed that "bad characters from south of the Boundary" were jeopardizing Canada's reputation "for the observance of the laws and maintenance of order."[54] Before the problem of jurisdiction over the liquor trade was resolved, the reputations of Canada and of British Columbia for maintaining law and order were somewhat tarnished.

The police force along the CPR route in British Columbia was small. Indeed the press in Victoria noted the area was "without any local authority" and that maintaining "the old British Columbia traditions of order and law abidingness in that busy eastern section of the province has become a pressing question." In the spring of 1885, Charles Todd, the federal commissioner of police and former provincial superintendent of police, was alone responsible for the line from the eastern border of the province to Kamloops. This included Farwell. Occasionally he could draw on the aid of two provincial constables and, when he was sure of the fine revenue to pay them, he appointed special constables. To supplement his own inadequate expense money, he served the provincial government as a stipendiary magistrate. Overwork and conflicts of interest were major problems. He found himself being

> obliged to spy around whiskey camps and try to talk some people into laying informations upon my own evidence in order to bring lawbreakers up before myself. In some instances I am obliged to serve my own summonses or else allow a quantity of liquor often amounting to two hundred and sometimes three hundred gallons to pass and be hidden in the woods contiguous to railways camps and then listen to bitter complaints about demoralized camps etc.

Nevertheless, he managed to keep "surprisingly good order." However, the illegal trade continued, especially in Farwell where in April, 1885, there were "probably twenty bars...selling spirits openly—without a shadow of a license." According to the *Inland Sentinel*, "when the Stipendiary Magistrate makes his visit there all the glasses and decanters are removed and no whiskey selling apparently goes on.

Half an hour after his back is turned the trade opens out in full blast."[55]

By the summer the problem at Farwell was a Dominion-Provincial squabble over jurisdiction. The federal government reminded the province that under the Peace Preservation Act, liquor could not be sold for twenty miles on either side of the rail line from the summit of the Rocky Mountains to a point 150 miles west. The province, which enjoyed the revenues from the sale of licences, promised it would "adequately enforce law & order in the district" if the Dominion police commissioner would stop interfering with the liquor traffic. The Dominion government, seeing no reason to withdraw the Peace Preservation Act, urged the province to instruct its officials to "prevent any conflict of authority."[56]

While the two governments sparred diplomatically, the men on the spot had been engaging in such a lively conflict that the Grand Jury complained that the dispute over liquor licences had "inflicted the greatest hardship and loss upon many respectable licensed hotel keepers and traders." By June, when the first phase of the quarrel began, the provincial government had appointed the ubiquitous Gilbert Malcolm Sproat as stipendiary magistrate at Farwell. Sproat's presence seemed to make Farwell more orderly. Although he did not close the liquor establishments, he did sell provincial licences to some vendors. Indeed, he publicly declared that the Peace Preservation Act was unconstitutional and promised to protect holders of provincial liquor licences from any action under it. Critics of the provincial government claimed Sproat issued licences as a bonus to buyers of town lots thus enriching the townsite owners who supposedly included himself and Provincial Secretary John Robson. Such allegations are plausible but cannot be proven. Supporters of the provincial cause countered by saying that Dominion police officials were taking bribes from unlicenced vendors who wished to avoid prosecution.[57]

The Dominion police at Farwell were not a well trained force. When the Mounted Police, who had been in the area during a strike of unpaid CPR construction workers, left to help put down the North West Rebellion, George Hope Johnston, who already held a commission as a provincial justice of the peace, was sworn in as a Dominion Commissioner of Police. His chief support were specials, known as "Cossacks" to Farwell residents, because they did "most outrageous acts." Indeed, the *Colonist*'s Farwell correspondent observed, "The Dominion police are the chief disturbers of the peace in this district. But for their partial, irregular and oppressive proceedings, everything would go on quietly in the old British Columbia fashion."[58]

Provincial officials had taken advantage of the situation. While Johnston was temporarily absent, Provincial Constable Kirkup, armed with a warrant from Stipendiary Magistrate Sproat, broke into the Dominion police barracks and seized liquor which the Dominion police had previously seized from John McGillies, the holder of a provincial licence. To add insult to injury, Sproat summoned the Dominion constable to appear before him on a charge of felonious stealing. Johnston instructed the constable not to appear in court; indeed the constable left town. Johnston, however, decided he did not want to get involved "in an altercation between constituted authorities." Possibly he was influenced by the recent decision of Chief Justice Matthew Baillie Begbie, who had been holding county court sessions at Farwell, that he could not pass judgment on several liquor cases until he had heard the legal arguments on the constitutionality of the relevant laws. In any event, Johnston "merely warned" local officials that he would hold them responsible for their actions and advised them that his constables "had instructions to prevent any such violation of the premises occupied by the Dominion police." He subsequently learned that his own name had been removed from the list of provincial justices of the peace. In announcing this, the *Colonist* remarked, "it was shown to the satisfaction of the ministry that these gentlemen [Todd also lost his commission] had been intent in guarding Dominion interests to the detriment and sacrifice of their provincial duties."[59] Thus ended the preliminary skirmish.

Throughout the summer, the Victoria papers carried reports of alleged maladministration of federal justice at Farwell but no specific incident arose until approximately 2:00 a.m. on July 29th. While Johnston was away, his constable, James Ruddick, seized 140 bottles of lager beer. Because of Johnston's absence, Ruddick did not have a warrant. When Johnston returned, he fined the owner $20 plus costs but withdrew an order for the destruction of the beer when he heard of an appeal. In the meantime, one of the men who had been transporting the beer charged Ruddick with larceny. Sproat remanded the case until Johnston's return but refused Johnston's claim that as a Commissioner of Police "he was a magistrate having equal jurisdiction" with Sproat as to Dominion law. After Sproat twice postponed the case, Johnston dismissed it and gave Ruddick, who had never been formally under arrest, a certificate of dismissal. Soon after Ruddick left the court room, two of Sproat's special constables, acting without warrant, "laid hands on Ruddick to arrest him." On instructions from Johnston, Ruddick resisted arrest and, along with another Dominion constable and a N.W.M.P. constable, arrested Hubbard, one of the two provincial constables. (The other ran away.) Within a half hour or so, Johnston had tried Hubbard, convicted him, and sentenced him to fourteen days in jail.[60]

Sproat soon retaliated. During one of Johnston's absences, his Constable Pennycook had arrested a man for fighting but had freed him on $15 bail until Johnston's return. Sproat, without consulting Pennycook, freed the man and charged Constables Pennycook and Shane with taking money under false pretences. On August 27, when Johnston went to Sproat's office to hear the Pennycook case, Sproat ordered that Johnston and Constable Orchard of the N.W.M.P. be charged with resisting the Provincial Police. Pending trial, he allowed them out on their own recognizance.

The advantage soon turned to the Dominion Police. The next day a special provincial constable attempted to arrest Ruddick. With the help of other Dominion police officers, Ruddick turned tables on the provincial officer, handcuffed him, and incarcerated him in the Dominion police station. According to Provincial Constable Kirkup, who warned of "bloodshed," the Dominion police had a number of armed men and boasted they were "going to lock up Sproat and the whole lot of us."[61]

Sproat prepared his revenge for what he believed was a "pure outbreak against the law of Canada respecting the administration of justice." After decrying Johnston and his men for their repeated defiance of the law and describing the incidents at the Dominion barracks which suggested the Dominion police "seemed frightened out of their wits," and admitting that the situation was tinged "with the burlesque," Sproat explained his next move to the Attorney-General:

> Recognizing that this was civil war, and that the situation created was military, I arranged to take the barracks with an overwhelming force of police and volunteers, under my personal command, at an early hour on Saturday morning; but having fortunately succeeded by a dash during the night in capturing the ring leaders, Johnston, Rhodes and a man called Fane, the necessity for an attack did not seem immediate; though two provincial policemen...still are imprisoned.

In fact, after arresting Rhodes, who was out walking, Sproat's men were able to arrest Johnston when he came to investigate and they soon overtook Constable Fane of the N.W.M.P. No warrants had been issued but the three federal police officers spent the night in a windowless 6' X 8' cell. The next day Sproat charged them with "aiding and abetting in the escape of a prisoner James Ruddick," remanded them for eight days but refused bail.[62]

The conflict might have remained a comedy on the frontier but the political superiors of Sproat and Johnston became involved. Justice Minister Langevin wisely counselled Johnston "to do nothing which will further complicate difficulty between Dominion and Provincial authorities" and asked the provincial government to co-operate in an investigation by Colonel Macleod, stipendiary magistrate at Ft. Macleod. The provincial cabinet did not welcome this suggestion. It blamed the Dominion police for the *contretemps*, warned of bloodshed, and advised the Dominion to withdraw its officials and not allow them to interfere with provincial authorities. Finally, the provincial cabinet warned that if Superintendent Steele attempted to enter the province with a posse of Mounted Police to assist Johnston, the action would be illegal and might "lead to severe trouble."[63]

By this time, the story had reached the Victoria newspapers and taken on political overtones. The *Colonist*, sometimes described as "the acknowledged organ of the provincial ministry," printed most of Sproat's despatch, provided some embellishment of its own, and, after complaining that "the Dominion officials were acting with a studied disregard for provincial courts and rights," suggested that "the arrogance, impudence and tyranny of the mounted police in the Northwest were the chief cause of the Riel outbreak...They adopted the same tactics at Farwell that made them objects of hatred and contempt in the Northwest, and have met with a wholesome check at the hands of Mr. Sproat, who is backed by the entire population at Farwell." In contrast, the *Times* expressed disbelief in reports that the Mounted Police were themselves defying the law and chastised the provincial government for its blunder in issuing liquor licences. Similarly the *Standard*, which was delighted to have an excuse to attack the Smithe government, considered the provincial government's attempt to control the liquor traffic on the line east of Kamloops to be "an insane step" which would "in all probability end in a real war with the Dominion." The incident, mused the *Standard*, was "one of the saddest pictures of lawlessness that has ever taken place in the province" and had caused laughter and ridicule in the outside world.[64]

Fortunately, Colonel Macleod soon arrived at Farwell on a mission of peace. Johnston immediately gave him "a full statement" but Sproat was disinclined to do so since matters were before the court. However, Sproat privately gave Macleod an account of "all the difficulties that had occurred." Subsequently, Macleod concluded that Johnston had been wrong in telling his constable to resist arrest. Macleod advised Johnston to submit to the court. Macleod persuaded Sproat, who had invited him to share the bench, to be as lenient as possible since Johnston had acted under legal advice, albeit improper advice. Thus the charges were reduced to common assault and Johnston was fined $10 on each of three charges plus $9.75 costs. The N.W.M.P. members were referred to their own officers for disciplinary action[65] and warrants were issued for some of the Dominion special constables who had already fled the country. Afterwards, Sproat and Johnston shook hands and thanked Colonel Macleod for settling the difficulty. On the broader question of authority, Macleod did not accept Sproat's contention that the province alone could maintain peace along the line of railway construction; he believed the presence of the Mounted Police was necessary. But Macleod proposed a compromise for the town of Farwell. Since construction through the town would be complete by the time his report reached Ottawa he recommended that the townsite be withdrawn from the Peace Preservation Act and that the Provincial Licence Act apply. With this solution to the problem, the *Colonist* boasted that once again in British Columbia, the law was supreme.[66] Indeed, one of the striking features of the Farwell affair was that, despite the nature of the population and the problems of the police, good order prevailed.

The "war" at Farwell can be partially attributed to the exuberance of inexperienced police officials. The Sproule murder case drew in American diplomats (Sproule was an American citizen), saw public opinion attempt to change a judicial decision, and raised such a conflict between judges of the British Columbia and Canadian Supreme courts that one British Columbia judge publicly suggested that two Canadian Supreme Court judges were like perpetrators of lynch law by condemning judges without trial.[67]

The Sproule case began as a conflict between Robert Sproule and Thomas Hammill, the murder victim, over the rights to the rich Blue Bell silver mine on Kootenay Lake. Sproule had recorded his claim in July, 1882 but in October, 1882, left it for more than the seventy-two hours allowed under the mining law although he had posted a notice stating two recognized excuses for extended absences, reprovisioning and illness. Hammill, however, decided that Sproule had abandoned the claim and took it up as his own. Sproule appealed to the gold commissioner, "Judge" Kelly. The subsequent "trial" suggests something of the crude nature of justice on the frontier. When the only available Victoria lawyer could not come at the last moment, William Baillie-Grohman, a land speculator who had invested in it, acted as legal counsel for the Sproule claim. Baillie-Grohman, who had no legal training recalled:

The largest of the three shanties in the two camps was selected as the court-house, where the trial took place. Every soul except the judge was, of course, deeply concerned in the issue of litigation; millions, we all thought, were at stake, and feelings therefore ran very high, for Sprowle's [sic] intense animosity had communicated itself to the witnesses as well as partners. That in such a rough crowd, composed to a great extent of men who had passed their lives in American mining camps, where men very frequently take justice into their own hands, a trial lasting some weeks that was not marred by a single affray was, under the circumstances, very creditable to the man who had to decide the issue. The Court opened on Aug. 31 [1883], and the first thing Judge Kelly insisted on was that all revolvers were to be deposited in a box at his side so long as the Court sat, a precaution which, alas, succeeded only for the time being to save the life of one of the two persons most concerned.

Finally, after six weeks, the gold commissioner ruled in favour of Sproule's claims. The Hammill interests appealed to the Supreme Court of British Columbia. Complaining of this "wearisome, expensive and mischievous litigation" the judge ruled in Sproule's favour in only one of four related cases. In the other three the court reversed the gold commissioner's decisions. As Baillie-Grohman later explained:

It was a terribly unexpected blow which affected one man most disastrously, more particularly so in consequence of the unfortunate but not uncommon sequel of costly litigation. As the winning side got the costs in three of the suits, and Sprowle [sic] could not settle the large amount that was now claimed...an attachment to cover their costs was issued against his remaining interest, and the latter was sold by the sheriff. This unfortunate ending unhinged Sprowle's over-excited mind altogether, and he now also turned against me...Hammil's [sic] and my life, he openly threatened, should pay for the loss of his mine.[68]

Baillie-Grohman narrowly escaped Sproule's rifle shot; Hammill was less fortunate.

Because of the litigation "no work of any consequence" was done on the claim until the spring of 1884. Meanwhile, Sproule went about declaring that he would kill Hammill if "that Cornish s—of a b—" ever worked the claim. On 1 June 1885, Thomas Hammill was found at the claim dying of bullet wounds in his back. Hammill's friends tracked down Sproule with the help of local Indians.[69]

The murder caused great excitement. Men talked of lynching Sproule and suggested the Government "were heavy on taxes but seemed indifferent to the protection etc. of the lives of persons who were trying to open up the country." Recognizing the difficulty in getting a fair trial for Sproule in the Kootenay, the Crown secured a change of venue to Victoria but not all of Judge Begbie's instructions about the change were properly recorded. This technicality later provided Sproule's lawyer, Theodore Davie, with an avenue of appeal and caused conflict among the judges.

The case was tried in Victoria in early December. Although the evidence was entirely circumstantial, for no one had actually seen the crime. Mr. Justice Gray told the jury he could not "define any other thing by which the crime could have happened than that adduced by the crown." The jury found Sproule guilty but recommended mercy. In pronouncing the death sentence a few weeks later, Gray took special pains to make it "understood that every American citizen who may come into the country will be as welcome as you yourself were...[but]...they cannot bring with them that looseness and laxity of administration which obtains in their own country."[70]

The case had drawn considerable attention in the United States. Some Washington and Oregon newspapers suggested that Sproule was a known bad character; Sproule's American friends claimed such stories were inspired by Portland, Oregon mining interests who wanted Sproule out of the way. Sproule's friends secured four to five hundred names on a petition demanding a new trial. More significantly, a private investigator, hired by Sproule's brother, found that some witnesses had perjured themselves; that one had accepted a bribe; that some of Sproule's enemies, who were "composed in most cases of the lawless and shiftless part of the community," were simply motivated by "personal animosity to Sproule"; that not all the jury had realized the death penalty applied; and that Sproule had been at some distance from the scene when the crime occurred.[71]

The American consul in Victoria, Robert Stevens, gradually concluded that Sproule was innocent. He lobbied Attorney-General A.E.B. Davie, who claimed he could do nothing in a federal matter. Stevens then persuaded Lieutenant-Governor Clement Francis Cornwall to forward evidence of "undue influence" on witnesses to Ottawa. As well, Sproule's friends convinced Mayor James Fell and other Victorians to doubt Sproule's guilt. Thus, the mayor called a meeting at City Hall "to consider what steps should be taken to call the attention of the Dominion Government to the necessity of postponing the execution of R.E. Sproule." The well-attended meeting unanimously called for the postponement of the execution to allow time for "a searching inquiry" and examination of new evidence since there were "good grounds for thinking that the said R.E. Sproule may be the victim of a conspiracy, and that the conviction may have been secured by perjured and unreliable testimony."[72]

Three days later the matter of political intervention became an academic question. Theodore Davie got Mr. Justice Henry and Mr. Justice Strong of the Supreme Court of Canada to issue an order of *habeas corpus* on the grounds that irregularities in the change of venue meant the court at Victoria had no jurisdiction and the trial was therefore a nullity.[73] When the sheriff refused to deliver the prisoner, Mr. Justice Henry ruled him in contempt and ordered Sproule's release.[74]

According to the Ottawa press, Judge Henry's decision meant that the British Columbia courts were "improperly constituted" and, if his decision were sustained, "the execution of every criminal in the province will be declared to have been murder." Mr. Justice Henry's explanation for granting the writ greatly angered Mr. Justice Begbie and his colleagues on the British Columbia Supreme Court who, as a result of earlier disputes over procedures in their court, were already sensitive to the interference of the Supreme Court of Canada. Now they had a new grievance. Not only had the federal judge overruled one of Begbie's decisions but he had indirectly impugned all of the British Columbia Supreme Court judges. As Mr. Justice McCreight told Mr. Justice Crease, "No doubt he virtually accused the C.J. of something like a forgery for the purpose of carrying out something like a judicial murder and accused us of being accessories to this. If another had so spoken in this Province we should have been obliged to send him to prison." Begbie feared that Henry's "unwarranted interference" gave "great encouragement to the criminal classes."[75]

The British Columbia judges, who had a tradition of speaking out in public on matters affecting their courts, took the matter to the people. At the Lytton and Victoria Assizes, Mr. Justice Walkem and Mr. Justice Crease respectively complained that the British Columbia bench had been "condemned of crime behind our backs" thereby diminishing the respect for the law. Eventually, the British Columbia judges were vindicated. When Attorney-General A.E.B. Davie appealed the *habeas corpus* order, the Supreme Court of Canada as a whole quashed Mr. Justice Henry's order. Indeed, Mr. Justice Taschereau noted that while *habeas corpus* was "one of the most effective safeguards of the liberty of the subject...society also has its rights...the courts...are bound to see that the writ is not taken advantage of for the protection of felons and convicts." The British Columbia bench was so bitter, however, that when Mr. Justice Henry visited Victoria that fall, they refused to see him socially.[76]

To the last, Sproule's friends interceded on his behalf. They had doctors investigate his mental condition; he was of sound mind. They appealed to Mr. Justice Gray of the Supreme Court of British Columbia; he offered legal advice but lacked the power of reprieve. They had influential people in the United States appeal to Sir John A. Macdonald. They circulated petitions in Victoria, Vancouver, and Nanaimo which Mayor Fell was to present in Ottawa as he lobbied for the commutation of Sproule's sentence. All efforts failed. On 29 October 1886, in the words of Consul Stevens, Sproule was "judiciously murdered."[77]

Within British Columbia there was but limited sympathy for Sproule. In commenting on the petitions the *Columbian* complained that the notion that the government should bow to public pressure and reverse the decision of a judge and jury was as "pernicious as lynch law itself, because it is disorganized force raising a hand against organized and constituted authority." The *Colonist* questioned the nonrecognition of the jury's recommendation of mercy. The

Nanaimo *Free Press* stated its opposition to capital punishment but was convinced that the eight reprieves and the appeals taken on Sproule's behalf demonstrated that "full justice had been done." Similarly, the Port Moody *Gazette*, which earlier had doubts about the case, concluded that the circumstantial evidence "was quite sufficient to satisfy any sensible man that the criminal deserved death."[78]

By this time the case had attracted widespread American attention. According to one report, President Cleveland had asked the Imperial government to intervene to save Sproule's life. The Chicago *Herald* called the execution a "judicial butchery" and "an act of unmistakable hostility to the American people." The New York *Tribune* said that the whole affair suggested "everything but justice," a contention which led the Victoria *Times* to declare that:

> the sooner our neighbours are given to understand that in British Columbia, as elsewhere in Canada, the punishment is made to fit the crime, be the criminal an alien or a native-born citizen, and that convictions or acquittals are not obtained through newspaper editorials or hanging accomplished by vigilance committees the quicker they will understand the difference between criminal jurisprudence as practised in the two countries.

The Portland *Oregonian* expressed a more modest sentiment that found some support in British Columbia when it observed, "Possibly they go to one extreme in the English possessions there; we certainly go to the other. That is, if they sometimes execute laws too vigorously, seldom do we execute them rigorously enough." A year later, Consul Stevens ironically commented, in connection with another matter, in Victoria, "it is claimed, that Law is always promptly paramount, and Justice unerring—it was so asserted at the time of the execution of the American Sproule."[79] The Sproule case had demonstrated that there was a basis for British Columbia's claim that law and order prevailed but not all were convinced that justice was firmly and fairly administered.

What can be learned from this brief examination of the state of law and order in British Columbia in the 1880s? The most obvious answer is the need for further research. Although some work has been done on the Supreme Court of British Columbia,[80] we need to know more about the minor courts, the justices of the peace and the stipendiary magistrates, and about the role of special constables, both Dominion and provincial. Although much has been written about such high profile incidents as those at Metlakatla and Fort Steele, we need to know more about less publicized events such as the displacement of the Songhees in Victoria (a fact of which the Metlakatlans were aware) and about the general administration of the law among the native people of the province who, during the 1880s, ceased to be a majority of the population. Similarly, although we know how the provincial government acted promptly to restore the peace after the anti-Chinese riot in Vancouver in 1887 and we know a little about the maintenance of law and order among the Chinese building the CPR,[81] we know very little about the place of the legal system in regulating the relatively large Chinese community. And, of course, problems in preserving the peace present aspects of a traditional Canadian subject, the relations between the federal and provincial governments. That matter is unusually significant in the 1880s because, with the coming of the CPR, British Columbia was becoming physically and psychologically, as well as constitutionally, a part of Canada.

Despite the many gaps in our knowledge, it is possible to draw some tentative conclusions from the evidence at hand. British Columbia was demonstratively anxious to make it known that law and order prevailed, that it was not part of an American-style "Wild West" where people shot Indians, were "bad characters," and accepted a loose and lax administration of the law. That was the image portrayed in the immigration literature; what was the reality? Did law and order prevail? Was justice fairly and firmly administered? From the point of view of the government—though probably not of those who came into conflict with the law or those who wanted it to be very strictly enforced, especially against the Indians—the answer was a qualified yes. Warnings about possible bloodshed were largely that, warnings. In spite of a shortage of efficient, well-trained policemen and uncertainties about jurisdictions, British Columbia, with the help at times of other governments, generally preserved law and order. This was often accomplished with considerable difficulty;

the hold on law and order was tenuous. The publicity given cases where the preservation of the peace was in question made advertising an image of law and order necessary but, on the whole, the advertising was true. The reality was not far distant from the image.

NOTES

1. Victoria *Daily Standard*, 1 and 7 May 1885; New Westminster *Mainland Guardian*, 21 March 1885; *Standard*, 18 April 1885; Victoria *Daily British Colonist*, 18 September and 2 May 1885; Victoria *Daily Times*, 27 April 1885.

2. British Columbians would have been more confident had they realized that the British Northwest Coast never figured in Russian plans. See Glynn Barratt, *Russian Shadows on the British Northwest Coast of British America, 1810–1890* (Vancouver: University of British Columbia Press, 1983), p. 117. Details of the actual state of the defences of the British Columbia coast are conveniently laid out in Chapter 7.

3. Col. F.C. Stanley to Lansdowne, 27 October 1885 and Minute of 20 November 1885 in National Archives of Canada (hereafter NAC), Records of the Department of Militia and Defence, RG 9 II A1, vol. 491.

4. For examples see New Westminster *British Columbian*, 18 March 1885; *Standard*, 18 April 1885; Nanaimo *Free Press*, 22 April 1885; *Colonist*, 18 March 1885; *Times*, 27 April 1885; Victoria *Daily Evening Post*, 20 April 1885; Port Moody *Gazette*, 2 May 1885. The American consul in Victoria reported that officers of the B.C. Garrison considered the situation "grave" but believed the only place subject to Russian attack was Nanaimo (Robert J. Stevens to James D. Porter, 22 April 1885 in United States, Consular Reports, Victoria. Microfilm in the Provincial Archives of British Columbia [hereafter PABC]).

5. *Colonist*, 11 September 1885; *Times*, 3 August 1885; *Gazette*, 8 August 1885. This intercity rivalry over defence installations was not confined to this period of "war scare." On 18 November 1882, the *Mainland Guardian*, which was boosting Port Moody lands, suggested that because of the possible Russian attacks if would be "absurd" to construct the Pacific railway terminus at an exposed location such as Coal Harbour or English Bay. The rivalry continued. In 1888, for example, the Vancouver Board of Trade advised General Middleton that the defence of Esquimalt was "of no use to the Mainland" and called attention to Vancouver's defence needs (David Oppenheimer, President, Vancouver Board of Trade to Major-General F.D. Middleton, 8 October 1888, NAC RG 9 II A1, vol. 494).

6. This was particularly true of the two New Westminster newspapers. The

Victoria papers seem to have had a better wire service and received some news apparently direct from the Territories.

7. *Times*, 13 August 1884; *Standard*, 1 April 1885; *Free Press*, 16 May 1885; *Columbian*, 30 May 1885; *Colonist*, 12 May 1885; *Mainland Guardian*, 20 May 1885; *Post*, 18 May 1885; *Gazette*, 23 May 1885; *Columbian*, 4 April 1885; Kamloops *Inland Sentinel*, 4 June 1885; *Colonist*, 13 and 15 November 1885; *Free Press*, 18 November 1885; *Standard*, 16 November 1885; *Colonist*, 28 July 1885.

8. *Colonist*, 1 January 1885 and 1 January 1886; *Times*, 31 December 1884.

9. *Resources of British Columbia*, Victoria, vols. I and II (April 1883-March 1884); *Illustrated British Columbia* (Victoria: J.B. Ferguson, 1884); "Questions and Answers on the Geography, Climate and Resources of British Columbia," PABC, GR 1198, vol. I, file 3; Canada, Department of Agriculture, *Province de la Colombie Britannique: renseignements Pour les Colons qu'on l'intention d'y émigrer* (Ottawa, 1885), p. 31; Hubert Howe Bancroft, *History of British Columbia, 1792–1886* (San Francisco: The History Company, 1887), p. 706; R.E. Gosnell, *British Columbia. A Digest of Reliable Information Regarding Its Natural Resources and Industrial Possibilities* (Vancouver: News-Advertiser, 1890), p. 43.

10. *Times*, 23 July 1885; *Columbian* and *Mainland Guardian*, 4 July 1885.

11. Molyneux St. John, *The Province of British Columbia Canada* (n.p. [1886]), p. 16.

12. Chas. Hayward to E.C. Baker, 30 November 1885, PAC, Records of the Secretary of State, RG 6 A1, vol. 54, file 13305–14743. See also *Colonist*, 24 October 1885. Establishing a university was somewhat premature. In 1886 there were only three high schools in the province with a total of 157 students. F.H. Johnson, *A History of Public Education in British Columbia* (Vancouver: University of British Columbia Publications Centre, 1964), p. 61. Indeed, the question of whether or not high school education should be free had not been fully settled.

13. Canada, *Census*, 1881, Vol. I, pp. 198–99. See also Robin Fisher, *Contact and Conflict: Indian-European Relations in British Columbia, 1774–1890* (Vancouver: University of British Columbia Press, 1977), p. 202.

14. *Information for Intending Settlers* (Ottawa, 1883), p. 21; *The West Shore*, September 1884, p. 275.

15. *Columbian*, 6 August 1884; *Mainland Guardian*, 3 June 1885; *Colonist*, 26 August 1885.

16. British Columbia, Legislative Assembly, *Journal*, 25 January 1886.

17. E. Palmer Patterson II, "A Decade of Change: Origins of the Nishga and Tsimshian Land Protests in the 1880s," *Journal of Canadian Studies* 18 (Fall, 1983), p. 41.

18. *Colonist*, 27 July 1882; *Columbian*, 17 January 1883; cf. *Mainland Guardian*, 20 January 1883. The background of the dispute is well analyzed in Jean Usher, *William Duncan of Metlakatla: A Victorian Missionary in British Columbia* (Ottawa: National Museum of Man, 1974).

19. F.C. Cornwall to Secretary of State, 10 February 1883, PABC, GR 443 vol. 32.

20. *Columbian*, 17 January 1883; *Colonist*, 12 January 1883. See also Barry M. Gough, *Gunboat Frontier: British Maritime Authority and Northwest Coast Indians, 1846–1890* (Vancouver: University of British Columbia Press, 1984), pp. 182–83.

21. Mackenzie Bowell to Lieutenant-Governor, 18 July 1883 and Rear Admiral Lyons to Secretary of the Admiralty, 2 August 1883, both quoted in *Colonist*, 8 January 1884. See also Gough, *Gunboat Frontier*, p. 183.

22. C.W.D. Clifford to Attorney-General, 13 October 1883, PABC, GR 429, Box 1, file 12.

23. William Smithe to John A. Macdonald, 24 October 1883, PABC, GR 441, vol. 381a.

24. Usher, *Duncan*, p. 125.

25. David Leask to J.W. McKay, 30 November 1883 and Leask to I.W. Powell, 26 November 1883, quoted in *Colonist*, 28 March 1884.

26. Smithe to Macdonald, 7 March 1884, PAC, John A. Macdonald Papers, vol. 38, pp. 14245ff. Also in British Columbia, *Sessional Papers* [hereafter BCSP], 1885, p. 2.

27. *Colonist*, 25 June 1884.

28. *Standard*, 5 November 1884; *Times*, 31 January 1885; *Post*, 27 January 1885.

29. A.E.B. Davie to Alexander Campbell, 22 October 1884, PAC, Macdonald Papers, vol. 38, pp. 14861–2.

30. *Colonist*, 28 and 29 October 1884.

31. *Columbian*, 1 November 1884; *Colonist*, 30 and 31 October and 6 November 1884; *Standard*, 5 November 1884. See also letters to the editor, *Colonist*, from Robert Tomlinson, 15 November 1884 and James Dean, 22 November 1884.

32. Usher, *Duncan*, p. 126.

33. Metlakatlah Commission, *Report*, BCSP, 1884, pp. 135–36.

34. *Post*, 30 January 1885; British Columbia, Legislative Assembly, *Journal*, 10 February 1885, p. 32; *Times*, 11 February 1885; *Post*, 10 February 1885; *Colonist*, 20 March 1885.

35. *Colonist*, 20 March 1885.

36. Usher, *Duncan*, pp. 131–33.

37. Smithe to Ridley, 22 October 1886, PABC, GR441, vol. 404; *Colonist*, 28 October 1886.

38. Gough, *Gunboat Frontier*, p. 185.

39. Usher, *Duncan*, p. 133; *Colonist*, 20 and 21 November 1886.

40. Patterson, "A Decade of Change," pp. 44–46; Robert E. Cail, *Land, Man and the Law: The Disposal of Crown Lands in British Columbia, 1871–1913* (Vancouver: University of British Columbia Press, 1974), pp. 224–25.

41. A.E. Green to John Robson, 14 March 1888 and P.A. Irving to Constable Anderson, 31 March 1888. All in PABC, GR677, vol. 1, file 1.

42. Anderson to Attorney-General, 5 April 1888; S.Y Wooton to Attorney-General, 3 April 1888; and C.W.D. Clifford to Wooton, 6 April 1888. All in PABC, GR 677, vol. 1, file 1.

43. Anderson to Attorney-General, 10 April 1888 and Constable Washburn, Report, 27 June 1888; PABC, GR 677, vol. 1, file 1.

44. Wooton to Attorney-General, 7 July 1888 and N. Fitzstubbs to Attorney-General, 15, 24 and 27 July 1888; PABC, GR677, vol. 1, file 1.

45. Jno. Field et al. to Attorney-General, 1 July 1888, PABC, GR 677, vol.1, file 1; "Minute of the Executive Council of British Columbia relative to the Indian Troubles on the Skeena River and the expenses of the Expedition in that locality." [October 1988], PABC, GR1198, vol. 1, file 1; *Colonist*, 13 July 1888.

46. Executive Council to Lieutenant-Governor, 12 July 1888 and Lieutenant-Governor to Secretary of State, 12 July 1888, PABC, GR429, vol. 2, file 1.

47. Mackenzie Bowell to Lieutenant-Governor, 17 July 1888 and L. Vankoughnet to I.W. Powell, 16 July 1888, PABC, GR 677, vol. 1, file 1; *Colonist*, 17 July 1888.
   The provincial cabinet had been insulted because a deputy minister, not a cabinet minister, had refused to order Powell to form the expedition. "Such conduct as this, from the Federal Government, is not what a Province has a right to expect, either under the Terms of Union or the B.N.A. Act." However, before sending its commentary to Ottawa, the provincial government struck out a second sentence: "Indeed, an appeal for assistance to the adjacent territory of the United States would undoubtedly have met with a more favourable answer." ("Minute of the Executive Council of British Columbia relative to the Indian Troubles on the Skeena River..." [October 1888], PABC, GR 1198, vol. 1, file 1.) The province claimed the cost of $8,095.61 was not a case of ordinary police supervision and should be wholly borne by the senior government. The Dominion government would not accept any responsibility for the disturbance but, because of its desire to make a general settlement with the province and the recognized difficulty of applying the Militia Act "in an uncivilized and uninhabited part of the country," it was agreed to pay the $5,441.08 cost of sending "C" Battery to the Skeena. (Minister of the

Interior to the Privy Council, 10 December 1888, printed in BCSP, 1889, p. 161.)

48. *Colonist*, 15 July 1888; Attorney-General to H.B. Roycraft, 16 July 1888, PABC, GR 677, vol. 1, file 1.

In one case, the provincial police readily admitted that a chief, Man-ah-hau, had committed justifiable homicide when he killed Tobias, "a raving maniac with homicidal tendencies." (Washburn to Attorney-General, 16 July 1888, PABC, GR 677, vol. 1, file 1.)

49. *Times*, 12, 16 and 26 July 1888; *Columbian*, 14 and 23 July 1888; *News-Advertiser*, 18 July 1888; *Colonist*, 13 July 1888.

50. *Inland Sentinel*, 21 July 1888; Ottawa *Free Press* quoted in *Colonist*, 26 and 27 July and 1, 5, and 16 August 1888; *Times*, 19 and 26 July 1888; *News-Advertiser*, 21 July 1888.

51. *Colonist*, 30 July 1888; Hugh Nelson to Secretary of State, 30 July 1888, PABC, GR 443, vol. 32.

52. Nelson to Secretary of State, 30 July 1888, PABC, GR 443, vol. 32; Jno. Field to Roycraft, 6 August 1888, PABC, GR 677, vol. 1, file 1; Roycraft to A.E.B. Davie, 14 August 1888, PABC, GR 429, vol. 2, file 1; *Colonist*, 16 August 1888; *News-Advertiser*, 31 July 1888; Robert Stevens to G.L. Rives, 16 August 1888, Records of the United States Consul, Victoria; Fitzstubbs to A.E.B. Davie, 30 September 1888, PABC, GR 677, vol.1, file 1. Nelson to Secretary of State, 11 June 1889, PABC, GR 443, vol. 32.

53. For details of this incident see Carol MacLeod, "Fort Steel [sic]," Parks Canada, National Historic Parks and Sites Branch, Manuscript Report Number 161, [1975–75], pp. 131–71.

54. G.M. Sproat, quoted in *Colonist*, 6 September 1885; J. Ross to William Van Horne, 27 October 1884; C. Drinkwater to Van Horne, 27 October 1884; Van Horne to Minister of the Interior, 8 November 1884, PAC, Department of Transport Records, RG 12, vol. 2106.

55. *Colonist*, 23 April 1885; Charles Todd to J.H. Pope, 4 March 1885, PAC, RG 12, vol. 2106; *Inland Sentinel*, 16 April 1885.

56. J.A. Chapleau to Lieutenant-Governor, 1 June 1885, PABC, GR 443, vol. 42; Lieutenant-Governor to Secretary of State, 23 June 1885, PABC, GR 443, vol. 32; Chapleau to Lieutenant-Governor, 26 June 1885, PABC, GR 444, vol. 51, file 6.

57. *Colonist*, 4 July 1885; C. Todd and G.H. Johnson to J.W. Trutch, 24 August 1885, PAC, RG 12, vol. 2106; *Standard*, 7 September 1885; *Mainland Guardian*, 9 September 1885; *Colonist*, 8 July 1885.

58. T.D. Regehr, "Letters from the End of Track," in Hugh A. Dempsey, ed., *The CPR West* (Vancouver: Douglas and McIntyre, 1984), p. 51; *Colonist*, 19 June and 3 July 1885.

59. G.H. Johnston to J.H. Pope, 15 July 1885; Johnston to Pope, 26 July 1885, PAC, RG 12, vol. 2106; *Colonist*, 28 July 1885.

60. *Times*, 13 August 1885; *Colonist*, 15 August 1885; Johnston to Pope, 28 August 1885 and A.G.M. Spragge to Pope, 30 August, 1885 PAC, RG 12, vol. 2106.

61. Spragge to Pope, 30 August 1885, PAC, RG 12, vol. 2106; J. Kirkup to Roycraft, 29 August 1885, PABC, GR 444, vol. 51, file 6.

62. G.M Sproat to Attorney-General, 30 August 1885, PABC, GR 996, vol.1, file 3. Much of this letter was published in the *Colonist*, 6 September 1885; Spragge to Pope, 30 August 1885, PAC, RG 12, vol. 2106.

63. H.L. Langevin to Johnston, 7 September 1885; Langevin to Lieutenant-Governor, 7 September 1885; Cornwall to Langevin, 5 September 1885, PAC, RG 12, vol. 2106.

64. Trutch to Pope, 7 September 1885, PAC, RG 12, vol. 2106; *Colonist*, 6, 7, and 8 September 1885; *Mainland Guardian*, 9 September 1885.

65. Even before Macleod arrived, Superintendent W.M. Herchmer of the N.W.M.P.'s Calgary District, had briefly visited Farwell and determined that the N.W.M.P. were "not inculpated either by direct charge, or substantial rumour, in the allegation[s]...that are freely made against the special constables or some of them." However, a few days later, Sproat told the Attorney-General of several cases "within the past fortnight" of drunkenness and disorderliness among the N.W.M.P. He recommended "That the detachment of North West Mounted Police...should be withdrawn forthwith...as their presence in dangerous to the public peace." Sproat was willing to accept the services of a few N.W.M.P. constables to escort the C.P.R. paymaster provided that when they "were not so employed" they would "be at the disposal of the Provl. authorities." Presumably that meant that at Farwell they should be under Sproat's direction. (Sproat, "Memo re visit of Col. Herchmer," 10 September 1885; Sproat to Attorney-General, 14 and 24 September 1885; PABC, GR 996, vol. 1, file 3.)

66. James F. Macleod, "Report," 7 October 1885, PAC, RG 12, vol. 2106; Sproat to Attorney-General, 24 September 1885, PABC, GR 996, vol.1, file 3; *Colonist*, 3 October 1885; see also *Times*, 31 December 1885.

67. David R. Williams, "...The Man for a New Country": Sir Matthew Baillie Begbie (Sidney, B.C.: Gray's Publishing, 1977), pp. 261–62.

68. W.A. Baillie-Grohman, *Fifteen Years' Sport and Life in the Hunting Grounds of Western America and British Columbia* (London: Horace Cox, 1900), pp. 238–41; I British Columbia *Reports*, p. 44 (Kootenay Mining Cases).

69. A.S. Farwell to Commissioner of Lands and Works, 31 December 1883 quoted in *Standard*, 16 January 1884; A.W. Vowell to P.A. Irving, 21 Sep-

tember 1885, PABC, GR 996, vol. 1, file 3; *Colonist*, 12 and 28 June 1885; *Standard*, 3 December 1885.

70. A.W. Vowell to Smithe, 2 July 1885, PABC, GR 441, vol. 1, file 3; Williams, '...*The Man for a New Country*,' pp. 260–61; *Standard*, 10 December 1885; *Colonist*, 10 December 1885 and 6 January 1886.

71. Robert Stevens to J.D. Porter, 10 February 1886; Sproule to U.S. Consul, c. 1 March 1886; Stevens to Porter, 11 and 20 April 1886; U.S. Consular Reports, Victoria.

72. Stevens to Porter, 12 April 1886, U.S. Consular Reports; Cornwall to Secretary of State, 21 April 1886, PABC, GR 443, vol. 32; *Colonist*, 30 April and 2 May 1886; *Times*, 29 April 1886.

73. Davie sought the writ as a means of gaining time to lure a perjuring witness from the United States and prosecute him. He believed a successful prosecution for perjury would force the federal cabinet to reprieve Sproule and re-open the case. (*Colonist*, 5 May 1885; Stevens to Porter, 13 May 1886, U.S. Consular Reports).

74. Supreme Court of Canada, *Reports*, vol. 12 (1886), pp. 169–75.

75. *Times*, 14 August 1886; J.W. McCreight to H.P.P. Crease, 27 September 1886; Begbie to John A. Macdonald, 1 October 1886; PAC, Macdonald Papers, p. 2106485 ff. On the background of the conflict between the two supreme courts see Hamar Foster, "The Struggle for the Supreme Court: Law and Politics in British Columbia, 1871–1885," in Louis Knafla, ed., *Law and Justice in a New Land: Essays in Western Canadian Legal History* (Toronto: Carswell, 1986).

76. *Times*, 13 October and 22 November 1886; Supreme Court of Canada, *Reports*, vol. 12 (1886), p. 250; Williams, "...*The Man for a New Country*," p. 261.

77. Stevens to Porter, 2 and 29 October 1886, U.S. Consular Reports.

78. *Columbian*, 18 October 1886 (The *Colonist*, 30 April 1886 and *Times*, 1 May 1886 had expressed similar sentiments about the idea of a public meeting on Sproule's behalf.); *Colonist*, 29 October 1886; *Free Press*, 30 October 1886; *Gazette*, 22 September and 6 November 1886.

79. San Francisco *Alta* quoted in *Times*, 29 September 1886; *Colonist*, 20 November 1886; *Times*, 5 and 10 November 1886; *Oregonian* quoted in *Colonist*, 4 November 1886; Stevens to G.L. Rivers, 24 September 1887, U.S. Consular Reports.

80. Hamar Foster, "The Struggle for the Supreme Court." See also his "Law Enforcement in Nineteenth-Century British Columbia: A Brief and Comparative Overview," *BC Studies*, no. 63 (Autumn, 1984), pp. 3–28.

81. Patricia E. Roy, "The Preservation of the Peace in Vancouver: The Aftermath of the Anti-Chinese Riot of 1887," *BC Studies*, no. 31 (Autumn,

1976), pp. 44–59; and "A Choice Between Evils: The Chinese and the Construction of the Canadian Pacific Railway in British Columbia," in Hugh Dempsey, ed., *The CPR West* (Vancouver: Douglas and McIntyre, 1984), pp. 17–21.

ROTA HERZBERG LISTER

5 A Distinctive Variant
1885 in Canadian Drama

For a century Canadian history has taken its course of expansion and consolidation since the bitter and bloody confrontation between the Western indigenous forces and the military power organized by the Dominion government put a stop to the hopes of Louis Riel and his followers. The events of the North West Rebellion have provided dramatic imaginations with stimulating materials for the development of character and motive during two widely separated periods of our political and cultural history; the first and immediate dramatic responses came from both the side of the victors and that of the vanquished and exhibit substantially different interpretations and treatments of these tragic experiences. The sixty-five years which elapsed between the first and second phase of dramatizations are reflected in the greater sophistication of representation of character and motive. It is the purpose of this discussion to examine in some detail the orientation and treatment brought to bear upon the common historical source materials in each of the dramatizations under consideration.

The three early responses, Staff Sergeant George Broughall's musical and dramatic burlesque, *The Ninetieth on Active Service: Campaigning in the North West* (1885), Professor Charles Bayer and E. Parage's *Riel: Drame historique en quatre acts et un prologue* (1886) and Dr. Elzéar Paquin's *Riel: tragédie en quatre acts* (1886)[1] emphasize triumph over adversity, whether in military victory or defeat. The sheer physical endurance tests of soldiering in the North West are presented in terms of patriotism and loyalty to the British Empire in Broughall's celebration of the fall of Batoche:

> OFFICER: Well men I know that you have poor fare. Hard biscuit and salt pork are not what you have been accustomed to and I think with you, that you should have, at least, what the Government sets down in regulations as your rations...Still, we have all come out here in defence of our country and institutions; and we should patiently and willingly submit to many blunders of a commissariat and the hardships of a campaign. We are here to do our duty; and we can at least tolerate many grievances, on a campaign in which so much is at stake...(20–21)

Very different is the hardship endured and the loyalty proved in the Bayer and Parage treatment of the same historical situation:

> RIEL: Je suis décidé. Si je suis victime de la perfidie de nos enemies; si au lieu de pardon, c'est l'échafaud qui m'attend, mon martyre sera utile à notre cause; il servira à démasquer leur politique de fourbes, et mon sang répandu sur leurs têtes les couvira d'opprobre. Du reste, dans toute pays civilisé, on ne condamne pas sans jugement. Ma soumission désarmerer mes enemis. Je subirai mon procès devant les juges impartiaux. La grand publicité des débats, où la légitimité de notre révolte sera discutes, où tous nos griefs seront mis à jour, fera peut-être plus de bien a notre cause qu'un lutte désespérée. (55–56)

The Paquin interpretation describes the events of the years from 1869 to 1885, including Riel's commitment to the asylums of Longe Pointe and Beauport and his exile in Montana, and takes the play beyond the execution of the protagonist to the outraged reactions of Quebec and world newspapers and a discussion of the likely political consequences between Gabriel Dumont, Senator Trudel and other French Canadians. It is a story of suffering and betrayal, ending in the prediction of future vindication:

TRUDEL: My dear friends, since the day we were so ignominiously insulted on the gallows of Regina, I haven't ceased filling my newspaper with the most outspoken documents along with the most irrefutable arguments, together with the most categorical proofs, to demonstrate that the ringleaders of the disorders and uprisings—that the enemies of law and justice, of peace, prosperity and the glory of our country, between 1869 and 1870, and 1884–85—were the Federal ministers themselves and their subalterns in the North-West. (268)

Such interplay of victory and defeat, past and present, and future, belongs to the tradition of classical epic and of the interwoven history plays of the Shakespeare canon. The dialectic of historical forces finds its appropriate dramatic form in the conflicts of opposing armies and their leaders, each challenging the legitimacy of the other.

That the events of 1837 in both Upper and Lower Canada have inspired only a few dramatizations, Robertson Davies's *At My Heart's Core* (1950), Rick Salutin's *1837: The Farmer's Revolt* (1974), and Louis-Honoré Fréchette's *Papineau*, indicates the lesser impact upon the national memory of these struggles for Responsible Government. What was at stake in 1885 as it had been to the same extent in 1869–70 was the nature of the future Canadian polity: was it to be a Dominion within the British Empire or a series of smaller, autonomous states such as those that developed in Latin America? The hindsight of history is not the kind of destiny the dramatist probes: he or she, in tracing character in action, must create the illusion of real choice, of major alternatives, to engage the audience in the conflict of significantly opposing visions of the future.

It was surely this recognition of a major turning point in Canadian history which drew John Coulter to the same set of circumstances three times. When Coulter arrived in Canada in 1936, he was already a successfully-produced Irish playwright and decided to turn his skills to the creation of Canadian plays. As Geraldine Anthony records, he "found it necessary to frequent the corner drugstores, to listen to the chatter of young Canadians, then go home to spend long hours trying painfully to reproduce what he had heard."[2] Eventually he discovered a congenial subject in an aspect of Canadian history which resembled in its tensions those familiar Irish struggles between Catholic and Protestant, English landlord and Irish crofter. Louis Riel's kaleidoscopic personality held more than a little of the Dionysian qualities of the Celtic spirit. Coulter recalls:

> I feel sympathy for him in his suffering, and admiration for his moral courage and integrity. He had these qualities, and with them a spark of political genius complicated by mental instability...If he was fortunate in anything, I have believed it to be in the singular confluence of historical circumstances which combined to give him heroic stature.[3]

The earliest of his three dramatizations, *Riel*, covers the Red River Resistance as well as the North West Rebellion and links them together in terms of tragic causality: the execution of Thomas Scott, presented as necessary to demonstrate the effectiveness of the Provisional Government, brings about the demand for revenge in Orange Ontario. In the manner of Shakespeare's history plays, the prophecy of retribution, that blood will have blood, is assigned to Riel himself as response to the volley of the firing squad which rids him of Thomas Scott but not of the consequences:

> RIEL: (*Overcome*) Me too. My life too is taken. This will be. Oh there is blood and blood.[4]

The connection between the two violent deaths is explicitly completed in Act Two, Scene Fifteen, set in Prime Minister Macdonald's office:

> MACDONALD: Hang! Reprieve! Hang! Reprieve!...Oh hang the whole confounded boiling of them!
> CHAPLEAU: It is not a comfortable position: horns of a dilemma!
> MACDONALD: It's the very dickens of a position. But as we must somehow resolve the dilemma, let's examine the horns.
> CHAPLEAU: If he hangs, Quebec revolts.

MACDONALD: Aye, every flag in Quebec will fly half-mast for him; and we may march behind his hearse into the wilderness perhaps for generations. R.I.P. Riel, R.I.P. Conservative Party. *And*, my dear Chapleau...R.I.P. your political career, never to speak of my own...what with this bawling for clemency—petitions, petitions, petitions, pleas, demands, threats—your entire French Catholic population, priests, people, press (*He tosses a handful of clippings.*) backed up by all the hysterical and sentimental public blatherers in the press of New York, Boston, Washington, Dublin, London, and even Paris and God alone knows where else besides—all determined, by a sort of inverted lynch law, to see that he doesn't hang.

CHAPLEAU: It demonstrates again the widespread revulsion, especially in America, against capital punishment for what is regarded as a political offence.

MACDONALD: A political *offence*, if we hang Riel, but a political *necessity*, when Riel shot Thomas Scott. An obliging sort of logic...By the way, why *must* people associate the trial of Riel with the shooting of Scott?

CHAPLEAU: A most *dis*obliging sort of logic.

MACDONALD: However, if we take our cue from Quebec and *don't* hang him...

CHAPLEAU: Then, of course, Ontario revolts.

MACDONALD: Ontario votes against us to an Orangeman. And we're back where we started from...Chapleau—by another pleasant little masterstroke of irony—the hangman at Regina is to be one, Jack Henderson—a former chum of the late lamented Thomas Scott at Fort Garry. I understand he actually applied—(*Mischievously.*) and to your brother the Sheriff out there—for the privilege, and I'm sure pleasure, of officiating.

CHAPLEAU: How the shade of Thomas Scott will laugh!

MACDONALD: An ugly laugh that will echo around Ontario and go cackling at Quebec till the very mischief is let loose...Hang? Reprieve? One way or the other we must now decide and advise Her Majesty.

CHAPLEAU: If Whitehall would make the decision and save us the embarrassment.

MACDONALD: What else is Whitehall for? However, this time, Her Majesty's Imperial Government flatly refuses to play catspaw for us. Most inconsiderate of them. But this time we must risk burning our own paws—or should I say boats? No, my dear Chapleau, this wretch Riel is actually forcing us to take responsibility and govern Canada. How odd! The outlaw once more shapes the law. Henceforth, Louis Riel's name is scribbled across a chapter of our Constitutional law!...When all has been considered and weighed, I think, perhaps, the public good will be served if he hangs...

CHAPLEAU: I feel relieved. His death at least removes an endless menace and anxiety.

MACDONALD: And he goes down to history as (*Ironically, slightly burlesque and pompous.*) one of the mortal instruments that shaped our destiny! (128–31)

Neither of the sides in the national conflict, Coulter shows in his arrangement of political choices, can escape the foreseen disastrous consequences of an extremely unpleasant decision. Though, unlike the traditional history play, *Riel* does not deal with the internecine struggles of kings and princes, the fate of nations and the irresistible movement into the future is just as powerfully present in the crucial moments of democratic societies and their leaders.

The Canada Council, to whose eventual creation John Coulter had contributed substantially when he presented the artists' brief to the Turgeon Committee of the House of Commons in 1944, commissioned a trilogy about Riel in 1960 which resulted in the addition of *The Trial of Louis Riel* and *The Crime of Louis Riel* to the earlier historical tragedy. The first of these, a condensation of the documents of the Regina trial of 1885, has been staged in Regina every year since 1967, as an important commemoration of Saskatchewan's heritage. One is reminded here of the Christian cycle plays of the Middle Ages: each year, the sacred foundation stories must be revived, to integrate the living community with the mysteries of the tribe.

In several important studies of the nature and function of myth and its ritual re-enactment in numerous earlier, though not necessarily primitive societies, the French comparative religion scholar Mircea

Eliade has shown the integrative function of such revivals of the collective memory.[5] Two of the basic categories of these stories about the common past are creation myths, dealing with the beginnings of the world, and inspiring tales about "the marvellous adventures of the national hero, a youth of humble birth who became the saviour of his people."[6] When most of the summing up of the Prosecution's case against Riel as a traitor and the Defence's case for him through the plea of insanity has been completed, the protagonist of Coulter's *Trial* is finally allowed to speak in his own defence:

RIEL: Your Honours, Gentlemen of the Jury. (*He bows gravely to the Court.*) It would be easy for me today to play insanity, because the circumstances are such as to excite any man...(*To the wonder and embarrassment of the Court, Riel clasps his hands, closes his eyes and prays, with deep humility and simplicity.*)

Oh my God, help me through thy grace and the divine influence of Jesus Christ. Oh my God, bless me. Bless this honourable Court. Bless the honourable jury. Bless my good lawyers who have come seven hundred leagues to try to save my life. Bless also the lawyers for the Crown. They have done what they thought their duty...(*He opens his eyes and looks around, then begins to speak in an intimate, tender voice.*)

On the day of my birth I was helpless, and my mother took care of me and I lived. Today, although I am a man, I am as helpless before this Court in the Dominion of Canada, and in this world, as I was helpless on the knees of my mother on the day of my birth.

The Northwest is also my mother. It is my mother country. And I am sure my mother country will not kill me...any more than my mother did, forty years ago when I came into this world. Because, even if I have my faults, she is my mother and will see that I am true, and be full of love for me.

When I came into the Northwest in July, the 1st of July 1884, I found the Indians suffering. I found the half-breeds eating the rotten pork of the Hudson's Bay Company. They were getting sick and weak every day. I also saw the whites. Although I am a half-breed, the greater part of my heart and blood is white. So I wanted to help also the whites to the best of my ability. I worked for them here, as I worked for them in Manitoba fifteen years ago. I can say that by the grace of God I am the founder of Manitoba. I worked to get free institutions for Manitoba. I was exiled for my pains. But today in Manitoba they have those institutions and I—I am here, hounded, outlawed, on trial for my life, forgotten in Manitoba as if I were dead.

But I am not dead. Not yet. When the glorious General Middleton fired shells and bullets thick as mosquitoes on a hot summer day, I knew that only the grace of God saved me. I said, "Oh my God I offer you all that I am. All my existence I offer you to save my people. Please make my weakness an instrument to help my people, my country." In hope and humility I prayed that prayer. And my prayer was heard.

And I was given a mission. I say humbly the God—who is in this box with me—made me his prophet. Prophet of the New World. God directed me to lead my people. I have led them. (57–58)

Eliade deals with the traditional coping structures concerning the inevitability of misfortune in history by bringing together an awareness of the normality of suffering with conceptualizations of history as theophany and as destiny, in a variety of ancient cultures, as well as modern cultures built upon their foundations: "It has been said that one of the great superiorities of Christianity, compared with the old Mediterranean ethics, was that it gave value to suffering: transforming pain from a negative condition to an experience with positive spiritual content...But if pre-Christian humanity did not seek out suffering and did not grant value to it...as an instrument of purification and spiritual ascent, it never regarded it as without meaning."[7] North American Native religions, though not immediately apparent in Riel's summary of his mission and his mortification, appear in veiled form, in Riel's prayer and ceremonious address, as well as his obvious awareness that a hunter's life, always filled with danger, may become that of the hunted.[8]

This role reversal is the issue confronted in the third part of Coulter's Riel trilogy, *The Crime of Louis Riel*, as the Prologue makes clear: "when a man's people—his tribe—his nation—are menaced, is it a criminal act punishable by death to organize resistance, armed resistance, and fight? As Riel did."[9] What Coulter also addresses in his most recent dramatization is the archetypal and universal nature of the struggle dramatized:

> I see the Métis leader and the rebellions which he led as precursors of the later and present uprisings all over the world, particularly the so-called Third World—armed resistance by small nations against forcible take-over by some powerful neighbour, an impassioned rejection of even greatly enhanced material well-being in order to be free—free of the humiliation of paternalistic government by an outsider, free to develop in their own way from their own roots,

he writes in his Foreword to the play. The change in perspective from suffering servant to angry challenger is evident in the revised version of the protagonist's address to the court:

> RIEL: (*Now alight with passion.*) The Government to which we were subject was an alien Government. Sitting—oh so smug—in their Parliament a thousand miles away. Tools of the Parliament sitting in London—the other side of the world. Nothing to do with us and our kind of life here in our country. They would not allow us to regulate our own lives and property in our own way. Nor would they themselves do anything whatever to assure the rule of law. Common justice for all our people. Petition after petition was sent to that alien Government. With what result? So irresponsible were they, so deaf and so callous to all appeals, that in the course of several years, besides doing nothing to satisfy the just claims of my people, they hardly bothered even to reply. All they did was to send police and more police. That fact indicates absolute lack of responsibility. Insanity of government. Insanity complicated by

paralysis! I was elected by my people to lead them in their struggle against this insanity. To that end I set up our Provisional Government. (53)

Other recent dramatizations find their position somewhere between religion and politics, myth and history. Frederick G. Walsh's *Trial of Louis Riel*, a contribution of the North Dakota Institute for Regional Studies to its University's diamond jubilee, introduces a Narrator who interprets the significance of the events in universal terms.[10]

NARRATOR: How does one measure an event? By numbers? Was Waterloo where thousands died more important than Calvary where one man bled out his loneliness alone? Or by who's involved? Can one man diminish the efforts of the citizen farmers on the village green at Lexington? Did the Plantagenet line of kings accomplish more at Agincourt? What then is the measure of the Riel Rebellion? And of the man who stood trial for high treason? Each of us has his own basis for measurement...The night of the twenty-third of April was a cold one, and all night long the two forces had huddled by their camp fires in restless sleep. Riel's scouts told him that when morning came, his fewer than two hundred Métis would have to do battle with the entire Canadian army. So be it. He called his military leader, Gabriel Dumont, to prepare for battle against the young lads who had left farm and home to fight for Queen and country, for Sir John A. Macdonald and the Canadian Pacific Railroad [sic]. (5–6, 62)

Mavor Moore and Jacques Languirand wrote the bilingual libretto for Harry Somers's Centennial three-act opera, *Louis Riel*.[11] Like Paquin's *Riel* and Coulter's first dramatization, it brings together the major events of the years from 1869 to 1885. Riel's address to the court, compressed into thirty-eight lines of verse, incorporates the same opening selection from the transcript of the trial which had generated great pathos in Coulter's *Trial* documentary play: the helpless childhood of the hero is a most effective part of the myth of the birth, sufferings and achievements of the hero.[12] None of Riel's lengthy and detailed grievances recorded in the transcript appears in the operatic version, only the sufferings and tribulations of the protagonist, the defender of his people, showing, in Coulter's words, "the theme of Louis Riel as an emerging Canadian legendary hero."[13] The rest of the historic cast, from Sir John A. Macdonald to Canada First's Dr. Schultz and Charles Mair, play their now well-defined roles. Schultz and Mair, for example, return to Toronto from Fort Garry to call for revenge for the execution of Thomas Scott:

MAIR: You've read my letters in the Globe!
(*Cheers*)
You know what's been happening in the West!
(*Angry boos*)
SCHULTZ: My dear friends, true Canadians all,
We have come on a grim pilgrimage:
no less than another holy crusade
to rescue yet another land from savages...
(*Cheers*)
...and no less savage under the mask
of the Pope and American republicanism!
(*Cheers*)
Our cause now has a martyr: Thomas Scott!
(*Cheers*)
Thomas Scott was murdered for his faith!
(*Boos*)
Thomas Scott was slain for Canada!
(*Cheers*)
Will you forget the name of Thomas Scott?
(*No! Never!*)
See, here is the rope which tied the martyr's hands
(*Sensation*)

(*As soon as he felt unobserved, Schultz...brings from a carpet bag a whole fistful of short blood-stained ropes...and hands them to Mair.*)

SCHULTZ: Give one of these to every Orange lodge,
and get the posters printed at the Globe
Thomas Scott alive
was a pain in every ass
but his corpse'll be a hero by and by. (24–25)

Jean-Louis Roux subtitles his *Bois-Brûlés* (1968) a "reportage épique,"[14] focussing more on the heroic struggle and less on the noble suffering of Riel, Dumont and the Métis. As he notes in his preface, "Je ne veux pas que raconter l'histoire d'un homme, mais également chanter la saga de la nation métis."(10) This acknowledgement of the mythical dimensions of the events, of the saga of a brave but doomed minority, shows the extent to which the dramatic treatment of these materials has approximated the development of the English history play of the Tudor period. More than one literary scholar has identified the hero of Shakespeare's two tetralogies as England itself and the sequence of plays as a national epic. This heroic cycle was founded on the Tudor myth of Providential agency and the rebirth of King Arthur in the Tudor line shows it to be an even clearer precursor, on a grand scale, of the recent treatments of the North West Rebellions.[15] Riel, on the morning of 12 May 1885, cheers himself with an epic parallel from the Old Testament:

RIEL: J'ai vu Goliath s'avancer, sous un ciel assombri. J'ai vu la frêle David faire tournoyer sa fronde au-dessus de sa tête. J'ai vu Goliath lever son sabre menaçant. J'ai tremblé pour David; j'ai maudit sa faiblesse. J'ai pleuré sur la victoire du géant! Mais, j'avais tort de douter de Dieu. (175)

But Providence has designated this day and the fall of Batoche for other purposes; for Riel has sinned and must be brought to repent and return to the true religion of the Catholic Church, as Père André tells him in prison:

PÈRE ANDRÉ: Louis, un chagrin profond me dévore l'âme...Vous vous êtes révolté contre les hommes et vous leur en avez rendu comptes. Mais, vous vous êtes aussi révolté contre Dieu, en mettant en doute l'autorité de ses représentants du terre. (193)

Resembling Saul more than David, and Shakespeare's Richard II more than his triumphant Henry V, Riel must expiate his sin of pride and justice must be done.

While the survivor of 1885, Gabriel Dumont, appeared in many of the earlier dramatizations, though he was omitted from Coulter's trilogy, George Woodcock, biographer of Dumont, has centred his play about the North West Rebellion on the military leader, not the politician-prophet. It was broadcast in 1975 by the CBC as "Six Dry Cakes for the Hunted," published in 1976 as *Gabriel Dumont and the Northwest Rebellion* and reprinted in 1977 as *Six Dry Cakes for the Hunted* with the subtitle "A Canadian Myth."[16] George Woodcock, anarchist literary essayist, sees Gabriel Dumont as a political revolutionary whose consciousness conflicts with the dominant ideology of Canada. Because of this, he is exiled: "From the earliest days of settlement in Canada, those who have adhered to their ties to colonial power have consistently demanded the banishment of all those whose vision originates in a commitment to the particulars of the 'new land.'"[17] Dumont has the last word in the play and also the last word about reality:

DUMONT:....You have already heard, Monsieur le Commandant, what happened at Tourond's Coulee, which the English call Fish Creek. I planned it all like a buffalo pound....In Batoche we heard that Poundmaker and his Assiniboines and Crees had beaten the English outside Battleford. We expected him to march to our aid, but though we sent messengers, the Indians never arrived, nor did the Métis from Montana and Fort Edmonton. We faced the redcoats alone. On the ninth of May they reached Batoche. We fought four long and bitter days. Old men and boys lay in the rifle pits beside the hunters....Women picked bullets from the ground for their men to use again. At the end we were firing stones and nails from our muskets while the powder lasted. Riel foretold victory, and all the time he prayed for it, and there was victory, but we did not win....

RIEL: My voice has lost its power. My people are scattered and those who are with me do not hear what I say.

DUMONT: They know it is the end. Batoche is finished, Louis. And there is nowhere else to make a stand. You know what the English say, "He who fights and runs away, lives to fight another day." There is a time to fight and a time to run. To stay here is death.

RIEL: You are telling me we are beaten.

DUMONT: Napoleon himself could not fight without men or bullets.

RIEL: Beaten! Defeated! I cannot believe it.

DUMONT: When you talked of war and we took up arms, you should have thought of that, Louis. I knew from the beginning that two sides cannot win the same battle.

RIEL: Why did you fight, then?

DUMONT: Defeat seemed better than submission. There was a chance, and I was content with a chance.

RIEL: God spoke to me, Gabriel. I know he spoke.

DUMONT: You may have misunderstood him.

RIEL: What can we do now?

DUMONT: I know what I shall do. I have ninety cartridges and I am a dead shot. I shall stay in the woods and pick off the redcoats when they come to hunt me. When my ammunition is finished I shall go south like a migrant bird. (104–7)

One of the emergent Canadian thematic myths is "survival." Margaret Atwood, who dealt with the subject in great detail in 1972, examined Don Gutteridge's narrative poem, *Riel*, and the Coulter dramatic versions along with the Somers/Moore opera. Riel, "the perfect all-Canadian failed hero," while he represents the authentic life of the land, cannot prevail against the imposed culture. He does not know how to be a creative nonvictim; Gabriel Dumont does.[18] In fact, though not in his soldier's courage, he resembles the archetypical survivor of the Elizabethan history play, Falstaff. While the tragic hero, subject to the law of necessity, must bear responsibility for "the flaws in the nature of things," the comic hero escapes such fatalism. He or she functions as "chief tactician in a permanent resistance movement, or rebellion, within the frontiers of human experience."[19] The comic hero is a natural anarchist.

Franco-Manitoban Claude Dorge's memory-play *Le Roitelet*, produced by the Cercle Moliére of Saint Boniface in 1976, commemorates
Riel's days in the Montreal Asylum in 1876. In its production date it
thus coincides with the publication of Thomas Flanagan's edition of
The Diaries of Louis Riel, though Dorge's contribution to the theatre of
Riel was not published until 1980.[20] The drama of the mind, the self-
disclosures of the famous, these are the modern works which, like
Maeterlinck's theatre of stasis, take us beyond the old epic task of the
history play. Here soliloquy becomes the whole dramatic action and
psychology reconciles the contradictions which courts of justice could
not. Here, not only Bishop Bourget but also Thomas Scott hail the
protagonist as the New Christ:

> SCOTT: Tu es béni, car tu es le nouveau sauveur. Béni es-tu, Louis
> David. Va, maintenant. Marche la tête haute. Va sans crainte vers
> tes adversaires. Je suis la, à tes côtés. Je te défends et te second. Je
> suis ton précurseur. Le nouveau Baptiste. Et toi, tu es le nouveau
> Christ....
> RIEL:....Je suis le nouveau Christ! (85)

As editor Flanagan notes in his comments following a series of divine
revelations recorded by Riel in his diary, 1876 was the beginning of
Riel's public mission.[21]

The tentative conclusions to be drawn from these diverse dramatizations are that each of them, however limited, has made it possible
for contemporaries as well as for future generations of Canadian
readers and audiences to establish an immediate and felt relationship
to these characters in conflict. As my findings show, the perceptive-
ness and skill with which each of the playwrights has created this
impression of immediacy vary considerably. The three early playwrights, Broughall, Bayer and Parage, as well as Paquin, are too close
to the events dramatized in time as well as in unilateral sympathies to
be able to create the kind of genuine suspense and believable charac-
terization which we associate with the best kind of theatrical works.

Among the "new wave" of mid-twentieth century dramatizations,
the Coulter trilogy stands out for thoroughness of exploration as well
as grasp of the political, cultural, economic, and religious tensions

represented by the opposing forces. Coulter's growing awareness of the dynamics of his hero's character makes his Riel a valuable mediation of the historical figure in terms of the possibilities of dramatization. The Roux and Dorge French language dramatizations are impressive in their originality of approach and theatricality of conception, making them both eminently performable. Both the Walsh and Woodcock treatments are innovative in their perspective, choice of method of presentation and treatment of Riel. By choosing Gabriel Dumont as his titular hero, George Woodcock has made it possible for audiences to become immediately aware that there was a genuine alternative. The result need not have been the catastrophe of the West: one of the options a historical dramatist has is, indeed, that of counter-factual history. Yet Woodcock does not speculate he merely presents the events, the choices, the outcome, from the point of view of him who ran away, not to fight another day but to survive, to continue his life in another political and social context. He, like millions of immigrants, demonstrates the ability to accept the inevitable, to adjust, to change. This is not the choice of the tragic hero, it is the choice of ordinary Canadians in their daily struggles to prevail. We love and admire Louis Riel for his courage, his devotion to a cause, his willingness to stake his all; we love Gabriel Dumont as a fellow survivor, a role model for times of crisis. There is the way of the hero and there is the way of rational compromise.

NOTES

1. George Broughall, *The Ninetieth on Active Service* (Winnipeg: George Bishop, 1885); Charles Bayer and E. Parage, *Riel* (Montréal: L'étandard, 1886); Elzéar Paquin, *Riel* (Montréal: Beauchemin, 1886), tr. Eugene and Renate Benson, in Anton Wagner, ed., *Canada's Lost Plays*, Volume IV (Toronto: Canadian Theatre Review Publications, 1982).

2. Geraldine S.C. Anthony, *John Coulter* (Boston: G.K. Hall and Co., 1976), p. 60.

3. John Coulter in Geraldine S.C. Anthony, ed., *Stage Voices* (Toronto: Doubleday Canada Limited, 1978), p. 13.

4. John Coulter, *Riel* (Hamilton: Cromlech Press, 1972), p. 37; *The Trial of Louis Riel* (Ottawa: Oberon Press, 1968); *The Crime of Louis Riel* (Toronto: Playwrights Co-op, 1976).

5. Mircea Eliade, *Myth and Reality* (New York: Harper and Row, 1968); *Cosmos and History* (New York: Harper and Row, 1959).
6. *Myth and Reality*, p. 8.
7. *Cosmos and History*, p. 96.
8. Ruth M. Underhill, *Red Man's Religion* (Chicago: University of Chicago Press, 1965), p. 48.
9. *The Crime of Louis Riel*, p. 1.
10. Frederick G. Walsh, *The Trial of Louis Riel* (Fargo, N.D.: Institute for Regional Studies, 1965).
11. Harry Somers, Mavor Moore and Jacques Languirand, *Louis Riel* (Toronto: Canadian Music Centre, 1967).
12. D. Morton, ed., *The Queen v. Louis Riel* (Toronto: University of Toronto Press, 1974), p. 312. See also Otto Rank, *The Myth of the Birth of the Hero* (New York: Alfred A. Knopf, 1959).
13. *The Crime of Louis Riel*, Foreword.
14. Jean-Louis Roux, *Bois-Brûlés* (Montréal: Editions du jour, 1968).
15. See especially E.M.W. Tilyard, *Shakespeare's History Plays* (London: Chatto and Windus, 1944).
16. George Woodcock, *Gabriel Dumont and the Northwest Rebellion* (Toronto: Playwright's Co-op, 1976); *Two Plays* (Vancouver: Talonbooks, 1977), p. 57.
17. *Two Plays*, back cover.
18. Margaret Atwood, *Survival* (Toronto: Anansi, 1972), pp. 167–69; 38–39.
19. Wylie Sypher, "The Meanings of Comedy," in Robert W. Corrigan, ed., *Comedy: Meaning and Form* (San Francisco: Chandler Publishing, 1965), pp. 49; 54.
20. Claude Dorge, *Le Roitelet* (Ottawa: Editions du Blé, 1980); Thomas Flanagan, ed., *The Diaries of Louis Riel* (Edmonton: Hurtig Publishers, 1976).
21. *Diaries*, p. 168.

E. BRIAN TITLEY

6 Hayter Reed and Indian Administration in the West

I HAVE HEARD talk about this new man Reed. They say he brags about being able to tell just exactly how much work an ox can do by looking at it. Then he feeds it enough to keep it going—not one bit more. Well, that may be all right for oxen but not for men—tell me...why do they put men like this over us?[1]

In her fictionalized biography of Poundmaker, Norma Sluman attributes these observations about Hayter Reed to the Cree chief during the early months of 1881. Although the words are the products of the writer's imagination, they nonetheless convey well the discouraging first impressions which the Battleford Indians formed of their newly appointed agent. Reed's incumbency as agent was to be short, tempestuous and, in the eyes of the Indian Department, successful. For he brought to his work an unusual combination of talent and temperament; qualities that had been forged in an earlier career in the military and which were all the more remarkable in a department conspicuous for the mediocrity of its personnel. Promotion came rapidly: to Assistant Commissioner, to Commissioner and ultimately, in little more than a decade after joining the service, to Deputy Superintendent General of Indian Affairs. This spectacular advancement was a consequence not only of ability and hard work, but also of good fortune and shrewd politics. For Reed's rise in the department coincided with a lengthy period of Conservative ascendancy in Ottawa and his loyalty to that party and to one its luminaries, Edgar Dewdney, worked greatly in his favour. His belief that the Indians benefitted under his supervision and his success in conveying such an impression to his superiors also helped.

Hayter Reed was born on 26 May 1849 in L'Orignal, Ontario, the son of George D. and Harriet Reed, immigrants from Surrey, England. Education was received at Upper Canada College and the Model Grammar School, Toronto. The 1860s was the decade of the American Civil War and the Fenian raids on British North America. The sense of insecurity arising from these events and the evident unwillingness of London to commit adequate forces to the defence of Canada, prompted the organization of many local militia units. The young Reed was caught up in the patriotic excitement of the time and in 1865, at the age of sixteen, he joined the Kingston Rifle Battalion. Within two years he had become a full-time drill instructor.

Reed evidently found the military life congenial and in 1870 he was appointed Brigade Major of the 6th Brigade Division. In the following year he accompanied the force to Manitoba where it took up garrison duty at Fort Garry. The militia had afforded the energetic officer the opportunity of developing his talents in other directions. He had been studying law for some time and in 1872 was called to the Manitoba Bar. A year later he was made Adjutant of the garrison and held that position until the force was disbanded in 1878. Shortly afterwards he was asked to inaugurate the land guide system in the province, and remained in charge of that operation until offered the post of Indian agent at Battleford in 1881.[2]

These were difficult times for the Indians of the North West. During the previous decade the first seven of the numbered treaties had been signed and the buffalo herds had declined to the point of virtual extinction. This latter calamity raised the spectre of starvation for the hunters of the plains and the federal Indian department was obliged to supply rations as a measure of relief. Rations were but a temporary expedient, however, as far as the department was concerned. Under the direction of Edgar Dewdney, Indian Commissioner for Manitoba and the North West Territories, it was decided that the Indians should be settled on their reserves, encouraged to adopt agriculture, and thereby achieve economic self-sufficiency.

Many Indians were prepared to make an honest effort at this new way of life. The treaty negotiations show that they regarded these agreements as the means by which the government would supply them with the knowledge and equipment to do so. Nevertheless, there were some leaders, such as Big Bear, Piapot, and Little Pine who wished to perpetuate the hunting culture for as long as possible, and who initially refused to take treaty.[3]

The task of settling the Indians on their reserves and initiating them into the mysteries of tillage and animal husbandry fell to those intrepid sentinels of civilization: Indian agents. By 1881 the area encompassed by Treaty 6 had been divided into three agencies with headquarters located at Edmonton, Battleford and Prince Albert. When the position of agent at Battleford became available in 1881, Hayter Reed was selected to fill it.

When informing Reed of his appointment, Commissioner Dewdney issued instructions in accordance with prevailing policy. The new agent was advised that every inducement should be made to get Indians settled on their reserves. Rations of flour and either beef or bacon should be distributed to the destitute but, whenever possible, "work should be exacted in return." Luxury items such as tea, sugar and tobacco were not to be supplied, except at treaty payment time. Expenditure was to be minimized as much as possible. The efficient operation of the Indian farms and the supervision of the work of the farming instructors was to be one of the agent's principal responsibilities. While the transition to agriculture was deemed essential, it was recognized that the Indians could still partially support themselves in the interim by hunting deer, moose, rabbits, and any game animals that remained abundant.[4]

Shortly after arriving in Battleford in May, Reed set out on a tour of his fiefdom. He found that the Indians regarded their rations as inadequate and expected them to be increased. Instead he reduced them, explaining that assistance would now be strictly limited to those who worked. He did, however, issue some tobacco to the chiefs in order to humour them.[5]

Most of the Indians were unwilling to submit to the harsh regimen which Reed wished to impose. Reserve life was monotonous and the lure of the open plains irresistible. Big Bear and his followers were camped in the Cypress Hills and many wished to join him. Some of Poundmaker's band threatened to take government cattle with them to the south and Reed only prevented them from doing so "by a show of firmness." But in spite of the agent's best efforts, by the end of May the majority of Indians belonging to the bands of Poundmaker, Thunderchild, Moosomin and Strike-Him-On-The-Back had left for the plains. Only a handful of men remained on the reserves to do the agricultural work. Reed identified Poundmaker as the principal troublemaker and the cause of much of the unrest. The chief had apparently circulated a rumour that 800 soldiers had landed at Prince Albert with the intention of imprisoning male Indians and abusing their women. This had hastened preparations for the exodus to the south.[6]

Those who remained on their reserves that summer worked hard. This came as a big surprise to Reed, who had already formed a low opinion of "Indian character." While expressing cautious optimism about the future, he warned his supervisors that the present generation would only make progress toward self-sufficiency under careful and constant supervision. And yet it was difficult to find men who were prepared to provide such tutelage. He had found that the farm instructors preferred to do the work themselves, rather than subject themselves to the "monotony of teaching." Most of them spent little time among the Indians.[7]

Reed struggled on throughout the summer against this frustrating indifference. And when the crops were brought in that autumn, there was further cause for disheartenment. Poor seeding techniques, heavy rains, and early frosts brought poor yields and resultant discouragement to those who had toiled so assiduously.[8]

Although Reed was willing to persevere in the face of such adversity, he evidently found several features of his role as agent unpalatable. Many years later, he characterized the Indians under his charge as some of the worst in Canada and "the scum of the Plains."[9] And on one occasion he complained to Dewdney of the manner in which they pestered him in his office during working hours. He was often obliged to retreat to his living quarters "in order to obviate the constant nagging, noise and stench."[10]

The dislike was mutual. Reed confessed to the Commissioner that his strict adherence to the work for rations rule had earned him the name "Iron Heart" among the Indians. He warned his superior that should he set foot in the agency he would be greeted by a barrage of complaints about the policy pursued. Headquarters in Ottawa was informed of the hard line adopted by the Battleford agent and it not only approved, but urged that all other agents do likewise.[11]

Dewdney showed his growing appreciation of Reed's efforts and abilities in 1882 when he appointed him one of the official members of the North-West Council.[12] It proved to be a wise choice, for a year later the Commissioner reported to Prime Minister Macdonald that Reed had "been of good service, his legal training being of much assistance" to him.[13] Reed remained a member of the Council until it was superceded in 1888 by an elected assembly.

Fortuitous circumstances brought further opportunities. Towards the end of 1882, Elliot T. Galt, the Assistant Indian Commissioner, decided to abandon the federal service in order to devote himself fully to his family's prospering coal business.[14] Reed was the logical candidate to succeed him. He left his post at Battleford in December and spent a few months making himself conversant with the routine of the Assistant Commissioner's office in Winnipeg under the guidance of the outgoing incumbent.[15] Galt's resignation took effect on 15 March, 1883 and Reed was appointed Acting Assistant Commissioner on the same day.[16]

Indian administration in the West was facing a crisis of alarming magnitude at the time. About 3,000 Cree and Assiniboine Indians under the leadership of Big Bear, Little Pine, Lucky Man, and Piapot had gathered in the Cypress Hills area where they conducted raids across the border and received rations from the Mounted Police post at Fort Walsh. Should it be acceded to, their demand for contiguous reserves would have created a large Indian territory which would have been difficult to control. Dewdney was determined to resist this demand and he had resolved to resettle the Indians in the Qu'Appelle, Battleford, and Fort Pitt districts.[17]

Reed was dispatched to carry out the Commissioner's wishes in April. By his own account, it took three months of "hard labour" and "not a little risk of life" to accomplish the task.[18] The Mounted Police cooperated closely with him in the difficult negotiations that were necessary. Fort Walsh was closed, rations were cut off, and promises of assistance were made to those who agreed to settle in the desired areas. Among the assurances made by the Assistant Commissioner was that fifteen Indians imprisoned in the Manitoba Penitentiary for horse-stealing would be given reduced sentences.[19] By the end of the summer Big Bear and the other chiefs had reluctantly led their followers northwards in accordance with government wishes.

The Cypress Hills episode confirmed in Dewdney's mind that Reed had the tenacity and martial ardour necessary to bend Indians to his will. During the years that followed, the Assistant Commissioner became his trusted aide, tirelessly traversing the countryside with a vigilant eye for potential difficulties and informing his superior of the lie of the land.

The resettlement of the Indians along the Saskatchewan and Qu'Appelle Valleys had not produced the subservience that officialdom had anticipated. Big Bear continued to agitate for a large Indian territory and for renegotiation of the treaties. Winters were hard, crops were poor, and the general hardship spawned ready support for his campaign. The Métis were also disaffected, and the return of Louis Riel from the United States was a further unwelcome development to the authorities.

The situation was an explosive one, and yet, in spite of the many portents of impending disaster, Reed and Dewdney grimly persisted with a policy that was punitive rather than conciliatory. Admittedly, their hands were tied somewhat by the budget reductions imposed upon the Commissioner's domains by Deputy Superintendent General Lawrence Vankoughnet after his visit to the West in September 1883.[20] Nonetheless, they maintained their faith in the efficacy of the rations for work rule, and Reed's inflexibility on the question earned him a notoriety that was legendary.

But flexible he could be, especially when an arsenal of loaded rifles was pointed at his head. Such was the case in the well-known confrontation that took place in the Crooked Lakes agency in February, 1884. In that incident, a group of armed Indians led by Yellow Calf beat up the local farm instructor, raided the storehouse and barricaded themselves in their dance hall in defiance of the police. In order to resolve the dispute, Reed was obliged to promise leniency for the offenders and an increase in rations. An earlier directive of his to reduce rations had been the cause of the problem in the first place.[21]

Reed's tactics were not just the infliction of punishment upon those he considered troublesome; he was equally concerned to reward those making genuine attempts to adjust to reserve life and to the wishes of the government. On a tour of the Saskatchewan District in October and November of 1883, he observed that the settled Indians at Duck Lake, Battleford, and Fort Pitt had produced grain for which there was no market. He recommended that the government purchase it and arrange to have it milled. This would encourage the Indians in future agricultural endeavours and enable them to buy badly needed items such as clothing.[22] Moosomin's band was one marked out for special commendation by the Assistant Commissioner. After an visit to these Indians in September 1884, he informed Dewdney that they owned about fifty pigs, mostly purchased by themselves, and were planning to buy sheep. He urged that they be supplied with additional livestock as encouragement to keep up the good work.[23]

The prosperity of Moosomin's band tended to reinforce in Reed's mind the notion that the evident hardship visited upon other Indians was of their own making. As he toured the Treaty 4 and Treaty 6 agencies during 1884 he tended to minimize in his reports to the Commissioner the extent of the widespread suffering.[24] Starvation, he believed, was a product of laziness or moral turpitude. Gratuitous assistance would merely foster dependency upon the government.

Reed was far more concerned about the political activities of Big Bear than he was about the prevalence of misery. The Cree chief organized a major council of Indians at Duck Lake during the summer of 1884 at which he advocated strong measures against government policy. Reed warned Dewdney that a council would be troublesome and that it should be prevented by the police. He also suggested finding some pretext for arresting Poundmaker, "the worst moving spirit in the country."[25]

To Dewdney's credit, he refused to act on some of the more draconian proposals emanating from his assistant. By temperament he tended to be more conciliatory and his views were shaped by reports from a variety of sources. Few of his other informants couched matters in such absolute hues of black and white. Yet it would be misleading to put much emphasis on the differences of opinion between the two men. That Dewdney valued Reed's efforts is beyond question. In April 1884, for instance, he strongly recommended to the Prime Minister that Reed's appointment as Assistant Commissioner be confirmed. He pointed out that not only was his subordinate thoroughly familiar with office work, but that he found him to be "energetic and hardworking, having a knowledge of the Indian character possessed by few in the country."[26] The appointment was confirmed on 5 May.[27]

There can be little doubt that the harsh policies supported by Reed and Dewdney were a major contributing factor to Indian participation in the Rebellion of 1885. The Indian role in the main consisted of raids on storehouses and acts of violence against obnoxious officials. The skirmish between the police and Métis at Duck Lake on 26 March was taken as a signal by angry, frustrated, and hungry young men to strike back at an oppressive system.

Reed remained in the Saskatchewan District throughout the disturbances. He moved about among the loyal Indians pressing upon them the good will of the government and counselling them to remain on their reserves. After the fall of Batoche on 12 May, Dewdney assigned him to assist General Middleton in an advisory capacity, because of his knowledge of the country and of the Indians. With the surrender of Big Bear at Fort Pitt on 2 June, this role came to an end.

Throughout most of July, August and September, Reed remained in the Saskatchewan District supervising the readjustment of the Indians to more peaceful times in close co-operation with the military and the police. He hired more agents, believing that the lack of close supervision had contributed greatly to the recent hostilities. His frequent reports to Dewdney were optimistic in tone. The Indians were subdued and were unlikely to rise again. There were, however, some "reckless characters" on the loose and he had borrowed a revolver for his own protection. And to prevent even the possibility of further disturbances, he was attempting to confine former rebels to their reserves by requiring that they receive a pass from their agents before departing. The pass system, of course, had no legal validity.[28]

Reed's reports also betrayed a vindictive attitude towards those who had been in arms. He had been appalled to discover that some rebels were in receipt of rations and had arranged for such supplies to be either cut off completely or drastically reduced.[29] It was his earnest wish that Riel would "swing," for if he did not, it would have "a great prejudicial effect on the minds of the Indians."[30] In fact, he urged Dewdney to have Riel and those Indians convicted of murder at Regina returned to the Battleford area for public execution. The Indians should witness the spectacle as it would "cause them to meditate for many a day" and provide "ocular demonstration" of the "sound thrashing" that the government was inflicting.[31] Dewdney felt that such a course of action would be unwise. He feared that public hangings close to home would excite the superstitious nature of the Indians and cause them to leave the reserves.[32]

Reed's most lasting contribution to the post-Rebellion readjustment lay in a series of recommendations regarding the future management of the Indians which he submitted to Dewdney on 29 July. The Commissioner added his own observations (almost entirely supportive) in the margin and passed the document along to the Prime Minister. After some discussion of the proposals in Ottawa, they were endorsed with few exceptions. Among the principal recommendations that won the approbation of Macdonald were the following: that all Indians be disarmed either by persuasion or the withholding of ammunition; that the tribal system of government be broken up; that the work for rations policy be strictly adhered to; that the pass system be used to confine the Indians to their reserves; that rebels be denied their annuities until such time as the cost of the damage they had caused be recouped by the government and until they had displayed remorse for their actions; that the horses of rebels be confiscated and cattle substituted for them; that Big Bear's band be broken up and dispersed among others; that loyal Indians be conspicuously rewarded as an object lesson to those who had been in arms.[33]

These tactics were pursued with mixed results in subsequent years. Tribal organization proved particularly resilient, although elected chiefs gradually replaced those who had acquired leadership by traditional means. The disarmament of the Indians and the confiscation of their horses had to proceed with great caution, and was universally resisted. The pass system also proved ineffective. It constituted a denial of treaty rights and never became part of the Indian Act. It only served as a means of monitoring the movements of those who travelled from their reserves. The withholding of annuities was easy to accomplish and Reed believed that it had a salutary effect upon those so deprived during the years of its implementation.[34] And the loyal were rewarded. Gifts of cash, livestock, blankets, cookstoves, tobacco, and so forth, amounting to a value of $13,073, were bestowed upon those who had resisted the call to arms.[35]

The crushing of the Rebellion, the imprisonment of Big Bear and Poundmaker, and the flight of some of the more troublesome Indians to the United States brought an end to the agitation for greater Indian autonomy and a renegotiation of the treaties. It also ushered in a "coercive system of reserve administration" that survived until well into the next century.[36] In order to accomplish this, the larger agencies were subdivided and the administrative structure of the Indian department was firmly established.[37] Increasingly, agents came to regulate almost every aspect of Indians' lives, or at least attempted to do so.

During these critical years of transition, Reed continued to be Dewdney's right-hand man. The Commissioner's appreciation of his efforts was evident in the frequent representations he made to Ottawa seeking salary increases for his assistant. He described Reed as "a very faithful and hard-working officer" and, on another occasion, as "an indefatigable worker" and felt that it was unjust that his remuneration should be less than that of agency inspectors E. McColl, A.

McGibbon and T.P. Wadsworth. Nor was he completely satisfied when the Assistant Commissioner was granted the same salary as the inspectors ($2200) as of 1 July 1887.[38]

When Dewdney resigned as Indian Commissioner and Lieutenant Governor of the North West Territories in 1888, it was decided that the two positions should no longer be held by the same man. Reed was Dewdney's logical successor as Commissioner. Dewdney was certainly supportive, and, as he entered parliament assuming the portfolios of Minister of the Interior and Superintendent General of Indian Affairs, he was able to have his way.[39] Vankoughnet evidently favoured Wadsworth, an old ally of his, but was "squelched," as Reed put it, by the incoming minister.[40]

The intrigue surrounding the succession was complicated by the intrusion of ecclesiastical agitation into the question. The Roman Catholics, who felt that adherents of their faith were underrepresented in the department, campaigned for a Catholic appointee either as Commissioner or Assistant Commissioner. Rumours that such representations were being made aroused the ire of Protestant missionaries, who in turn attempted to ensure the appointment of one of their own. Several, in fact, openly favoured Reed, who was of the Anglican persuasion.[41] Reed himself felt that if Amedee E. Forget, clerk of the North West Council, were given the position of Assistant Commissioner, it would "certainly satisfy the Catholics."[42] This suggestion of his was acted upon.

Reed's elevation to the Commissionership brought a deluge of congratulatory messages to his doorstep, many of them from the Indian agents of Manitoba and the North West Territories to whom he was known personally. To interpret this as evidence of universal enthusiasm in the department for his promotion would, however, be misleading. R. Newberry Toms, a Presbyterian missionary at File Hills, confided to the new Commissioner that many under him regretted his appointment, as they felt he was "too stingy."[43] Their premonition that he would prove a demanding taskmaster was to be accurate indeed.

Reed's administration showed that he was a firm believer in the department's long-established policy of "protection, civilization and assimilation." "If the Indian," he said, "is to become a source of profit to the country, it is clear that he must be amalgamated with the white population." Before this goal could be accomplished the Indian would have to acquire an occupation and become "imbued with the white man's spirit and impregnated by his ideas." In the process of learning to "provide for their own requirements," Indians would, "inculcate a spirit of self-reliance and independence which [would] fit them for enfranchisement, and the enjoyment of all the privileges, as well as the responsibilities of citizenship." Reed was critical of the unseemly haste with which the Americans were pursuing enfranchisement. He preferred the more gradual Canadian approach. While admitting that keeping Indians on reserves would ultimately delay their assumption of citizenship, he felt that it was preferable to immediately dispersing them "unprotected among communities where they could not hold their own, and would speedily be down-trodden and debauched."[44]

Although the department had three inspectors in the prairie region to supervise the work of its agents, the new Commissioner insisted on making regular tours of the agencies to keep a personal eye on things. The tours were gruelling ordeals on horseback and required lodging in agents' houses or camping out, sometimes during the winter months.[45] But they kept Reed in touch with reserve conditions and enabled him to offer encouragement, reward, or reprimand as he saw fit.[46]

Among the rewards which he saw fit to bestow upon the Indians was the gradual restoration of annuity payments to those who had been deprived of them because of insurrection. In 1888 between ten and fifteen per cent of the former rebels were thus restored to departmental favour. And the Commissioner promised that the number would be increased in the following year should enough be found worthy. He explained his strategy in language that could readily be mistaken for that of a stern parent or school teacher dealing with recalcitrant children:

Although....clemency may too readily be construed by Indians as indifference or fear; on the other hand, to continue a punishment too long cannot fail to suggest the idea of vindictiveness; and if, as is being done, the restoration of their privileges be made dependent upon the practical evidence of sincere contrition, furnished by cheerful application to the pursuit of industry, the best results may be anticipated; for not only will those rewarded be stimulated to perseverance, but other will be encouraged to follow their good example.[47]

Reed had reason to be pleased with his program of behaviour modification, for in the following year he was able to report that it was working wonders.[48] And in 1890 he proudly announced that all payments had been resumed and that traces of disloyalty had evidently vanished.[49]

The gradual restoration of annuities of former rebels and the distribution of rations to all Indians were key elements in the agricultural policy that the department pursued in the post-Rebellion years. Farming operations increasingly owed little to Indian initiative as they came to be carefully supervised in every respect by agents and other officials. The relentless pursuit of agriculture was in some ways curious, as the suitability of the North West for tillage was by no means clearly established. In fact, seed varieties and cultivation practices amenable to prairie conditions would not make their appearance until the turn of the century.[50] That progress of any measurable degree took place in the 1880s was remarkable indeed.

Reed was cognizant of the difficulties facing agriculture in this untried terrain, but the abundant harvest of 1888 convinced him that the North West had a great future as a grain producing region. He was particularly pleased that several bands, most notably those in the Moose Mountain, Muscowpetung, Assiniboine, Touchwood Hills, and File Hills agencies, were virtually self-sufficient in flour throughout the subsequent winter. With two or three more good harvests in succession, he believed, the department would not have to support the majority of the bands outside of Treaty 7 for at least half of each year.[51] But the produce of the soil was disappointing in subsequent years and his predictions of progress were modified accordingly.

Apart from these harsh realities, Reed did not conceive of the Indians becoming prosperous farmers but rather frugal, self-sufficient peasants in the European sense. The aim was to expand slowly the acreage under cultivation, encouraging each family to work an individual piece of land. The Commissioner believed that if a family had an acre of wheat, an acre of roots and vegetables, and the product of a cow or two, it would be well on its way to independence.[52]

The transformation of the Indians into a peasant class was deliberately fostered by ensuring that they engaged in their work using hand tools rather than machinery. Reed admitted that when his charges saw white farmers using labour-saving devices, they coveted such implements for themselves. But they did so, he surmised, merely to have more time to sit and smoke their pipes. He instructed his agents to teach Indians the use of hoes, scythes, cradles, and other simple devices which were readily available and which would allow everyone to be kept constantly busy.[53] Manual labour, it seems, was morally uplifting in itself, apart from its products.

This feature of the agricultural program was not adhered to, however, with rigid absolutism. Indians who were conspicuous for their productivity were permitted to buy reapers, mowers, wagons, and other useful articles. Reed believed that unless they derived some tangible material reward for their efforts there would be no incentive to persevere with the work.[54]

A key element of the program was the subdivision of reserves into individual lots, a process that Reed initiated and pursued vigorously during his incumbency as Commissioner. The rectangular survey system employed throughout the West was thus applied to Indian lands with one important difference. Each section was divided into sixteen lots of forty acres, rather than the standard four quarter-sections of 160 acres. Reserve hay and wood lands continued to be held in common. Certificates of ownership were granted by the department for the forty-acre lots and Reed believed that they would do much to develop the "spirit of individual responsibility" and undermine the "tribal communist system."[55]

Raising livestock was the other major component of the department's program of reserve economic development. Cattle and other domestic beasts would provide an alternative source of food when crop returns were disappointing. Some livestock had originally been given to the Indians as a treaty right. These animals had been of poor quality and most had either perished or been killed within a few years. During his time as Commissioner, Reed promoted the establishment of government-owned herds of cattle that would be tended by the Indians under supervision as if they were their own. This policy had complementary aims: first, it would enable the department to raise its own beef rations rather than purchase them from whites; and second, it would serve to awaken "that sense of proprietorship, which renders [Indians] strongly averse to countenancing anything having a tendency to disturb existing law and order."[56]

By the early 1890s Reed was pronouncing his animal husbandry program a success. Cattle-killing by Indians was virtually a thing of the past and the natives were learning to avoid brutality to the beasts.[57] The Commissioner was most anxious to create livestock herds on the reserves of Treaty 7 as that region was considered unsuitable for cultivation and there was much idleness among the men which cattle would cure. But his enthusiasm for herding was not shared by all officials in the department's headquarters in Ottawa. Headquarters wished to proceed with greater caution until the success of the stock already purchased had been more fully established. To Reed's annoyance, his estimates for 1891, and especially an item to enable the purchase of cattle for Treaty 7, were reduced by Ottawa.[58] And a plan of his which involved exchanging the Peigans' ponies for cattle failed to win the Deputy Superintendent General's approval.[59]

In spite of the obvious frustrations in dealing with a distant and indifferent bureaucracy, Reed could claim some success in the promotion of agriculture and ranching among his minions in Manitoba and the North West Territories. Between 1888 and 1893, livestock in the hands of Indians increased from 10,488 to 19,492 head. During the same time period, land under cultivation expanded from 10,228 to 16,327 acres.[60] These latter figures suggest a more modest increase, but this was in line with Reed's policy of the gradual expansion of cultivation.

The ultimate measure of the success of Reed's agricultural policies lay, of course, in their ability to produce food for the Indians and thereby reduce and perhaps eliminate the necessity of providing rations at public expense. Rations had always been viewed as merely a temporary measure during a period of transition and there was a constant effort to minimize this unprecedented example of state-sponsored charity. The insistence that Indians work for all they received was ideologically in harmony with the prevailing neo-mercantilist economic outlook and it was a necessary foil to constant parliamentary criticism of profligate government spending.[61]

It has been observed that in his days as Indian agent and Assistant Commissioner, Reed had acquired a deserved notoriety for the ruthlessness with which he restricted rations only to those whose behaviour was in accordance with department wishes. During his term as Commissioner this adamancy persisted. There were predictable complaints and not just from Indians, but from settlers and from the Mounted Police as well. Fears were expressed that ration reductions would not prompt the Indians to work, but rather to kill settler's cattle.[62] But Reed clung tenaciously to his principles and, as the following figures demonstrate, was able to produce the sort of results which appeared to vindicate his tactics.[63]

Rations reductions therefore went hand in hand with an increase in Indian agriculture and animal husbandry. While the Commissioner was reasonably pleased with this evidence of progress, he believed that more could have been accomplished but for unavoidable contingencies. Game continued to decline during these years, placing many on the ration list who had hitherto supported themselves at least in part by the chase. And then there was that lingering generation of old warriors whom Reed believed would have to be supported until they died off. Only then could total self-sufficiency be accomplished. In the interim an economic system akin to feudalism was to be maintained. Confined increasingly to their reserves and forced to labour under the supervision of agents and farm instructors, Indians found themselves in circumstances that bore an uncanny resemblance to serfdom.

In attempting to impose his will upon his domains, Reed found himself hampered somewhat by a perceptively growing lack of cooperation by the department's headquarters in Ottawa. When the Commissioner's office had been established in 1879, poor communication between east and west dictated that it operate in an independent manner. But with the completion of the railway in 1885 and the subsequent improvement in postal service, Ottawa's toleration of

TABLE 6.1.   Ration Reductions in Manitoba and the North West
Territories

	1890–91	1896–97	decrease
Indian Population	24,157	23,683	1.96%
Indians on the Ration List	12,155	8,853	27.16%
Flour (sacks)	17,453	12,861	26.31%
Beef (lbs.)	2,029,697	1,409,266	30.56%
Bacon (lbs.)	245,742	149,266	39.26%

such autonomy began to fade. Deputy Superintendent General Vankoughnet was determined that all decisions of any significance, and
especially those involving expenditure, should be referred to him for
approval.

Superintendent General Dewdney, who was no admirer of Vankoughnet, felt that the dignity of the Commissioner's office should not
be undermined. After all, he had filled the position himself for nine
years. Shortly after taking up his cabinet post in 1888, he warned
Reed that he should keep up the credit of his office, or some excuse
would be made to centralize its work in Ottawa.[64] Two years later,
when he heard complaints at headquarters about the size and
expense of the Regina staff, he advised the Commissioner to make
reductions lest "radical changes" be insisted on.[65]

Extravagance had never been one of Reed's vices and he was quite
prepared to effect economy in his administration. But he resented
having it forced upon him, especially by men whom he regarded as
ignorant of western conditions. He considered his budget estimates to
be reasonable, and when they were reduced by headquarters, which
happened on occasion, he made little effort to conceal his irritation.
He was annoyed even more by the petty manner in which Ottawa
insisted on approving almost all expenditures beforehand and requiring receipts for even insignificant items.[66] He argued, plausibly
enough, that such requirements hampered his ability to negotiate
with Indians, as he could never be sure that promises he might make
would be upheld by headquarters. Vankoughnet was unmoved by

appeals of this nature, and continued to insist that all expenditure, except for routine and emergency matters, be subject to his office's approval.[67]

Nor was Reed impressed when he heard of remarks made by the Deputy Superintendent about his office to the Civil Service Commission in 1892. Vankoughnet claimed that a Commissioner had been appointed in 1879 merely to humour the Indians and to assure them of the government's good will. The Regina office, he said, was no longer necessary and should be abolished, as it was just duplicating the work and expense. This prompted Reed to write a spirited defence of his office, which he submitted to the Minister. Drawing upon the memorandum that had originally established the post, he stressed the extensive powers of the Commissioner, showing that he was directly responsible to the Superintendent General and that Indian Agents were under his immediate jurisdiction. There was a lot more to the job than just humouring the Indians. The abolition of the Regina office, Reed argued, would not reduce administrative costs significantly and "would be ruinous to the proper management of Indian affairs in the West for, at any rate, a few years yet..."[68]

The Commissioner was nonetheless cognizant that some changes were necessary in his administration, both for the interests of economy and for the appeasement of critics at headquarters. The roles of school inspectors J.A. Macrae and A. Betournay were therefore sacrificed to meet this end. In fact, Reed had found them both insubordinate, unpleasant to work with, and unwilling to subject themselves to the indignity of office routine. Some thought was given to offering their services to the public schools, but that system declined. In 1892 Macrae was transferred to Ottawa and later Betournay was given clerical duties in the Winnipeg office. Costs were thereby reduced somewhat, but school inspection was added to the responsibilities of agents and agency inspectors.[69]

That Indian agents were singularly unfit for such a task must have struck the Commissioner upon occasion. The earliest agents in the North West tended to be former policemen, militiamen, and Hudson's Bay Company personnel, backgrounds which Reed regarded as unsuitable.[70] In the years following the Rebellion, however, they were increasingly recruited from the ranks of clerks and farming instructors.[71] Such men were likely to make better agents as they were familiar with department policies and were used to working with Indians.

Reed, as a former agent himself, had no illusions about the difficulty of the job. And he was quick to defend the salaries and benefits that agents received when these were subject to public criticism. By the early 1890s they were earning annual salaries of around $1200 and were granted a house, rations and travelling expenses in addition to this. The Commissioner believed that this was reasonable compensation for having to live in "a state of practical exile." As he explained:

> You might say that he (the agent) is debarred from all the pleasures of the world, from society, from civilization, from educational facilities for his children, etc.; and he is often put to great expense in sending away his family to be educated, etc.[72]

The job obviously had its disadvantages. Even so, it was well paid by the standards of the day and by 1890 it was acquiring some of the status of a plum appointment. The question of political interference in the process therefore naturally arose. Reed was later condemned as a faithful servant of the Conservative party whose administration was rife with sordid patronage. Yet there is considerable evidence to suggest otherwise. Undoubtedly, partisanship was present in department appointments and promotions, but competence was the principle criterion.[73] The Commissioner was prepared to reject representations from the Minister himself when the individual in question did not measure up to the requirements of the job.[74]

In reality, few agents at this time were of the calibre of men that Reed desired. The Commissioner was often obliged to make do with employees whose human failings were embarrassingly conspicuous. Inefficiency and even laziness had to be tolerated. Even a predilection for intoxication had occasionally to be overlooked. A fondness for Indian women, however, was a distinct taboo. In fact, the department preferred its employees to be married, believing that the matrimonial state offered a bulwark against such temptations. A fondness for Indian boys was even more likely to be fatal to one's career in the service, as Blackfoot interpreter Jean l'Heureux discovered to his chagrin in 1891.[75]

Circumstances dictated that only the most degenerate and dishonest officials be fired. Mere incompetence brought sanctions, but they tended to take the form of demotion rather than dismissal. Agents unable to meet the standards set by Reed often found themselves back at the clerk's desk from whence they had come. And there was a considerable shuffling about of officials. All agencies were not equally demanding on the nerves and energies required for successful management and an agent who had performed dismally at Battleford might be satisfactory at Morley.

Reed's relations with his subordinates were, in the main, good. While he was a demanding taskmaster, and this could be a source of aggravation to the less energetic, he was respected by agents as one of their own. He, after all, had once served in a most difficult agency and he remained in touch with developments on reserves through his frequent tours of inspection. In fact, the Commissioner's correspondence with the various agents suggests a level of camaraderie that was unusual in the public service. The Indian department in the West was no cosy sinecure; rather, it comprised a group of men who struggled together under trying circumstances to attain an unquestioned goal.

The department's greatest allies in its attempt to incorporate the Indians into the dominant society were the missionary Christian churches: Anglican, Methodist, Presbyterian and Roman Catholic. The principal contributions of the churches lay in the provision of educational services. The school system that emerged for Indian children in the aftermath of the treaties was largely financed by the federal government, but was managed and operated by missionaries or their nominees. Three categories of schools appeared: day, boarding and industrial.

Day schools enroled the majority of Indian children, but they suffered from irregularity of attendance and the inability to find and maintain competent teachers. Neither church nor state officials put much faith in their ability to sever the children from their ancestral culture.

Like day schools, boarding schools were located on or near reserves. They offered the advantage of residence, which ensured some isolation of the children from home influences. Regular attendance was another advantage. These schools were the property of the missionary organizations that built them. Operating costs were subsidized by an annual per capita grant of $60 (later $72) by the Department of Indian Affairs.

Industrial schools were also residential, but they were deliberately located in centres of white settlement such as Battleford, Regina, Calgary and Red Deer in order that the inmates might more readily forget their origins. They were built and equipped by the federal government and were managed by the churches with per capita subsidies that ranged from $100 to $140. A joint program of academic studies and instruction in trades and agriculture was offered.[76]

The attitude of Indian parents towards the white man's schools was ambiguous. Most appeared to be ready to accept the necessity of formal instruction for their children that they might better adapt to a world without buffalo. But they could muster little enthusiasm for a system which deliberately sought to denigrate and destroy their own beliefs and traditions. They were particularly suspicious of industrial schools in this respect, and with good reason. For both churchmen and Indian department officials viewed these institutions as the most persuasive of assimilative agents. The difficulties that most industrial schools experienced in attempting to attain full enrolment is a clear indicator of parental misgivings.

Hayter Reed was a great champion of the industrial schools. In his frequent tours of the agencies he usually attempted to secure some children for the schools, using whatever bargaining power was at his disposal. He took a personal interest in the progress of the more successful students, corresponding with a number of them over the years.

In 1889 he visited the Mohawk and Mount Elgin institutions in Ontario and also spent some time at Carlisle Industrial School in Pennsylvania. These were earlier prototypes of the schools that were built in the West. In a subsequent report he indicated his disapproval of the Mohawk Institute practice of allocating two-thirds of the school day to the academic program. The half-day system in vogue at Carlisle was preferable. As he explained, "Unless it is intended to train children to earn their bread by brain-work rather than by manual labour, at least half of their day should be devoted to acquiring skill in the latter." Reed, it seems, had a rather clear notion of where he wished to see the Indians placed in the occupational hierarchy. In fact he proposed hiring some of the students out to settlers at intervals as farm labourers or as domestic servants in order to provide them with practical experience in civilization. This idea, known as the outing system, was adopted at a number of the schools in the 1890s with limited success.

Reed's enthusiasm for the type of education provided in these institutions led him in April of 1892 to propose an amendment to the Indian Act which would empower the department to keep Indian children in industrial schools in violation of parental wishes. He cited a recent incident in which parents withdrew their daughter from the Battleford school after one year as justification for this new measure. But Deputy Superintendent Vankoughnet opposed compulsory attendance as premature. He felt it was wiser to continue with the prevailing policy of persuasion.[77] This was but another instance in which Reed felt that his better judgment was overruled by distant bureaucrats in Ottawa without good reason. It served to exacerbate the already strained relations that existed between himself and Vankoughnet.

While employing the resources of the churches in providing educational services was a tremendous boon to the department, it also brought its own peculiar difficulties. Denominational rivalry, although useful, required Indian Affairs to be absolutely neutral in its treatment of the various church bodies. By and large, it succeeded in doing so, but rarely to the satisfaction of the feuding ecclesiastics.

A persistent Roman Catholic complaint was that few Indian agents in the West were of their persuasion. This, they reasoned, worked to their disadvantage in educational matters.[78] Reed responded to this criticism by sending a letter to all agents in October 1890, insisting that they observe strict neutrality in religious affairs. He warned them that parents should not be pressured into sending their children to a school run by a denomination to which they did not belong, even if it were the only school available. He further advised that missionaries should not be obstructed in their work of proselytism. He demanded, however, that he be consulted prior to the construction of church or school buildings on a reserve, in order to ensure that the wishes of the Indians were adhered to. Archbishop Taché of St. Boniface agreed that should such procedures be followed, most of his church's grievances would be removed.[79]

Anglican missionaries did not accuse the department of being prejudiced against them; rather they inferred that its officials were soft on the Roman Catholics and did little to restrain the aggressive tactics of the priests. Cyprian Pinkham, Anglican Bishop of Saskatchewan and Calgary, was dismayed to discover late in 1888 that the department had permitted the Catholics to build a school at Running Wolf's camp on the Blood reserve. He complained to Reed about this invasion of his missionary domains, pointing out that the Rebellion had shown the limitations of the Catholic work, a favourite Protestant jibe.[80] The Commissioner refused to discuss the relative merits of the work of the various missionaries. As far as the Blood reserve school was concerned, he pointed out that it had first been offered to the Anglicans but that the Indians had "refused point blank" to agree to this. The Indians favoured a Catholic school and the department could hardly refuse them.

Reed was prepared to admit that the Catholics had to be credited for their energy in such matters while "our church" was sometimes less diligent. He reminded the bishop that it was the department's policy to take a vote on reserves in order to ascertain the will of the Indians on the question of religion in education. This was a treaty right that could not be denied.[81] Dealing with temperamental ecclesiastics whose bitter prejudices against beliefs and practices of rival denominations often exceeded their zeal in combatting native "paganism," demanded from Reed the most judicious application of diplomacy.[82] In this he was generally successful.[83]

Reed had reason to be satisfied with his performance as Commissioner. He had won the grudging respect of agents and churchmen; he had protected much of the autonomy of his office from the centralizing designs of headquarters; and the Indians appeared to be sub-dued. His star was evidently in the ascendant. But before it could reach the zenith of its brilliance, an odious scandal almost snuffed it out.

It began in June of 1887 when David Mills, Liberal M.P. for Both-well, mentioned Reed's name in the House of Commons in connec-tion with the confiscation of furs during the North West Rebellion. The "looting," as Mills described it, had taken place at the instigation of General Frederick Middleton and the plundered furs had been divided among the general, Reed, and S.L. Bedson, the warden of the Manitoba Penitentiary. The confiscated property had belonged to Charles Bremner, a resident of the Bresaylor half-breed settlement, who was now seeking compensation for his loss.[84]

This incident became a minor *cause célèbre* for some Liberal M.P.s in the following years, as they demanded justice for Bremner and an investigation of the conduct of Middleton and his associates. In sup-port of their campaign for redress, the opposition produced in the House a letter purported to have been written by Reed on 4 July 1885, in which he asked the quartermaster at the Battleford police barracks to pack two bales of furs for the general, one for Bedson, and one for himself.[85] These revelations were probably not prompted by any sense of animosity towards the accused parties, but rather were per-ceived as a convenient stick with which to beat the government. They were, nonetheless, damaging to the individuals involved.

At the time Middleton held the post of General Officer Command-ing of the militia and was intending to retire soon to become presi-dent of a Canadian insurance company. The bad publicity was ruin-ing his plans and in 1890 he agreed to a parliamentary inquiry which he believed would clear his name.[86] Before the committee of inquiry met, Middleton interviewed Reed in Ottawa and tried to persuade him to accept responsibility for the confiscation. The Commissioner, realizing that his own career was in jeopardy, refused.[87]

The Committee hearings, held between 19 March and 23 April 1890, were a disaster for the general. His testimony was confused. At first he denied all recollection of the confiscation but later, under cross-examination, admitted to a certain amount of looting. And he foolishly tried to justify the pillage on the grounds that it was not his duty to protect the property of rebels.[88]

Reed was also called to testify and acquitted himself well. He admitted to writing the letter quoted in parliament, but claimed he had done so on orders from Middleton, who had instructed him to keep the matter secret. This revelation was particularly damaging to the general's case. Middleton would not have counselled secrecy had he not harboured doubts about the legality of his instructions. The Commissioner pointed out that when his own bale of plundered furs had arrived in Regina, he had questioned the propriety of the confiscation and had returned the bale to Battleford.[89]

This action by Reed, and the consistency of his evidence, impressed the committee members and they exonerated him of all blame in the incident.[90] Middleton was not so fortunate. The report of the committee of inquiry concluded that he had "acted under an unfortunate misconception as to his powers" and that the appropriation of the furs had been "highly improper."[91] Shortly thereafter when Prime Minister Macdonald described the confiscation as "an illegal and improper act" which could not be defended, it was obvious that Middleton's days in the government service were numbered.[92] He resigned from his command of the militia on 1 July and later left for Britain in an angry and bitter mood.

Reed did not escape entirely unscathed. Throughout the summer of 1890 he had to endure a campaign of vilification against his character in the Liberal press. Stories with headlines proclaiming "Hayter Reed to Blame" were, he surmised, instigated by friends of Middleton in an eleventh hour attempt to shift the responsibility to his shoulders.[93] This effort to re-open the case failed, however, and the adverse publicity faded quickly. Reed's role in the affair was not entirely forgotten. It was referred to briefly in the House of Commons in March 1893, when the Commissioner was denounced as a "blood-sucker" by opposition for attempting to claim travel allowances to which he was not entitled.[94]

These remarks accomplished nought, for the wheels were already in motion to bring Reed to Ottawa that he might assume the top position in the department, that of Deputy Superintendent General. The long-serving incumbent, Lawrence Vankoughnet, was only in his mid fifties and had no intention of stepping down. His relations with Reed and Dewdney had been strained over the years, but his close friend-ship with John A. Macdonald had given him an impregnable niche in the corridors of power. The death of the old chieftain in 1891 made Vankoughnet vulnerable to the intrigues of his enemies. His ill-con-sidered criticism of the Indian Commissioner's office before the Civil Service Commission in 1892 likely hastened his demise.

During the early months of 1892 Vankoughnet became ill and requested four months leave of absence in order to recuperate. Super-annuation was suggested instead, but he would not hear of it. The proposal evidently made him nervous, for he only took two months leave rather than the four that were granted. He remarked before his departure that the department would sink into a deplorable state should he ever forsake the service.[95]

Dewdney left the cabinet that year to become Lieutenant Governor of British Columbia. His successor, T. Mayne Daly, was also of the opinion that Vankoughnet would have to go. By March 1893, the decision had been made and it was only necessary to convince the Privy Council to give its approval. There was some hesitancy at first to support a change that appeared to be based on purely personal considerations, but in the end the Council agreed. Vankoughnet was superannuated against his will on 2 October, and Reed moved to Ottawa to assume the position of Deputy Superintendent.[96]

The appointment appeared to be the crowning pinnacle in the career of Hayter Reed. He had joined the department in 1881 and now, just twelve years afterwards, and at the relatively young age of forty-four, he had succeeded to its top position. It was a heady moment of triumph and was marred only by the predictably hostile attitude of the *Globe*, which remarked that Vankoughnet's retirement had been "a disgraceful job perpetrated to make room for hungry supporters" of the government.[97]

Reed's tenure as Deputy Superintendent was brief and unremark-able. Much time had to be spent acquiring familiarity with Indian conditions outside of the prairie region, a task accomplished through frequent tours. But he did find time to attend to some outstanding business from his days as commissioner.

It will be recalled that a proposal of his to make school attendance compulsory had been overruled by Vankoughnnet in 1892. He was now in a position to secure such legislation. Clause 11 of the Indian Act, as amended July, 1894, empowered the Governor General in Council to make regulations to enforce the attendance of Indian children at school with appropriate fines or imprisonment for those parents refusing to co-operate.[98] The legislation reflected Reed's belief in the vital role that education was playing in the cultural transformation of the Indians. And he was quite prepared to spend money on it. Education, he asserted, was "an excellent investment."[99] In fact the industrial schools, the most expensive components of the educational system, reached their maximum influence during his years as Deputy Superintendent.

Reed was aware from his experience in the West that certain Indian customs hindered the department's program of civilization by interfering with work and school. The most prominent of these customs were the potlatch of the Pacific coast and the sun and thirst dances of the prairies. The potlatch had been prohibited in 1884, but the law had become a dead letter. In 1895 an amendment to the Indian Act rephrased Section 114 making both the potlatch and the prairie dances indictable offences. To ensure that Indians were effectively brought under the restraints of the law, Section 117 gave agents the powers of justices of the peace with respect to the Act and certain sections of the Criminal Code of 1892.[100] This is by no means a complete catalogue of amendments to the Indian Act brought about at Reed's instigation. But they illustrate a trend with which he can be readily identified: the imposition of a system of increasingly close supervision over the everyday lives of Indians.

Ottawa meant more to Reed than the joys and frustrations of a deputy ministership. His personal and social life also experienced a dramatic improvement. He had first married in June, 1888, but his wife, Georgina A. Ponton, had died in the following year without issue. His second venture into matrimony occurred on 16 June 1894 when he chose as his bride Kate, the eldest daughter of Justice J.D. Armour of Toronto. Kate had been previously married to Grosvenor Lowry, a member of the New York bar and had had two children with him, Grace and John Douglas.[101] With Reed she produced

another son, Gordon, who was born in September 1895, and was pronounced "an exceptional specimen" by the proud father.[102]

The marriage was an exceedingly happy one. The second Mrs.
Reed was already a well-known figure in the federal capital for her
involvement in charitable and cultural events. In fact her connections
went as far as a personal friendship with Lady Aberdeen, the wife of
the Governor General. Reed was swept into the glittering social life of
the Ottawa elite by his charming new wife and he evidently found it
to his liking. The rough-hewn world of Battleford and Regina seemed
eons away. But it could be resurrected at will for the amusement of all
when the occasion warranted. At the Governor General's Ball in January 1896, Reed made his appearance wearing the feathers and buck-
skin of a plains Indian chief and leading an entourage of similarly
attired men and women. Their parade was the highlight of the
evening.[103] Presumably the irony of this spectacle was lost on its
observers.

Such were the rewards of high office. But they rested on a shaky
foundation. The federal Conservative Party, to which Reed owed so
much, had been crumbling since the death of Macdonald in 1891, and
in the summer of 1896 it surrendered the mantle of power to Laurier's
Liberals. The Deputy Superintendent received an anonymous hate
letter from Edmonton in July gloating at the prospect of his imminent
demise.[104] And a press report which accused Reed of "fixing up" his
friends with secure positions in Ottawa before the new minister was
appointed, was hardly reassuring.[105]

The new Superintendent General was the Manitoba maverick, Clifford Sifton, who did not arrive to take up his duties in the capital
until December. It quickly became obvious that Sifton was determined to purge the interior and Indian departments of Tory partisans
and open positions for his own supporters.[106] Reed was an obvious
target and he knew it. He was alarmed to discover that some of his
subordinates within the department, led by J.A. Macrae, had
"caballed" against him and were searching the files for damaging evidence to present to the minister. He attempted to counter this campaign of vilification by presenting to Sifton a number of documents
which undermined Macrae's credibility, but in vain.[107] During Janu-

ary and February of 1897 he received a series of sharply worded letters from the minister demanding information "at once" about a number of suspect transactions involving the department in recent years.[108] There could be no mistaking the hostile tone and implied criticism in these communications.

Sifton was in fact planning to dispense with both Reed and his counterpart in the Interior department, A.M. Burgess, and place both departments under a single deputy minister. James A. Smart, an old crony of Sifton's from Manitoba, had been selected for the job. It was unusual to dismiss deputies and the move was debated intensely in cabinet. By mid-February it was reluctantly approved.[109]

The end could not have been a surprise for Reed, but when it came, foreknowledge did little to lessen the blow. He was informed by Sifton on 25 February that a reorganization of the department was to be implemented immediately and that it would no longer be possible for him to retain the position of Deputy Superintendent. The department was to be divided into three branches with a chief clerk at the head of each one. Reed could either accept one of these chief clerkships at a salary of $2000, or be placed on the retirement list.[110]

Superannuation was the preferred choice for, as Kate Reed confided to Lady Aberdeen, "the new conditions might (have been) most trying." Life would not be easy on a pension, she concluded but "we must just pretend that we are in our twenties instead of our forties and start out with youthful hope and courage and try to catch up again some other way."[111]

The fall of Hayter Reed did not go unnoticed. The *Globe*, which had always been unsympathetic to the man, observed that Sifton could not have been expected to continue with an administration that had been "reeking with scandals."[112] It suggested that the reorganization was necessary to purge the department of Reed's favourites whom he had brought to Ottawa from Regina.[113] When Sifton's actions were criticized in the House of Commons by Conservative members, he retorted that the transfer of Reed and McGirr to Ottawa in 1893 had been "only a subject of merriment in the North-West where these gentlemen (were) known." The department, he asserted, had been notoriously mismanaged for years.[114]

These comments were brought to the attention of an almost forgotten figure now resident in England, Lawrence Vankoughnet. He took the opportunity of airing the deep resentment he still felt at his own forced retirement by composing a long letter to Sifton in which he derided Reed's knowledge of the Indians and his administrative abilities. The Superintendent General was pleased at this unexpected source of support, and assured Vankoughnet that the department was rapidly assuming that level of efficiency which had characterized its operations prior to 1893.[115]

Reed's years in the Indian department had created enemies who were only too quick to gloat at his humiliation. But they had also created friends, among whom was William Van Horne, the railway tycoon. Within a short period of his departure from the federal service, Reed found employment with the Canadian Pacific as manager of the Chateau Frontenac, its hotel in Quebec City. In 1905 he was made manager of the CP hotels division. His new career also created employment opportunities for his wife, whose genius for interior decoration was discovered by Van Horne. Her talents were used to transform the decor of the hotels from coast to coast, making them "the most home-like of any on the North American continent."[116]

After retirement, the Reeds divided their time between their Montreal apartment and their cottage, "Pansy Patch," at St. Andrew's, New Brunswick. Mrs. Reed died in October, 1928[117] and he survived her until 21 December 1936. He was 89 years old at the time. His obituary in the Montreal *Gazette* described him as "a vigorous personality and widely known throughout the Dominion."[118]

The 1870s and 1880s were the decades during which Canada took practical steps to secure the North West for its expansionist designs. A military presence, surveys, settlement, Indian treaties, and a railway were the more obvious manifestations of this determination. The most critical factor, however, in attaching the region to the Dominion, was the migration west of an optimistic breed of young Canadians who shared an unbounded faith in the prospects of their new abode. They tended to be English-speaking, Protestant, and Ontario-born and sought to emulate the success of their counterparts south of the international boundary.[119]

Hayter Reed belonged to this enthusiastic band for whose restless spirits the West proved irresistible. Skilled with a gun and comfortable on horseback, he was ready for the physical challenges of the new land. And he possessed in abundance those characteristics essential for success on the frontier: energy, courage, ruthlessness, and lack of imagination.

Reed's contribution to the consolidation of Canadian claims to the West lay in the leadership he provided in Indian administration. It was generally agreed that Indians would have no role of any significance to play in the agricultural empire which the Dominion was carving out for itself. In many ways native people were regarded as an obstacle on the road to that hallowed dream. Nothing was more likely to deter potential settlers than the knowledge that warlike bands of Indians roamed the plains at will.

The most immediate aim of government policy was therefore pacification and the confinement of Indians to their reserves. There they were initiated into agriculture, but in a manner that was paternalistic and condescending. The work for rations rule, the pass system, the industrial schools, the extensive powers granted to agents, and the many restrictive and oppressive features of the Indian Act, all suggest that their condition was one of servitude.

Reed's initiative was critical in devising and implementing this policy. With a vision unclouded by self-doubt, he pushed relentlessly forward with a grand design to transform Indians into a self-supporting peasant class. That the tactics employed to this end frequently caused hardship was of little concern. For Reed, like many of his contemporaries in the upper echelons of society, was convinced that poverty was a consequence of depravity or laziness and could be banished by that ultimate Victorian virtue, hard work. Only a rigid regimen of reward and punishment could bring this message home to those whose horizons were supposedly limited by an inferior cultural inheritance.

It would be easy to dismiss Hayter Reed as a mere opportunist who advanced his own career in the public service at the expense of the Indians. But when all things are considered, he was probably the most competent official of the Indian service in his day. Of all the

Deputy Superintendents and Commissioners (with the exception in the latter instance of W.M. Graham), he was the only one who had served in the field as an agent. If it could not be said that he understood Indians, he at least knew them. But this advantage mattered little in the end. As a leading figure in the confident vanguard of expansionist English Canada, Reed could not conceive of programs or policies that involved meaningful consultations with the Indians or treated their traditions with respect. It was small wonder that they failed to embrace enthusiastically what he prescribed for them.

NOTES

1. Norma Sluman, *Poundmaker* (Toronto: Ryerson, 1967), p. 109.
2. The details of Reed's early life are somewhat sketchy, but they can be pieced together with some reliability from the following sources: National Archives of Canada [hereafter NAC], MG 30, D1, F.J. Audet, Biographical Notes, Vol. 25 and NAC Sir Wilfrid Laurier Papers, Vol. 141, p. 42225, Reed to Laurier, 9 February 1900.
3. John L. Tobias, "Canada's Subjugation of the Plains Cree, 1879–1885," *Canadian Historical Review* LXIV, no. 4 (December, 1983), pp. 522–25.
4. NAC, RG 10, vol. 3733, file 26743, E. Dewdney to Reed, 25 February 1881. Reed's appointment was to be effective 1 March 1881. His salary would be $1200 per annum.
5. NAC, RG 10, vol. 3753, file 30640, Reed to E. Dewdney, 29 May 1881.
6. *Report of the Department of Indian Affairs for the Year ended 31 December, 1881*, pp. xiv-xvi.
7. *Report*, 1881, pp. xvii-xviii.
8. *Report*, 1881, p. 77.
9. NAC, MG 29 E 106, Hayter Reed Papers, vol. 18., Personnel M-P, Reed to T.M. Daly, (date illegible), 1893.
10. NAC, RG 10, vol. 3949, file 126886, Reed to E. Dewdney, 17 March 1883.
11. NAC, RG 10, vol. 3755, file 30961, Reed to E. Dewdney, 18 June 1881 and headquarters to Assistant Commissioner E.T. Galt, 25 July 1881.
12. Lewis H. Thomas, *The Struggle for Responsible Government in the North-West Territories, 1870–1897*, 2nd Edition (Toronto: University of Toronto Press, 1978), p. 111.
13. NAC, MG 26A, John A. Macdonald Papers, vol. 211, p. 89923, E. Dewdney to J.A. Macdonald, 27 September 1883.
14. Galt had been appointed secretary and clerk to Dewdney in June, 1879 and had been promoted to Assistant Indian Commissioner for Manitoba

and the North West Territories in April 1881. See NAC, RG 10, vol. 3692, file 13955, P.C. 845, 12 June 1879 and P.C. 681, 21 April 1881.

15. NAC, MG 27 I C4, Edgar Dewdney Papers, vol. 5, p. 1207, E.T. Galt to Dewdney, 21 February 1883.

16. NAC, RG 10, vol. 3626, file 5675, E. Dewdney to Superintendent General, 5 March 1883.

17. This episode is discussed in detail in Tobias, "Subjugation of the Plains Cree." See also G.F.G. Stanley, *The Birth of Western Canada* (Toronto: University of Toronto Press, 1960), pp. 234–35.

18. NAC, Reed Papers, vol. 18, Personnel M-P, Reed to T.M. Daly, (date illegible), 1893.

19. NAC, Macdonald Papers, vol. 212, p. 90039, E. Dewdney to J.A. Macdonald, 16 February 1884.

20. Vankoughnet's interference was strongly resented by Reed. See NAC, Macdonald Papers, vol. 212. p. 90168, Reed to E. Dewdney, 10 September 1884.

21. Bob Beal and Rod Macleod, *Prairie Fire: The 1885 North West Rebellion* (Edmonton: Hurtig, 1984), pp. 81–85.

22. NAC, RG 10, vol. 3668, file 10644, Reed to E. Dewdney, 28 December 1883.

23. NAC, Macdonald Papers, vol. 212, p. 90168, Reed to E. Dewdney, 10 September 1884.

24. Beal and Macleod, *Prairie Fire*, pp. 88–90.

25. NAC, Dewdney Papers, Vol. 6, p. 1398, Reed to E. Dewdney, 4 September 1884.

26. NAC, Macdonald Papers, vol. 212, p. 90065, E. Dewdney to J.A. Macdonald, 11 April 1884.

27. NAC, RG 10, vol. 3626, file 5675, P.C. 972, 5 May 1884.

28. NAC, Dewdney Papers, vol. 5, p. 1232, Reed to E. Dewdney, 29 August 1885; Macdonald Papers, Vol. 212, p. 90322, Reed to E. Dewdney, 31 August 1885.

29. NAC, Macdonald Papers, vol. 212, p. 90303, E. Dewdney to J.A. Macdonald, 13 August 1885.

30. Ibid., p. 90322, Reed to E. Dewdney, 31 August 1885.

31. NAC, Dewdney Papers, vol. 5, p. 1240, Reed to Dewdney, 6 September 1885.

32. NAC, Macdonald Papers, vol. 212, p. 90330, E. Dewdney to J.A. Macdonald, 3 September 1885.

33. NAC, Dewdney Papers, vol. 6, p. 1414, Reed to E. Dewdney, 29 July 1885; RG 10, vol. 3710, file 19550-3, E. Dewdney to the Superintendent General, 1 August 1885 and L. Vankoughnet to E. Dewdney, 28 October 1885.

34. In April 1888, Reed reported to Dewdney that during a tour of the Saskatchewan and Alberta Districts those bands deprived of their annu-

ities had appealed for their restoration. He felt that it could now be done with those who had "expressed sorrow for their actions during the rebellion and who [were] now endeavouring to do what [was] right." He wanted them to understand, however, that payments would be cut off again in the event of bad behavior. Such an understanding, Reed believed, would give agents greater control. See NAC, RG 10, vol. 3796, file 47249, Reed to E. Dewdney, 5 April 1888.

35. NAC, RG 10, vol. 3710, file 19550–4, Reed to J.A. Macdonald, 25 January 1886 and E. Dewdney to Superintendent General, 8 October 1885.

36. Noel Dyck, "An Opportunity Lost: The Initiative of the Reserve Agricultural Program in the Prairie West," in F.L. Barron and James B. Waldram, eds., *1885 and After: Native Society in Transition* (Regina: Canadian Plains Research Center, 1986), p. 121.

37. A.J. Looy, "The Indian Agent and His Role in the Administration of the North-West Superintendency, 1876–1893" (Ph.D. thesis, Queen's University, 1977), p. 85.

38. NAC, Macdonald Papers, vol. 213, p. 90704, E. Dewdney to J.A. Macdonald, 13 April 1886; vol. 214, p. 90981, L. Vankoughnet to Macdonald, 13 December 1886; p. 91113, Dewdney to Macdonald, 21 September 1887. RG 10, vol. 3626, file 5675, Dewdney to the Superintendent General, 1 December 1887. Early in 1887 Reed had built a house in Regina in anticipation of a salary increase.

39. NAC, RG 10, vol. 3802, file 50319. Reed's appointment was made by an order-in-council dated 3 August 1888. His salary was $3200 per annum.

40. NAC, Dewdney Papers, vol. 5, p. 1301, Reed to E. Dewdney, 12 April 1888.

41. NAC, Macdonald Papers, vol. 327, p. 147879, Bishop C. Pinkham of Saskatchewan to Macdonald, 31 March 1888 and p. 147899, Bishops of St. Boniface and St. Albert to Macdonald, 4 June 1888.

42. NAC, Dewdney Papers, vol. 5, p. 1301, Reed to E. Dewdney, 12 April 1888.

43. NAC, Reed Papers, vol. 16, Church-Agency Relations, 1888–1892, R. Newberry Toms to Reed, 2 November 1888.

44. *Report of the Department of Indian Affairs for the Year ended 31 December, 1889*, p. 165.

45. NAC, RG 10, vol. 3844, file 73083, Reed to L. Vankoughnet, 24 February 1891.

46. NAC, RG 10, vol. 3847, file 74567, Reed to L. Vankoughnet, 9 January 1891.

47. *Report of the Department of Indian Affairs for the Year ended 31 December, 1888*, p. 124. See also NAC, RG 10, vol. 3806, file 52332, Reed to E. Dewdney, 28 October 1888.

48. *Report of the Department of Indian Affairs for the Year ended 31 December, 1889*, p. 160.

49. *Report of the Department of Indian Affairs for the Year ended 31 December, 1890,* p. 138.
50. Noel Dyck, "An Opportunity Lost," p. 125.
51. *Report of the Department of Indian Affairs for the Year ended 31 December, 1889,* p. 160.
52. *Report of the Department of Indian Affairs for the Year ended 31 December, 1891,* p. 193.
53. Ibid.
54. *Report of the Department of Indian Affairs for the Year ended 31 December, 1890,* p. 132.
55. Ibid., p. 136. See also NAC, RG10, vol. 3806, file 52332, Reed to E. Dewdney, 28 October 1888.
56. NAC, RG 10, vol. 3853, file 78004, Reed to L. Vankoughnet, 24 April 1891.
57. *Report of the Department of Indian Affairs for the Year ended 31 December, 1891,* p. 194.
58. PAC, RG 10, vol. 3853, file 78004, Reed to L. Vankoughnet, 24 April 1891. Reed argued in response to the reduction that cattle were an investment that could not lose. But someone at headquarters scribbled in the margin of his letter, "If not lost either by theft, blizzard or the Indians killing them on the sly."
59. NAC, RG 10, vol. 3879, file 92338, Reed to L. Vankoughnet, 6 July 1892.
60. Tabular statements in the department's annual reports. These statements also provide data on crops taken from the land. These statistics are somewhat meaningless in this context as they fluctuated greatly from year to year depending on climatic conditions and other variables.
61.. Noel Dyck, "An Opportunity Lost," p. 125.
62. NAC, RG 10, vol. 56, file 696, S. Steele to NWMP Commissioner, Regina, (undated), 1891; Reed Papers, vol. 16, Cattle-killing 1889–1893, H.M. Cochrane to T.M. Daly, 30 December 1892.
63. NAC, RG 10, vol. 3653, file 6567, F. Pedley to C. Sifton, 24 March 1904.
64. NAC, Reed Papers, vol. 18, Personnel H-L, E. Dewdney to Reed, 16 November 1888.
65. NAC, Reed Papers, vol. 18, Regina Office 1887–1893, E. Dewdney to Reed, 2 June 1890.
66. NAC, RG 10, vol. 3844, file 73083, Reed to the Deputy Superintendent, 24 February 1891.
67. NAC, RG 10, vol. 3870, file 88557, Reed to L. Vankoughnet, 7 April 1892; memo of D.C. Scott, 25 March 1892; Vankoughnet to Reed, 4 May 1892.
68. NAC, Reed Papers, vol. 17, Inspection of Agencies, 1885–1896, W. McGirr to Reed, 2 June 1892; memo by Reed (undated), 1892.
69. Ibid., Reed to E. Dewdney, 29 April 1892; W. McGirr to Reed, 31 May 1892.

70. NAC, Reed Papers, vol. 18, Personnel A-G, Reed to L. Vankoughnet, 21 November 1889.

71. A.J. Looy, "The Indian Agent," p. 96. Of seven agents in Treaty 6 in 1893, five had begun their department careers as clerks or instructors.

72. NAC, Reed Papers, vol. 17, Inspection of Agencies, 1885–1896, undated memo by Reed (circa June 1892).

73. This contention is supported by J. Douglas Leighton, "The Development of Federal Indian Policy in Canada, 1840–1890," Ph.D. Thesis, University of Western Ontario, 1975, p. 367.

74. NAC, Reed Papers, vol. 18, Personnel M-P, T.M. Daly to Reed, 31 October, 1892; Reed to Daly, 15 November 1892.

75. NAC, Reed Papers, vol. 18, Personnel A-G, J.W. Tims to Reed, 27 October, 1891; J. l'Heureux to Reed, 17 November 1891.

76. For a full discussion of these institutions, see Brain E. Titley, "The Industrial Schools: An Experiment in Canadian Indian Education Policy," paper presented at the annual meeting of the Canadian Historical Association, Montreal, May, 1985.

77. NAC, RG 10, vol. 3947, file 123764–1, Reed to L. Vankoughnet, 8 April 1892; Vankoughnet to E. Dewdney, 13 April 1892.

78. NAC, RG 10, vol. 3841, file 71345, Archbishop Taché to the Governor General in Council, 28 July 1889; Reed Papers, vol. 16, Church-agency relations 1888–1892, Father Lacombe to Reed, 11 November 1888.

79. NAC, RG 10, vol. 3844, file 73070, Reed to all agents, 31 October 1890; Reed to Archbishop Taché, 31 October 1890; Taché to Reed, 5 November 1890.

80. NAC, Reed Papers, vol. 16, Church-agency relations, 1888–1892, C. Pinkham to Reed, 5 January 1889.

81. Ibid., Reed to C. Pinkham, 8 January 1889.

82. For example, the Rev. Samuel Trivett, an Anglican missionary, informed Reed that his church would not tolerate Protestant Indian children being sent to High River Roman Catholic Industrial School to learn trades, as they would be taught "Idolatrous Acts that are worse than their own religion." NAC, Reed Papers, vol. 16, Church-department relations, 1887–1895, S. Trivett to Reed, 23 May 1889.

83. One such diplomatic success occurred in June, 1890, when Reed made an appearance at a Methodist church conference in Brandon, Manitoba, and convinced the assembled delegates that his department would do its best to ensure that their church would not be disadvantaged vis-a-vis others in the amount of state funds it received for Indian education. Winnipeg *Free Press*, 9 June 1890.

84. Canada, House of Commons, *Debates*, 31 May 1887, pp. 659–60 and 22 June 1887, p. 1237.

85. *Debates*, 17 May 1888, p. 1517.
86. Desmond Morton, *Ministers and Generals: Politics and the Canadian Militia, 1868–1904* (Toronto: University of Toronto Press, 1970), pp. 91–93. Morton's account of this incident does not mention Reed.
87. NAC, Reed Papers, vol. 16, Bremner Fur Case, Reed to F. Middleton, 5 March 1890.
88. Canada, Sessional Papers, *Report of the Select Committee re Charles Bremner's Furs* (Ottawa, 1890), pp. 13–22.
89. Ibid., pp. 22–27.
90. NAC, Reed Papers, vol. 16, Bremner Fur Case, A. Ferguson (Reed's lawyer) to Reed, 14 May 1890.
91. *Report re Bremner's Furs*, Appendix 1.
92. *Debates*, 12 May 1890, p. 4756.
93. Winnipeg *Free Press*, 11 June 1890, p. 4; Toronto *Globe*, 11 August 1890, p. 4 (editorial); Ottawa *Free Press*, 11 August 1890, p. 1. See also NAC, Reed Papers, vol. 16, Bremner Fur Case, memo by Reed, 22 August 1890.
94. *Debates*, 29 March 1893, pp. 3383–85.
95. NAC, Reed Papers, vol. 18, Personnel M-P, W. McGirr to Reed, 27 June 1892.
96. NAC, RG 10, vol. 3960, file 142119. P.C. 2599, 2 October 1893, appointed Reed as Deputy Superintendent at an annual salary of $3200, identical to that which he was receiving as Commissioner. For further details on the fall of Vankoughnet, see Douglas Leighton, "A Victorian Civil Servant at Work: Lawrence Vankoughnet and the Canadian Indian Department, 1874–1893," in I.A.L. Getty and A.S. Lussier, eds., *As Long as the Sun Shines and Water Flows* (Vancouver: U.B.C. Press, 1983), pp. 114–17.
97. Toronto *Globe*, editorial, 8 November 1893.
98. *An Act to further amend the Indian Act*, S.C. 1894, c. 32 (57–58 Vict.), assented to 23 July 1894.
99. *Report of the Department of Indian Affairs for the Year ended 30 June, 1894*, p. xxi.
100. *An Act to further amend the Indian Act*, S.C. 1895, c. 35 (58–59 Vict.) assented to 22 July 1895.
101. NAC, MG 30 D1, F.J. Audet, Biographical Notes, vol. 25; MG 29 D61, H.J. Morgan correspondence, vol. 18, pp. 6874–76. Madge Macbeth described Kate Reed as "a popular and brilliant woman and conspicuously artistic" whose hobby was collecting shoes. See Madge Macbeth, *Over My Shoulder* (Toronto: Ryerson, 1953), p. 26. A contemporary newspaper account portrayed he as follows: "Tall and of an easy grace of manner, with a humorous mouth just touched with cynical good nature, well-set sensitive eyes and a well made nose, distinguish Mrs. Hayter Reed in almost any company." See Winnipeg *Free Press*, 11 August, 1913, p. 3, "Canadian

Women of Note: Mrs. Hayter Reed." Margot Asquith was a little less flattering, ascribing to Mrs. Reed "a masculine face, with an earnest and beautiful expression." See Margot Asquith, *My Impression of America* (New York: G.H. Doran, 1922), pp. 99–100.

102. NAC, Reed Papers, vol. 17, Inspection of Agencies, 1885–1896, T.P. Wadsworth to Reed, 3 October 1895; Reed to Wadsworth, 12 October 1895.

103. Sandra Gwynn, *The Private Capital: Ambition and Love in Age of Macdonald and Laurier* (Toronto: McClelland and Stewart, 1984), p. 288. Gwynn inaccurately describes Reed as Superintendent General of Indian Affairs.

104. NAC, Reed Papers, vol. 17, Miscellaneous Correspondence 1887–1896, anonymous letter to Reed from Edmonton, 6 July 1896. The following excerpt from the letter is indicative of its tone: "Good day Mr. sweet truth loving Hayter. How do you feel now? Do you think that with all your passive turpitude summoned up you can get all you little 'jobs on the side,' now that your friends(?) are at hand. Ah poor swine we do not think you can. We know too much..."

105. NAC, Laurier Papers, vol. 21, pp. 7525–27, unidentified news clipping dated 21 August 1896, "Fixing Up Their Friends." The report specifically mentioned A.W. Ponton, Reed's brother-in-law from his first marriage who was a surveyor with the department. But A.E. Forget, who knew Laurier well, came to Reed's defence, pointing out to the Prime Minister that the family connection had nothing to do with Ponton's advancement in the service. See A.E. Forget to W. Laurier, 31 August 1896, same file.

106. D.J. Hall, *Clifford Sifton*, Vol. I (Vancouver: U.B.C. Press, 1981), pp. 124–25.

107. NAC, MG 27 II D15, Clifford Sifton Papers, vol. 31, pp. 20363–64, Reed to C. Sifton, 25 January 1897.

108. NAC, Sifton Papers, vol. 216, p. 342, C. Sifton to Reed, 20 January 1897; p. 375, Sifton to Reed 22 January 1897; p. 663, Sifton to Reed, 30 January 1897; p. 706, Sifton to Reed, 1 February 1897.

109. Hall, *Sifton*, Vol.I, p. 126.

110. NAC, Sifton Papers, vol. 217, p. 633, C. Sifton to Reed, 25 February 1897.

111. NAC, MG 27 I B5, Lord Aberdeen Papers, vol. 4, Kate Reed to Lady Aberdeen, 1 March 1897.

112. Toronto *Globe*, p. 5, "At the Capital."

113. Toronto *Globe*, 5 March 1897, p. 2, "At the Capital." The report referred to two of Reed's sympathizers, W. McGirr and J.J. Campbell, who were also to be retired.

114. *Debates*, 4 May 1897, pp. 1709–19.

115. NAC, Sifton Papers, vol. 221, p. 526, C. Sifton to L. Vankoughnet, 19 July 1897.

116. Winnipeg *Free Press*, 11 August 1913, p. 3, "Canadian Women of Note: Mrs. Hayter Reed."
117. NAC, Aberdeen Papers, vol. 4, Reed to Lady Aberdeen, 26 October 1928.
118. Montreal *Gazette*, 22 December 1936, "Hayter Reed dies; served with CPR"; 24 December 1936, "The Late Major Hayter Reed."
119. D. Owram, *Promise of Eden* (Toronto: University of Toronto Press, 1981), p. 5.

JOHN F. GILPIN

7 The Edmonton and District Settlers' Rights Movement, 1880 to 1885

THE LITERATURE ON the development of Edmonton concentrates on its years as a fur trade post prior to 1870 and its emergence after 1900 as a major urban community by virtue of the construction of Canada's second generation of transcontinental railways. The neglect of the period from 1870 to 1900 in the history of Edmonton derives in part from a preoccupation with the Riel Rebellion and the construction of the Canadian Pacific Railway; events to which it was largely a spectator. What literature does exist consists to a large extent of biographies of its early business and religious figures whose individual lives are described in great detail as they laboured to lay the foundations of what would become the city of Edmonton. Two exceptions to this general trend include an article entitled "The North Saskatchewan River Settlement Claims, 1883–1884" by E.A. Mitchner and a second article on the land claims issue by Margaret R. Stobie entitled "Land Jumping."[1] The former article contains a short description of the land claims issue as it evolved in the Edmonton Settlement from 1872 to 1884. In this summary, Mitchner emphasizes the problem of delineating the boundaries between some of the claims, rather than any disputes within the settlement as to who had the right to the claim. In his view "the community had kept its members' land rights inviolable until title could be granted."[2] Stobie's article concentrates on the events which occurred between February and July of 1882

149

when L. George tried to take over the Sinclair claim (River Lot Twelve) and Joe Bannerman attempted to take over the mission property (River Lot Six). The confrontation between the community and the two claim jumpers is described in great detail along with the trial that followed. Although it provides important evidence of the community solidarity noted by Mitchner, this article presents the series of events as an isolated incident in the history of Edmonton which was amicably resolved in a very short period of time. The broader issues raised by this dispute in terms of the development of the West are not discussed.

The literature dealing with this period gives very little indication that the 1880s was a period of fundamental change in Edmonton as the Hudson's Bay Company's monopoly gave way to a free market economy in which a number of entrepreneurs competed for access to the commerce and resources of the region. This competition centred around a number of issues including land claims and led to the citizens of Edmonton and area taking certain steps to protect their interests in this regard. The land claims question was one of a series of issues concerning resource development and Federal Government policy which preoccupied the citizens of Edmonton and district from 1880 to 1885. The community's actions with respect to these issues will be referred to as the Edmonton Settlers' Rights Movement.

The Edmonton Settlers' Rights Movement began on 15 January 1880, when a meeting of area residents was held at Fort Edmonton to consider the working of the Crown Timber laws as they affected the settlement.[3] No information is available about who organized the meeting but it was chaired by an individual who typified the changing circumstances of Fort Edmonton after 1870. Donald Ross, who claimed what would eventually become River Lot Four in the Edmonton Settlement, was a former gold miner and Hudson's Bay Company employee. He was one of the first Company employees to establish himself as an independent businessman beyond the walls of Fort Edmonton. His particular economic endeavour was the construction of a log house on his claim which would eventually become Edmonton's first hotel. In addition to this commercial use of his claim, Ross also exploited the coal deposits on the property and made use of a portion of it as a market garden.

The Crown Timber laws which led to the calling of the meeting were contained in an order-in-council passed on 20 March 1878, which included "certain Instructions and Forms of Permit embracing regulations for the guidance of those persons in the North-West Territories who may be appointed for the management and protection of the Timber on Dominion Lands."[4] The Minister of the Interior noted further that the regulations were "in a form as suggested by the Lieutenant-Governor of the North-West Territories..."[5] The regulations represented the first effort to devise a policy for the utilization of the forest resources of the North West Territories. Two types of permits were described, the first of which was available free of charge to any resident in a locality who wished to cut building timber, fencing, or fuel on crown land. The maximum allowable cut under this permit was twelve pieces of hardwood, two hundred pieces of poplar or softwood, two thousand fence poles and fifty cords of firewood. Oak, birch, tamarack, or softwood suitable to be used for lumber could not be cut for firewood. The only individuals not eligible for these permits were those whose farms contained a supply of timber. The first type of permit was thus designed to meet the wood requirements of homesteaders who lacked these resources on their own land. The regulations were not clear, however, as to how they would be applied to squatters on land claims who did not have title to their property or who were not homesteaders in terms of the Dominion Lands Act.

The regulations also described a second category of permit referred to as special permits which were to be given out in limited numbers to "parties on application to cut timber, fence poles and cordwood for purposes and wants not covered by the preceding class of permits."[6] This class of permits was designed to generate revenue for the Dominion Government as a result of the commercial utilization of the forest resources of the North West Territories. These permits would presumably be issued to capitalists engaged in the timber trade. They were distinguished from the first category by the quantity of lumber which could be cut and by the payment of duties. Under the terms of this kind of permit, one hundred pieces of hardwood, three hundred pieces of poplar or softwood, five thousand fence poles, and three thousand cords of firewood could be cut. The duties levied by the Dominion Government were two cents per lineal foot for hardwood, one cent per lineal foot for softwood, one dollar for every thousand fence poles and fifteen cents per cord of firewood.

The implications for the citizens of Edmonton of the way the regulations were drafted were significant. In the first place these regulations did not distinguish clearly who was eligible for which kind of permit. The Crown Timber Agent could arbitrarily decide which permit was appropriate, thus determining who paid and who was permitted free access to the timber resources of the region. A second problem was that it was inappropriate to apply timber laws when the settlement of the land claims of various settlers had yet to delineate what was and was not Crown land. A third problem was the imposition of a system of fees on a community which had the traditional problem of all frontier regions, namely a lack of currency.

In addition to the regulations outlined in the order-in-council, sections 47 to 73 of the Dominion Lands Act as amended to 1879 also dealt with timber resources. These sections covered a variety of issues including the liability of persons cutting timber on Dominion Lands without authority. The sections covering this subject authorized the Crown Timber Agent in any district to seize arbitrarily timber which he suspected had been cut without the necessary permits. Any victim of this arbitrary use of Federal power who wished to contest the seizure had to give notice within one month of the seizure that he intended to institute proceedings in a court of law. Failure of the settler to meet this deadline or to obtain redress in court permitted the agent to dispose of the timber by public auction. The act further stated that any interference with the actions of the Crown Timber Agent was to be considered a felony. The absolute authority of the agent and his protection under the act was summarized in section 63:

And whenever any timber is seized for the non-payment of Crown dues, or for any cause of forfeiture under this Act, and any question arises whether the said dues have been paid on such timber, or whether the said timber was cut on other than any of the Dominion lands aforesaid, the burden of proving payment, or on what land the said timber was cut, shall lie on the owner or claimant of such timber, and not on the officer who seizes the same, or the party bringing such prosecution.

The provisions of the Dominion Lands Act thus reinforced the arbitrary system established by the regulations.

The meeting called to deal with the regulations was dominated by Frank Oliver, who was another member of Edmonton's new business class. He had arrived in Edmonton in 1876 following three years as an employee of the *Globe* newspaper in Toronto and two years in Winnipeg as a general merchant. By 1880 he had established a small mercantile business in the settlement and would soon launch Edmonton's first newspaper, the *Bulletin*. In 1879 he was appointed as a government agent with the responsibility of issuing licences for cutting timber on Crown lands. Oliver opened the meeting with a public declaration of his intention not to accept the position. His decision can be explained in part by his own previous contacts with the Department of the Interior and by the overwhelming hostility shown toward those people who held this position. This hostility was evident not only at the Edmonton meeting, but also in reports which had appeared in the *Saskatchewan Herald* of previous holders of the office being shot. As Oliver explained to the meeting, he had applied to the agent at Winnipeg for a licence to obtain lumber and shingles for a house and had been informed that one would be granted on payment of the sum of twenty-five dollars on account. Oliver indicated that he was too poor to pay any such sum and so were the great bulk of the settlers in the district. He went on to point out that as he understood the regulations the actual settler had no right whatever to cut timber even on his own claim, except for firewood, without first paying the rates required by the law. In Oliver's opinion, the effect of these regulations would be to discourage the settlement of the country.

Since further details concerning Oliver's application for a timber licence are unavailable, one can only assume that the special permit provisions of the order-in-council were being applied. From Oliver's point of view, he was a new settler who was applying his own time and labour to the resources of the region thereby generating economic development. He was not the kind of capitalist to whom the provisions of the special permit should apply. Oliver's comments at the meeting reflected the deficiencies in his own knowledge of the timber regulations as well as the problems in the approach the Federal Government was taking to their application. Contrary to Oliver's statement, settlers did have access to certain quantities of free wood from Dominion land. Oliver's experience with the Department of the Interior, however, indicated that it was not prepared, at least in this instance, to utilize this provision in the regulations. In Oliver's case the department was dealing with his application as though he was directly involved in the timber trade. Oliver's indignation at being treated in this manner ensured that he would be sympathetic to the point of view of the settlers and would emerge as a severe critic of the government's policy and the way it was being implemented.

Oliver's introductory remarks set the tone for the meeting despite William Leslie Wood's efforts to defend the government against Oliver's charges that it was being unfair in its treatment of settlers. Wood argued that the settlers had relatively free access to timber resources by virtue of the government's recognition of their rights as squatters on their land claims. They could, by virtue of this recognition, cut all the timber they wanted on these claims free of charge and without requiring a permit. Additional timber could be obtained by paying a flat fee of fifty cents which permitted them access to Dominion lands. Wood considered the law a good one "for the settler and for protecting the timber lands and it was framed more with a view to put down speculators than to harm the settler."[7] Wood's observations, while correcting the technical error in Oliver's presentation, misrepresented the situation with respect to land claims. The land claims which had been made in the Edmonton Settlement since 1870 had received no Federal government assurance that they would be recognized.

Wood's comments were largely ignored and Oliver moved a resolution supporting the right of actual settlers to cut all the timber they required for their own use either on their own or government lands free of any charge, although the act as it stood should be enforced against all speculators. The speculators were not identified, but in view of Oliver's later comments they were probably eastern Canadian businessmen who owned or directed companies operating in the West, such as the promoters of the Canadian Pacific Railway and various colonization companies like the Edmonton and Saskatchewan Land Company. Oliver further suggested that the motion should include a request to the Dominion Government to have a survey "of the Edmonton district made without delay, as a good many new settlers were taking up claims, and there would be no end of complications if matters were allowed to run along as they were now doing."[8] Oliver's motion clearly defined the issue in terms of the right of the settlers versus those of the business interests of Eastern Canada who were making money in the region but not living there.

Despite a second plea, this time from Montague Aldous who was in charge of a survey crew which was then laying out the fourteenth base line through Edmonton, that the Dominion Government had the interests of the settlers at heart, the motion as presented was passed unanimously. The motion was strongly supported by Rev. Father Leduc of the St. Albert Settlement.

A committee consisting of Father Leduc, Richard Hardisty and Frank Oliver was appointed to draw up and forward a memorial to Sir John A. Macdonald in his capacity as Minister of the Interior. The memorial so drafted dealt primarily with the issue of timber duties. It began with an outline of the types and amounts of duties which were then being applied. The remaining portion of the memorial discussed the economic burden which these duties represented and the fact that the settlers were receiving very little in return in the way of improvements. In regard to the economic burden represented by these charges the memorial noted that "while most of your petitioners are very poor men and there being very little money in circulation, they are called upon to pay a tax upon the improvements they are trying to make higher than the local tax in large eastern cities."[9] In addition to their lack of money, the majority of these settlers had only begun to develop their farms; thus these additional costs had to be faced in the future. In regard to their concern that these payments were being made to a government which showed little interest in their situation, the memorial pointed out that:

> in the provinces except Manitoba the timber taxes go to the local Government and are laid out in the shape of public improvements. While here the land is as yet unsurveyed, no roads have been made, no bridges built, nor one ferry constructed at Government Expense.[10]

The memorial concluded with a request that the timber regulations be modified:

> to allow each actual settler, free, all the timber he may require for his own use to make improvements to his own land and that a heavy tax be levied on all timber of whatever kind cut for speculative purposes or for export and that the Government...at an early date have the surveys completed in this part of the country.[11]

The petition thus emphasized the inadequacies of the Federal Government which was on a par with the speculators in terms of its efforts to exploit the area as a source of revenue rather than developing it in the interests of those people who actually lived there.

With the timber duties question having been addressed, the meeting moved on to dealing with the raising of a volunteer rifle company. The creation of such an institution, in the words of the *Saskatchewan Herald*, was in the best tradition of the citizens of Edmonton who having "been left in the cold by the Government...have always managed to paddle their own canoe—having during a few months gone by got up the first Agricultural Association in the Territories and taken in the telegraph at their own expense from a point twenty miles south...."[12] The new company once approved would represent "as fine a corps of mixed English and French riflemen as there stands on Canadian soil and just as loyal."[13] While no list of the names of those who joined is available, it was presumably made up of Métis as well as white settlers from Edmonton, St. Albert and Fort Saskatchewan.

A third item discussed was a letter from Bishop Grandin of St. Albert concerning the need for financial assistance to the orphanages being operated in his diocese. Bishop Grandin felt that the children should be a priority because of the inevitable failure of the present adult generation to adapt to farming and who would soon "be a cause of serious trouble to the inhabitants of the country."[14] The meeting approved the request and responded with a motion which supported Grandin's view that such institutions played an important role in civilizing the native population. The discussion of the mission orphanage was the only direct reference to Indians. The significance of the discussion lies in the attitude towards Indians which was revealed. Indians were clearly perceived as having virtually no role to play in the new society until they had been resocialized. The implications of this attitude would become more evident in the land claims debate which occurred in the 1880s and particularly during the 1885 Rebellion.

The protest meeting of 15 January 1880, was concerned with land claims as well as timber duties. This other issue would in its turn become part of the Settlers' Rights Movement over the next five years. The meeting also served as a portent of future trends for a number of other reasons. The meeting brought together representatives from all three settlements despite the diverse ethnic background of St. Albert, Fort Saskatchewan and Edmonton. It demonstrated the prominent role which would be played by members of the Catholic clergy, in particular Father H. Leduc. It showed the effectiveness of the town meeting format that would be used to articulate these concerns. The agenda revealed that the rights to be protected were those of the Métis and the white settlers but not the Indians. The meeting carefully avoided any separatist tendencies. Finally, the meeting revealed the siege mentality which these frontier residents had developed as a result of what they considered to be gross neglect of their interests by the Federal government.

The Federal government's response to the memorial concerning the timber duties in the summer of 1880 simply stated that the regulations as drafted were adequate to meet the settlers' needs for wood.[15] While rejecting the settlers' request for unlimited access to timber on the frontier, the Federal government did take action with respect to some of the administrative problems which directly affected the Edmonton district. These initiatives began with the creation of an improved administrative structure for the enforcement of the regulations. On 4 July, 1881, Thomas Anderson was appointed Crown Timber Agent. From his headquarters in Edmonton, Anderson was "to supervise....all matters connected with the administration of timber, lumber and fuel and the collection of dues thereon, on the Saskatchewan, above and including Battleford..."

His duties were further clarified in a letter dated 3 September 1881, from A. Russel, Acting Surveyor General. In the letter Russel indicated that reports had been received at his office that large quantities of timber had been cut on the Saskatchewan River above Edmonton and floated down to Edmonton, Battleford, and Prince Albert. Anderson's first priority, therefore, was "to ascertain who the persons are that have been so cutting and demand from them sworn returns of the quantity cut and the locality."[16] Anderson was clearly being sent to deal with the large-scale operators in the timber trade rather than the small group of settlers at Edmonton. Having obtained the necessary information, he was to collect the appropriate duties. At the same time that he was apprehending those individuals and companies which had hitherto been breaking the law, he was to:

> notify all persons to desist from further cutting without authority as in future their offence will not be dealt with so leniently, it being the instruction of the government to put down all illegal cutting on Dominion Lands in accordance with the statute on that behalf....Should any person continue cutting on Dominion Lands without authority after being duly notified you will seize the timber so cut reporting your actions without delay and recommending the course that should be taken.[17]

By the time Anderson arrived in Edmonton in the latter part of November, the regulations which he was to enforce had been revised. On 10 October 1881, a new order-in-council was passed which consolidated the regulations governing the granting of permits to cut timber in Manitoba, Keewatin, and the North West Territories. The new set of regulations did not represent any drastic change from those which had been adopted on 20 March 1878. The new set of regulations, which used the terms "Homesteader's Free Permit" and "Permits Subject to Dues," more clearly distinguished between the needs of the homesteader and those businessmen involved in the timber trade. Under the provisions of the Homesteaders Free Permit, any occupant of a homestead quarter section having no timber could upon payment of a fee of fifty cents obtain a permit to cut "such quantity of building timber, fencing timber or fuel as he may require for use on his homestead. The amount that could be cut could not exceed 1,800 lineal feet of hard timber, 400 roof rails, 32 cords of dry wood or 2,000 fence rails." These regulations had the added provision that if the house lumber was sawn at a mill, payment for sawing could not be made by way of toll, as the full quantity of lumber cut from the logs was to be used on the permit holder's homestead. In order to protect themselves, owners of saw mills had to maintain the appropriate records.

The second category of permits was clearly aimed at those individuals who were involved in the commercial exploitation of the forest. Under these permits, which were obtained for a fee of fifty cents, duties were charged on various products. In addition to the fence poles and firewood noted in the 1878 regulations, the 1881 regulations included such items as telegraph poles, railroad ties, shakes, and shingles. These special permits also required that a certain proportion of the dues be deposited on issuance of the permit. The holders of special permits were also liable for any extra costs "incurred by the Department in survey, or other area, on the ground of the limits within which such permits are to be operative."

Presumably Thomas Anderson arrived in Edmonton with a copy of these new regulations. In any event, the 17 December issue of the Edmonton *Bulletin* provided a summary and commented that "Although more liberal than those previously in force we do not think them by any means as liberal as the peculiar circumstances surrounding the settlers here give then a right to expect, but such as they are we are bound by them." In addition to providing information on the regulations, the *Bulletin* in its 10 December issue also indicated that Anderson was operating out of the Hudson's Bay Company Fort. This information was provided because:

> as the Government from motives of economy or other wise does not allow Mr. Anderson to advertise except by permission of his superiors in Ottawa we give the above and will give what further notices may from time to time be deemed of public interest, free, for the double purpose of keeping our readers posted and doing an act of charity to a Government which is either very poor or very mean.

This was the last expression of sympathy Anderson ever received in the *Bulletin*.

Anderson immediately encountered problems in trying to carry out his responsibilities. The first indication of the difficulties he faced occurred when he seized the timber being used by William Humberstone in a coal drift on the grounds that he was trespassing on Donald McLeod's property on which he alone held a permit to cut. Anderson gave Humberstone the choice of compensating McLeod or going to court. Humberstone chose to go to court which raised the question of whether the trial was to be over "Trespass on the Government or Trespass on Donald McLeod" since McLeod's land claim had not been officially recognized. Given this confusion the *Bulletin* expressed the hope that "If the court can decide on whose claim the wood was cut—and thereby all such cases—it will not have existed in vain."[18] Magistrates Hardisty and Gagnon, however, decided that they had no jurisdiction in the matter and dismissed the legal proceedings started by Anderson. The trial clearly illustrated the need to clarify the land claims issue before the timber duties problem could be resolved.

Anderson's timber seizure precipitated a second general meeting, held on 3 January 1882. The public announcement was made in the 31 December 1881, issue of the *Bulletin* by F.M. Juneau on behalf of a group of others who were not identified. The citizens of Edmonton and vicinity were requested to attend the meeting:

> to consider the tax on timber which is now being imposed on them by the Dominion Government and to take measures to lay before

the Government a statement of what is considered to be the rights of the settler in the matter.

The announcement included a special invitation to Anderson to attend the meeting so that he could "inform the people in a public manner what the full intentions of the Government are." In response to the meeting announcement about 150 people gathered in McDougall's hall for the purpose of ventilating their grievances in regard to the timber law. Mr. D. Maloney of the Rivière Qui Barre settlement was appointed chairman while Frank Oliver served as secretary. Conspicuous by his absence was the Crown Timber Agent. The meeting began with various people comparing their permits which revealed inconsistencies in the manner in which they had been issued. It was decided that a deputation consisting of the chairman, secretary, and Father Leduc should visit Anderson to seek clarification on two points, the first being why the settlers were being taxed at all and the second why certain settlers were charged more than others.

Anderson, who was less intimidated than previous holders of his office, demonstrated very little sympathy for any of the arguments presented to him. He responded to the first question simply by indicating that this was the law. In regard to the second question, Anderson said that "he made it a rule to grant a free permit to new settlers who had no improvements made but that the government took the ground that those who had been for a considerable time in the country were able and should be made to pay for what more timber they required."[19] The meeting between the deputation of settlers and Anderson ended with a request that the agent return to the meeting and explain his position. Anderson, however, declined when he found out that certain slogans which had been written on the blackboard had not been erased. The slogans in question included "Free Fuel or Fight" and *"Sic Semper Tyrannus"* which he considered "rebellious and not to be countenanced."[20] Upon the return of the deputation the results of the meeting were explained in English, French, and Cree.

In response to Anderson's refusal Mr. J. Lamoreaux from Fort Saskatchewan proposed the formation of a league "the members of which should pay no timber duties and should help each other out of whatever difficulties such action might bring them into."[21] Although there was general support for this strategy, Father Leduc opposed the idea as being rebellious. Despite the popularity of some kind of policy of passive resistance the meeting opted for a compromise which avoided any overt confrontation with either Anderson or the police at Fort Saskatchewan. It was decided that the chairman and secretary and Mr. Lamoreaux be appointed a committee to draft and send a telegram to Ottawa explaining the meeting's views. The text of the telegram represented a slight shift in position, requesting that the tax imposed on actual settler timber be delayed until such time as improvements were made, since the settlers were not in a position to pay it. The telegram identified the underlying problem which had led to the seizure of the timber by Anderson in December of 1881. If the land claims issue were resolved, the people would have access to the timber on their own claims thus reducing the need to trespass on Dominion land. The response which was received the following day ignored the request that the timber duties be considered part of a more fundamental problem relating to land claims. The answer simply reiterated Ottawa's position that the new regulations governing timber provided actual settlers with the opportunity to receive free timber.

The confrontation between Anderson and Edmonton area residents played an important part in shifting the debate from the issue of timber duties to land claims. The land claims issue can be traced back to the beginning of the Edmonton settlement in 1870 when the transfer of Rupert's Land to the Dominion of Canada allowed for the private ownership of land. The first land claims were made by individuals and institutions closely associated with the Hudson's Bay Company. In 1870 The Reverend George McDougall staked out the first claim in the name of the Methodist Church which became known thereafter as the mission property. In the spring of 1872 McDougall, William Hardisty, Richard Hardisty, Ed McGillivray, Donald McLeod, Harrison Young, and William Roland staked out an additional seven claims each ten chains wide to the east of the mission property.[22] In March 1873, the first survey of land in the Edmonton area was undertaken by W.S. Gore who surveyed the 3,000 acre Hudson's Bay Reserve. As surveyed by Gore, the Reserve was a rectangular block of land running north-south. It therefore impinged upon the Methodist Church property staked out by McDougall in 1870. This conflict was relatively easily resolved when the Company agreed at McDougall's request to move the eastern boundary of its land some distance west leaving the mission property untouched. The church land and the individual claims, however, did not receive the benefit of a government survey, thus forcing the owners to make their own arrangements. In 1875 Richard Hardisty hired a Dominion Land Surveyor to survey a line between his claim and that of Donald McLeod. The line surveyed ran parallel to the eastern boundary of the Hudson's Bay Company Reserve and thus deviated significantly from the line agreed to in 1872. The response to Hardisty's action gave the first indication of pending difficulties as McLeod and his neighbour immediately protested.

The first official survey of the settlement was conducted by William King in 1878. He was in charge of a survey party which was determining by direct observation the latitude of various locations throughout the West. He attempted to obtain the longitude of Edmonton by the chainage on the CPR as located at that time. Based on his observations he made an outline survey of the Edmonton Settlement and also one of Big Lake, which was later named St. Albert Settlement. King also made a traverse of the settlement. At the time of his survey an additional seven claims had been made stretching eight miles east of the fort on the north side of the river.

By the early 1880s the land claims issue was becoming increasingly important as the process of urban land subdivision had been initiated both on the Hudson's Bay Reserve and in the river lots to the east. In addition to the subdivision of existing river lots, new claims were being made, a number of them by members of the various survey parties active in the area. After 1880 real estate in the Edmonton area began to attract the attention of outside investors. In 1881, for example, John A. McDougall purchased Colin Fraser's claim and resold it soon after for $10,000 to the Reverend Samuel Pritchard of Winnipeg.

This process led to a request from the settlers for an official survey of the settlement and recognition of their claims. The demand was raised as early as the meeting of 15 January 1880, at which time Frank Oliver warned that the issue would create discord in the community. This was evident as early as 7 June 1880, when it was reported that Reverend Dr. Newton, the Anglican missionary:

> was committed for trial before the Stipendiary Magistrate for threatening George Roth with a loaded revolver and was held on $400 bail. Roth was taking limestone off land that Dr. Newton claims when the Doctor ordered him off. Roth claims that as Dr. Newton's title is not recognized by the Government he was not trespassing in taking the stone.[23]

Despite the obvious problems created by lack of an adequate survey, no further action was taken until 1881 when the community decided to hire its own surveyor. R. Bourne, who was subdividing the Hudson's Bay Company Reserve, was chosen for the job.

The land claims issue as it evolved between 1871 and 1881 involved boundary disputes between various claimants. The right of these individuals to their claims, however, was never challenged. This situation changed dramatically on Saturday, 4 February 1882, when word spread that L. George, an American working as a clerk in the Villiers store, was a jumper on the former Sinclair claim. In the morning he had driven in boundary stakes and had hired some carpenters who had commenced construction of a house. Mr. George was immediately challenged by the new owners of the property, including Thomas Anderson, who was no doubt relieved that someone else was the object of the community's hostility. George continued the construction of the house. Nothing was done on Sunday, but rumours were heard about other jumps being attempted if this one succeeded. When construction of the house resumed on Monday morning, the proprietors of the claim began to cast about for some means of ejecting the intruder. Since no titles to the property had been issued to give them the legal right to remove George, they were determined to use force. By the time this decision had been reached the community was sufficiently aroused to provide the necessary manpower "to make this a test case and carry matters with as high a hand as might be necessary."[24] About four o'clock a crowd of 150 men gathered. The owners confronted George and requested that he remove the building within half an hour. George pulled a revolver and threatened to shoot the first man who attempted to molest his house. George was over-powered and the house dragged to the river bank and thrown over the edge.

After this immediate threat to the Edmonton land claims had been resolved a deputation consisting of Messrs. Kippen, Garneau, and others went to A. Macdonald and Company's store which occupied part of the same river lot. Prior to the sale of the lot to the syndicate, Macdonald had paid rent to the previous owner, R. Sinclair. Macdonald's store represented another potential threat to the property. The deputation demanded:

> to know the intentions of the firm in regard to the property—whether they intended to jump or not, and whether they intended to pay rent or not, adding the remark that if they intended to jump it they and their goods would be turned out inside of five minutes. Mr. C. Stewart on behalf of the firm, refused to answer, as he did not consider that the questioners had any right to ask. The deputation then left and the crowd dispersed.[25]

Following the confrontation, Charles Stewart departed immediately for Fort Saskatchewan to report the incident and to request protection from the "mob" which now ruled in Edmonton. The police arrived the next day to investigate but no charges were laid.

Following this episode a meeting was announced for the purpose of organizing a vigilante committee or mutual protection society. This represented a distinct escalation in the community's effort to protect its rights, since such a body had been rejected only a month earlier when the timber duties crisis had occurred. The meeting began with A.W. Ripper stating its objective and the appointment of J. Harris as chairman and G.S. Wood as secretary. Harris began the meeting by asserting that it had been called for action and not for discussion, but that a short time would be allowed for those who had anything to say. The principal point of discussion was whether or not the society should be secret. Thomas Anderson expressed his agreement with the objective of the society but thought it was probably illegal. He believed it would be generally supported in the community, thus negating the need for secrecy. A committee was then appointed to draft a resolution stating the necessity for, object and intentions of the society and to formulate an oath to be taken by the members on joining. A total of 47 men signed the roll and took the oath. Conspicuous by his absence was Frank Oliver who also objected to the need for a secret society in view of the degree of community support.[26]

The vigilante committee was no sooner formed than it was challenged by J.M. Bannerman. In a letter to the vigilante committee, he declared his intention to locate on and homestead the mission property. He further declared that he was not subject to any rules adopted by the committee and that he had been authorized by the Minister of the Interior to proceed. A meeting of the vigilante committee was called and came out in favour of ignoring Bannerman's alleged authorization from the Minister of the Interior and upholding the Methodist Church's eleven-year-old claim to the property. With little discussion, the committee resolved to "apply the necessary persuasion" to deal with the problem.[27] On the following day the Bannerman shanty was thrown over the bank close to the same location where the George shack had been disposed of.

Bannerman, unlike George, was not prepared to suffer in silence at the hands of an Edmonton mob. In late February, at his insistence, warrants were issued for the arrest of Frank Oliver, Matthew McCauley, D.H. Fraser, James McDonald, Joseph Lake, and A.W. Kippen, all of whom were charged with "malicious injury to property."[28] At the preliminary hearing, all but McDonald and Kippen were bound over for trial. Kippen and McDonald subsequently sued Bannerman for damages amounting to $20,000 for arrest without due cause. In May, Bannerman sued Matthew McCauley, Frank Oliver, Joseph Lake, Lawrence Garneau, William Henderson, and D.R. Fraser in civil court for damages resulting from the removal and destruction of the house. The plaintiff requested $125 to cover the cost of material and work on the house and $700 to cover the loss of time, injury to business, and other expenses.[29]

The community immediately rallied to the support of the defendants. One of the first expressions of this support came from Rev. Dr. Newton who, on 12 March delivered a well-attended public lecture in the school house on the morality of claim jumping and house moving. In the lecture he suggested that "the manner in which Abraham procured a family burial place in the land of Canaan by paying for it with honest money...was an example to be followed by all those who wish to acquire lands already in the occupancy of others."[30]

Newton's lecture was followed by a town meeting which adopted a petition to the Governor General explaining why law abiding and loyal citizens were forced by a particular set of circumstances to take matters into their own hands to protect the property rights of the community. During the discussion, Father Leduc conveyed the support of the entire population of St. Albert, including Bishop Grandin. Superintendent Jarvis, recently retired from the North West Mounted Police also attended the meeting. While expressing his opposition to claim jumping in principle and denying any connection with the claim jumpers he pointed out that those involved "had done so as a vigilante committee, an institution which the Government was down on."[31]

The criminal proceedings took place during the afternoon of 15 June 1882. The prosecution's case was based on the testimony of four witnesses who had seen the various defendants taking part in the house moving. Donald McKay and J.R. Burton further testified that they heard Oliver admit to Bannerman that what they were doing was probably illegal but that the house had to be moved. Burton concluded the prosecution's case by stating that Bannerman had shown a document to McCauley which, if verified, would have given Bannerman a legal right to the property. This document was never entered as evidence.

The case for the defence began with the testimony of Rev. John McDougall who testified that the property on which the shanty stood had been taken up eleven years before by Rev. George McDougall for the Methodist Missionary Society. He also indicated that Matthew McCauley was in charge of the property with his consent. R. Hardisty and J. Brewster provided further evidence about McCauley's right to the property and the improvements he had made during his occupation of it. The case for the defence was concluded by Frank Oliver who stated "that the law relating to the crime for which they were being tried provided that nothing contained in it should extend to any case where the party acted under a fair and reasonable supposition that he had a right to do the act complained of."[32] Since the defence had proven that McCauley had a right to the land, Oliver requested an acquittal for himself and his friends.

The *Bulletin* concluded its coverage of the trial with a summary of the magistrate's instructions to the jury prior to their deliberations on the verdict. This summary predictably favoured the defendants' case by emphasizing how the magistrate stressed the right of a person to resist with force any attempt to evict him from his property. After a short absence the jury returned with a verdict of not guilty.

Bannerman's civil suit against the vigilantes was dealt with the following day. By virtue of the decision in the criminal case, McCauley alone was held liable for the damage done to the building after it had been removed from his property. In the view of the magistrate, McCauley could have prevented the use of his team to transport the house to the point on the river bank where it was thrown over. He was ordered to pay Bannerman $40 to cover the cost of the lumber destroyed. The decision in the two cases represented the first official recognition of the property rights of the citizens in the Edmonton Settlement as they had interpreted them since 1870.

The success achieved in the courts during the spring was followed by the commencement of the long sought Federal Government surveys. In July, Michael Deane arrived to conduct the survey of the Edmonton Settlement. His instructions from William Pearce ordered him to make surveys showing all the improvements, cultivation, fences, and buildings and to place a fair value on those improvements. He was specifically instructed not to lay down any lot lines defining the limits of the various claims. When the time came to decide the question of title to the land, the boundaries between the various claimants could then be defined. William Pearce intended to adjudicate these land claims himself at a later date.

Frank Oliver's view of Deane's responsibilities was very different. According to an Edmonton *Bulletin* article, Deane had been commissioned by the Minister of the Interior to subdivide the river frontages in the Edmonton district with full discretionary powers. These powers permitted him to gather all the relevant information from the individual claimants and survey the river lots based on this information. Only disputed claims were to be forwarded to the Land Commission in Winnipeg. In spite of his instructions, Deane lived up to the expectations of the *Bulletin* which subsequently reported:

> Mr. Deane has been to considerable trouble in getting at a full knowledge of the original claims here, and as we have not heard any dissatisfaction expressed as to the result of the survey we presume that all parties will agree to abide by it.[33]

Deane completed his survey of the Edmonton Settlement and forwarded the results to Ottawa by October of 1882. Despite his irritation that Deane had exceeded his instructions, Pearce was prepared to excuse his conduct, arguing that "he was no doubt strongly urged by the claimants to lots to do what he did in the way of defining the land limits."[34]

Deane was only one of a number of survey parties active in the Edmonton area in 1882. In July of that year the *Bulletin* announced the arrival of George A. Simpson, Walter Beatty and David Reatty who had contracts to undertake township and section surveying in the Edmonton area. These township surveys were to extend across the St. Albert Settlement. St. Albert, much more so than Edmonton or Fort Saskatchewan, was an established agricultural community organized in the form of river lots along the Sturgeon River. It was therefore the type of community the settlement survey was designed to accommodate. The community, through Father H. Leduc, confronted the survey party who promised that their surveys would in no way compromise the rights of the St. Albert inhabitants to a river lot survey at a later date.[35] The citizens of St. Albert immediately sent a request to Ottawa for a Settlement Survey. Prior to a response being received by

St. Albert, Michael Deane arrived in the community and commenced a survey of the various claims on 1 November 1882. He was soon recalled, however, for exceeding his instructions. His recall coincided with a reply from the Deputy Minister of the Interior that the township survey prepared by Beatty and Simpson would not be altered.

The Edmonton district responded to their common grievance under the leadership of the St. Albert settlers. On 15 January 1883 a public meeting was held in the school house in St. Albert to decide on what action should be taken regarding the survey of their claims. Don Maloney and Father Leduc served as chairman and secretary respectively. The meeting resolved to emulate the approach used by the citizens of Prince Albert in their confrontation with the federal government by sending a delegation to Ottawa. A subscription list was opened and Maloney and Father Leduc were selected as delegates.

The public meeting in St. Albert was followed by a public meeting in Edmonton at which time various concerns were discussed that might be taken to Ottawa by the St. Albert delegation. The involvement of the other communities in the area was encouraged by Father Leduc in an open letter published in the 27 January 1883, issue of the *Bulletin*. In this letter addressed to the inhabitants of Edmonton and vicinity he promised "to work with might and main for all without distinction *viz.* for the general interest of St. Albert, Edmonton and other post that may think proper to place their confidence in me." Fort Saskatchewan took full advantage of this invitation to participate. When the delegation stopped in the community on their way to Ottawa they were presented with a cash donation of a hundred dollars and a petition from the settlers to the Federal government. The final result of the input from all three settlements was a document which emphasized the need for settlement surveys. This approach achieved immediate results. The Federal government agreed to a settlement survey at St. Albert which was completed 20 June 1883.

The final stage in the resolution of the land claims issue in the Edmonton area involved the issuance of certificates of title. This process began with the arrival of William Pearce in 1884. After spending two weeks in the community during which time he was commended by the citizens for the thoroughness of his investigations, he submitted a final report to the Land Board. A subsequent visit to Edmonton in 1885 dealt with the small number of objections to his decisions.[36] Pearce's effectiveness in dealing with the land claims ended the settlers' rights movement, in spite of Frank Oliver's effort to keep it alive. Some individual complaints continued to be recorded as late as 1904, but they were handled without an overall community response.

The settlers' rights movement in the Edmonton area was a response to a conflict between frontier residents, both Métis and white, against the perceived indifference of central Canada. Their approach to dealing with this conflict involved a series of protest meetings, memorials to government officials along with some minor use of force against those who violated community standards. These methods were ultimately successful in dealing with their concerns. The short-term implication of the resolution of their problems by 1885 ensured that Edmonton area residents would have little sympathy for those who participated in the Rebellion. From their point of view it was an Indian uprising caused by Federal government incompetence. The long term implication of the settlers' rights movement, at least in the case of Edmonton, was the creation of a vigilante tradition which would arise again in times of crisis in the community's relationship with the Federal government.

NOTES

1. E.A. Mitchner, "The North Saskatchewan River Settlement Claims 1883–1884," in Lewis H. Thomas, ed., *Essays on Western History* (Edmonton: University of Alberta Press, 1976) and Margaret R. Stobie, "Land Jumping," *The Beaver* (Winter, 1982).
2. Mitchner, "North Saskatchewan River Settlement Claims," p. 136.
3. *Saskatchewan Herald*, 19 February 1880.
4. P.C. 208, 20 March 1878.
5. Ibid.
6. Ibid.
7. *Saskatchewan Herald*, 29 February 1880.
8. Ibid.
9. Ibid.
10. Ibid.

11. Ibid.
12. Ibid.
13. Ibid.
14. Ibid.
15. Edmonton *Bulletin*, 13 December 1880.
16. Provincial Archives of Alberta, Acc. 69.305, file 66, Russel to Anderson, 3 September 1881.
17. Ibid.
18. Edmonton *Bulletin*, 24 December 1881.
19. Edmonton *Bulletin*, 7 January 1882.
20. Ibid.
21. Ibid.
22. University of Alberta Archives, William Pearce Papers, summary by Pearce of Edmonton situation.
23. *Saskatchewan Herald*, 7 June 1880.
24. Edmonton *Bulletin*, 11 February 1882.
25. Ibid.
26. Edmonton *Bulletin*, 13 February 1882.
27. Edmonton *Bulletin*, 25 February 1882.
28. Edmonton *Bulletin*, 4 March 1882.
29. Edmonton *Bulletin*, 20 May 1882.
30. Edmonton *Bulletin*, 15 March 1882.
31. Edmonton *Bulletin*, 25 March 1882.
32. Edmonton *Bulletin*, 17 June 1882.
33. Edmonton *Bulletin*, 19 August 1882.
34. UAA, Pearce Papers, 74–169–437.3.
35. The St. Albert surveys are discussed in detail in Donald W. Moddie, "The St. Albert Settlement: A Study in Historical Geography," M.A. Thesis, University of Alberta, 1965.
36. Mitchner, "North Saskatchewan River Settlement Claims."

JUDITH P. WIESINGER

8 The Evolving Urban West
An Analysis of Manitoba, 1870 to 1891

THE CANADIAN PRAIRIES became rapidly available
for intensive settlement from 1870 onwards. This was a period of
unprecedented economic and social change as industrialization and
urbanization spread; new areas were opened up for settlement, the
railway network penetrated formerly unsurveyed territory, and a
rapid increase in immigration to Canada resulted in an influx of settlers to the West, particularly in the 1880s. Agricultural settlers were
attracted by the large amount of land available for settlement and the
decline of settlement opportunities in the United States, but their
commercial success depended to a large extent on the development of
related settlements through which trade and communication were
organized to link them with their trade areas and to markets beyond.
Urban centres, such as towns, cities and smaller places, therefore
played a vital role in the changing economic and social life of the
prairies.

During this period of rapid development, urban places ceased to
be independent, isolated, organizing centres, both economically and
socially. Rather, they became parts of an increasingly well integrated
system. The urbanization and integration of the Canadian prairies
was influenced by three major institutional landholders: the Hudson's
Bay Company, the Canadian Pacific Railway Company and the
Canada North-West Land Company. These companies all created,

influenced and planned urban settlements which became settlement nodes in a system between which interaction might take place. It is the relations between settlement nodes which create a measure of influence and interdependence that enable an urban system to be defined. While some explanations for the changing character of this system of interacting places have been suggested, including work on the Canadian plains (Hodge 1965), little attention has focused on the role of institutions in creating and influencing such settlement. One notable exception is a study of the urban development of the American Upper Midwest, a region similar to the Canadian prairies (Hudson 1985). Hudson (1985), while not focusing on the development of an urban system *per se*, demonstrated that the strategies of several railway companies were crucial in determining the patterns of urban centres.

In this paper, the evolution of the urban system in the eastern prairies is analyzed for the period between 1870 and 1891. The emphasis is on those settlements established by institutions, stressing in particular the urban land sales of the three aforementioned companies in Manitoba, the first of the prairie provinces to become urbanized. In addition, an analysis of trade flows provides an actual measure of interrelatedness between nodes, enabling some conclusions to be drawn concerning the urban system of the eastern prairies and Manitoba in particular. Although urban centres located on transport routes are linked and thereby have the potential for economic interaction, it is only by analyzing economic flows between settlements, such as those of trade, for example, that an actual measure of interrelatedness can be ascertained. This paper begins with a summary of some of the existing literature on prairie urban settlement, then outlines the companies' urban land sale policies and analyzes the economic interaction within the system by means of a focus on trading relationships.

THE URBANIZATION OF THE PRAIRIES

The nature and degree of interaction between urban settlements both within and beyond the region over time provides evidence of the evolution of an urban system in the eastern prairies and of the integration and development of that region. Institutions had a significant impact on this change. Railway companies, such as the Canadian Pacific Railway Company for example, were involved not only in the expansion of the transport network, but also in the sale of agricultural lands and in the creation of urban settlements. Together with two other major landholders in the prairies, the Hudson's Bay Company and the Canada North-West Land Company, the Canadian Pacific Railway Company created settlement nodes in Manitoba which subsequently formed part of the urban system of the eastern prairies among which interaction could be established. Although several assumptions concerning the importance of the railway have been questioned (George 1968, 1975; Norrie 1979; Wiesinger 1985), the role of the CPR with respect to town creation and development within a system of settlements has not been assessed. Likewise, both the Hudson's Bay Company and the Canada North-West Land Company have received little attention regarding their urban land sale activities. In fact, although the number of studies of the urban West in the late nineteenth century is increasing (for example, Artibise 1981), it is the rural, agricultural themes that dominate historical settlement studies of the prairies. The commercial success of the agricultural population, arriving on the prairies from the 1870s onwards, depended on the organizing abilities of urban settlements, but only limited attention has been given to the nature of urban development in histories of the prairies (for example, Foster 1983; Friesen 1984).

Much of the existing literature relating to the urbanization of the prairies consists of biographical studies of individual urban centres (for example, Artibise 1975, 1977; Foran 1978), rather than studies of the prairies as a whole. Although two exceptions are provided by Artibise (1979) and Voisey (1975), neither author dealt systematically with the development of an urban system in the prairies. In their overviews of the urbanization of the region, however, both authors recognized that the advance of urban and agricultural settlement were closely related. It was acknowledged that the founding of towns and the progress of agricultural settlement took place simultaneously with the urban centres acting as shipping and distribution points for their surrounding hinterlands, but no attempt was made to determine the nature or degree of interaction between urban centres.

COMPANY URBAN LAND SALE POLICIES

Most companies provide few, if any, explicit written statements regarding their corporate strategies. This is also the case for the three companies in question. Following an outline of each of the companies' principal policies, as they have been discerned from government and company records, an analysis of their urban land sales is presented. Inferences about what appear to have been the corporate policies are made from this empirical evidence.

The Hudson's Bay Company

In 1869 under the terms of the "Deed of Surrender," the HBC ceded its proprietary rights to the Dominion government, receiving in return one-twentieth of the land in the "fertile belt" of the prairies, in addition to £300,000 in cash and 50,000 acres around its trading posts (Galbraith 1951). As a result, the company once again became a major landholder in the West. The origins of the company's land policies can be traced back to 1879. Only in that year did a policy become a necessity in response to the increased sale of town lots and the beginning of agricultural land sales (Galbraith 1951). Further, it has been suggested that the company's policies evolved in response to prevailing conditions both inside and outside the company (Selwood and Baril 1981). Land was regarded as capital; once sold, no further income could be provided by it. The policy was to sell the land, but to withhold it if it was likely to increase in value (Galbraith 1951). The earliest urban landholdings of the company were in Winnipeg and Portage-la-Prairie, but other new townsites were established at several locations where some settlement had already taken place or where it was anticipated. Their selection was on the supposition that they would develop, supported by their hinterlands, but in most cases their limited accessibility prevented this from happening. Some, including those at West Lynne and Colville (Fort Ellice), subsequently reverted to farm lands (Hudson's Bay Company Archives, A 12/L 92/1 fo. 26, 6).

The Canadian Pacific Railway Company
The impact of the CPR has been summarized as follows:

> The pattern of urban development in western Canada was strongly influenced by the railway, first in determining the very sites of hundreds of communities along its various lines, and then in contributing markedly to these centres' economic and spatial growth. (Foran 1984)

Many of the approximately 800 villages and townsites that were established by the company along its lines in the three prairie provinces in the late nineteenth and early twentieth centuries were located in anticipation of rural development, not in response to existing demand (Foran 1984). The first townsites created by the CPR were in Manitoba in the 1880s. The fact that the process of townsite selection, which was seen as a necessary part of its corporate planning, continued elsewhere on the prairies for a long time suggests that this aspect of the company's urban land policy was successful. The general policy was to establish a townsite in each township crossed by the railway (Munroe 1959). Where possible sites were located on railway land so that profits could be gained from expansion of the town (Hedges 1939). It has been suggested that townsites were planned with a view to achieving maximum profits and although Hedges (1939) did not identify the source of the profit, he did imply that it might be derived from the sale of urban land rather than from the traffic along the company's lines. Foran further contended that the CPR was interested in immediate profit and he suggested that the company had created too many small townsites on the prairies in order "to make the townsite business as lucrative as possible" (Foran 1984). By 1888 the company's annual report stated, with regard to the sale of town lots, that "the townsites along the [main] line which have, as far as possible, been secured for the benefit of the company are contributing handsomely to its revenues" (CPR 1889). It is probable, however, that one major aim of the company was to generate as much traffic along its lines as possible and that this influenced its urban land sale activities. The location of townsites and sale of town lots were likely made with this long-term goal in mind, rather than the short-term aim of achieving as high a return as possible by withholding the town lots from sale until such time as their value had increased. This would be in keeping with railway company townsite activity in the United States, where "revenue from the sale of town lots was a short-term prospect; more important was a series of viable, trade centre towns along a railroad line that would sustain a profitable volume of business into the indefinite future" (Hudson 1985). Thus, the traffic considerations took precedence over the sale of town lots and were the reason for railway company involvement in townsite development in the American Upper Midwest (Hudson 1985).

On 6 June 1882, the CPR entered into an agreement with the Canada North-West Land Company, selling all town and village plots that would be established between Brandon and the eastern boundary of British Columbia during the construction of the main line and within one year of its completion between Winnipeg and the Pacific coast. This agreement was made in order to obtain working capital to continue construction of the main line toward the coast. Joining with a land company was a strategy frequently adopted by railway companies in the United States (Hedges 1939) and this action by the CPR may be considered to have been a deliberate management device. The management, administration and selling of this land became the responsibility of four trustees. Two trustees were appointed by the CPR, R.B. Angus and Donald Smith, and two by the land company, E.B. Osler and W.B. Scarth, all men with much corporate administrative experience in railway and land matters.

The selection of the townsites by the company was facilitated by the Dominion government (Brennan 1981; Hedges 1939). The railway company was able to select its town and station sites ahead of speculators as a result of the decision of the Department of the Interior to withdraw all its even-numbered sections from settlement in the "mile belt" along the railway line between 11 March 1882 and 1 January 1884.

The Canada North-West Land Company

In the spring of 1882, the CPR entered into another agreement with the Department of the Interior, such that "each contributed an equal area of land to constitute the...townsites [of Virden, Qu'Appelle, Regina and Moose Jaw], which were laid out in townlots and sold, and an equal division made of the proceeds" (Canada, Order-in-Council No. 2778, 1900). These townsites were known as the "joint townsites" and were administered by the four aforementioned trustees. In view of the agreement between the CPR and the Canada North-West Land Company, the companies' interest in the four joint townsites was one-quarter each, the government holding the other half.

ANALYSIS OF THE COMPANIES' URBAN SALES PLANS

In order to determine the nature of the companies' urban land sale policies in practice, their urban land transactions must be examined and conclusions inferred therefrom with some caution. Since there appear to have been long-run company strategies, the volume, value and location of urban land sales are describe and analyzed for those settlement nodes created by the companies, in order to achieve a basis upon which to subsequently measure and define the urban system of the eastern prairies. Specifically, the focus is upon those town lots disposed of by sale and as free gifts in Manitoba. An analysis of the volume and value of cancelled town lot sales is not included. Most of the information upon which this section is based is derived from the three companies' urban land sales registers and annual reports.

The analysis relates to 44 townsites in Manitoba that were created by the three companies and which registered land sales between 1872 and 1891. In two of these, both the CPR and the Canada North-West Land Company sold land and they are therefore considered to have been established by both of these companies. When providing a breakdown of the number of townsites created by the company, these two townsites are therefore assigned to both. Thus of the 44 townsites, 32 are CPR townsites, six are of the Canada North-West Land Company, seven are of the Hudson's Bay Company and one is the joint townsite of Virden. These townsites are located throughout southern Manitoba, principally along the railway lines (Figures 8.1, 8.2, 8.3). Most of the townsites were established along the CPR main line and along its southwestern, Pembina Mountain, branch line, as well as along the Manitoba South Western Colonization Railway line. This latter line, which had been built with the aim of populating and developing southern Manitoba, was leased to the CPR in perpetuity from 1884 so that the company might maintain its monopoly of traffic originating in the southern part of the province.

Already by 1891, the objective of the CPR to create townsites at fairly regular intervals is apparent (Figure 8.3). The distribution of CPR townsites exhibits a regular spacing along the company's own and acquired lines. This is in contrast to the location of the Hudson's Bay Company townsites. While several of the HBC townsites were located along the Manitoba and North-Western Railway line, the majority were established prior to extensive railway construction (Figure 8.1). As expected, due to the terms of the agreement between the CPR and the Canada North-West Land Company, most of the townsites of the latter company were located on the CPR main line west of Brandon, a settlement reached by rail in 1881 and incorporated as a city as early as 1882 (Canada 1936). Like the CPR townsites, these, too, were spaced in a regular manner.

The first sales of lots in CPR townsites took place between 1882 and 1886. Five of the six townsites in which sales were registered during these years were along the Pembina Mountain branch of the CPR rather than along its more northerly main line (Figure 8.3). This evidence suggests that the CPR was actively promoting townsite development near the border with the United States in order to deter encroachment into its territory by American railway companies. This south-western branch line of the CPR had been built as a strategic line to deter international competitors from attempting to capture the trade of the southern part of the province. Parts of this area had been extensively settled by commercially oriented settlers as early as the 1870s, prior to Canadian railway construction in this area (Loveridge 1986).

FIGURE 8.1. Sale of lots in Hudson's Bay Company townsites, Manitoba, 1872–1891

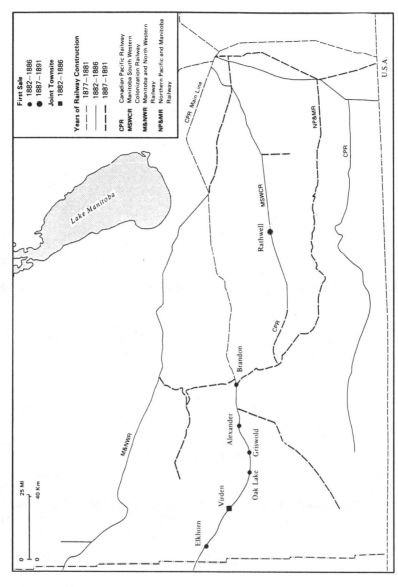

SOURCE: Hudson's Bay Co. Archives, Hudson's Bay Co. Townsite Land Sales Registers and Townsite Sales Registers.

FIGURE 8.2. Sale of lots in Canada North-West Land Company and joint townsites, Manitoba, 1882–1891

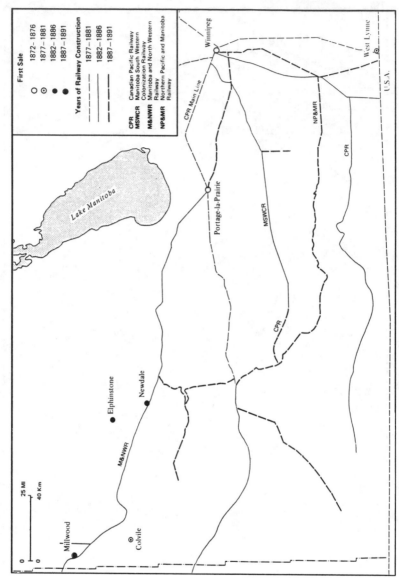

SOURCE: Glenbow-Alberta Institute, Archives, Canada North-West Land Co. Papers.

FIGURE 8.3.   Sale of lots in Canadian Pacific Railway Company townsites, Manitoba, 1881–1891

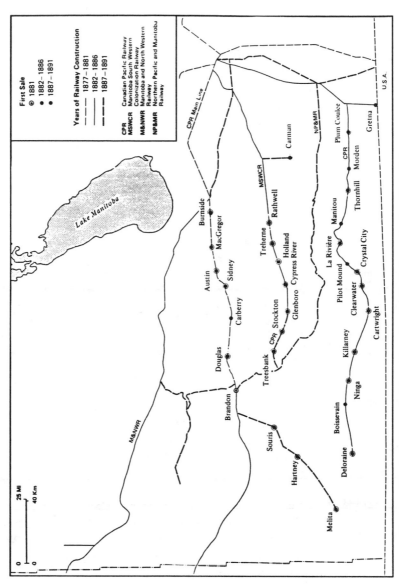

SOURCE: Glenbow-Alberta Institute, Archives, Canadian Pacific Railway Co. Land Sale Volumes.

TABLE 8.1.   Value of CPR Sales of Town Lots in Townsites Along the
Three Major Railway Lines in Manitoba, 1881 to 1891

CPR Main Line	$555,948.75
Manitoba South Western Colonization Railway	$13,662.50
CPR Pembina Mountain Branch	$60,946.50

SOURCE: See Figure 8.3.

TABLE 8.2.   Number, Value and Mean Price of Lots Disposed of by
Company in Manitoba Townsites, 1872 to 1891

Company Townsite	Years	Number	Value ($)	Mean Lot Price ($)
HBC	1872–91	1,615.25	652,628.23	404.04
CPR	1881–91	4038.50	639,051.75	158.24
CN-WLC	1882–91	1,047.00	424,416.22	405.36
Joint	1882–91	546.30	34,669.44	61.44
Total		7,265.05	1,750,765.74	

SOURCE: See Figures 8.1, 8.2, 8.3.

Over 63 percent of the total value of sales recorded by the CPR to 1891 were during the five-year period from 1882 to 1886, itself a likely reflection of rapid railway construction and migration to the area by intending settlers. The townsites were not accorded equal significance by the CPR with respect to the sale of town lots. This is suggested by the fact that although the majority of the company's townsites were located along its southwestern branch line, the total value of lot sales along this line was just over ten percent of that along the main line to the east of and including Brandon (Table 8.1). This implies that, in terms of the value of urban land sales, the townsites along the main line were of greater importance to the company than those along the southwestern branch line. There is considerable variation in the number and value of town lots disposed of by the three companies and in the joint townsite of Virden (Table 8.2).

Between 1872 and 1891, 7,265.05 lots were disposed of by these companies in their Manitoba townsites for a total of $1,750,765.74. While the CPR recorded the greatest volume of sales of the three companies and in the joint townsite, the greatest value of sales was obtained by the Hudson's Bay Company. This company sold its lots for an average price of $404.04 during the period of analysis, compared with the average price of $158.24 per CPR lot (Table 8.2). The difference in the average price obtained by the HBC and the CPR reflects the latter company's need for rapid sale at a lower price in order to finance its railway building activities. In addition, there was likely a desire on the part of the company to sell its lots in order to stimulate development and to generate trade and railway traffic, whereas the HBC was able to retain its lots until a higher return might be obtained.

The companies' annual urban land transactions are portrayed in Figures 8.4 and 8.5. These graphs illustrate the relationship between the number of lots sold and the amount obtained therefore. Of particular note is the large return obtained for the relatively small number of HBC lots sold. Apart from the sales made in 1872, the number of lots disposed of annually by the Hudson's Bay Company until the late 1870s was less than fifty (Figure 8.4). Until 1878, its sales were confined to only two townsites, Winnipeg and Portage-la-Prairie, with the majority of sales being recorded in the former centre. From the late 1870s, the volume of sales of town lots increases to a peak of just over 600 in 1881, of which more than three-quarters were in Winnipeg, probably to speculators anticipating rapid economic growth of the prairies. This peak possibly reflects the arrival of the CPR main line in the province and the anticipated subsequent economic development. The decline to the pre-1878 level by 1882 was as quick as the rapid increase to 1881 had been. This boom period of sales by the HBC bears out the company's need for a land sale policy from 1879 as the volume of land transactions increased. The number of town lots disposed of was small in 1883 and 1884 and nonexistent in 1885, reflect-

FIGURE 8.4. Number of lots sold in the townsites of the HBC, the CPR and the CN-WLC and in the joint townsite of Virden, Manitoba, 1872–1891

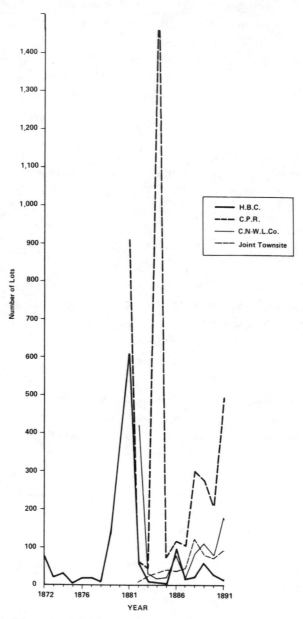

SOURCE: As for Figures 8.1, 8.2, 8.3.

ing the company's changed policy of withholding land from sale until conditions improved (Naylor 1975; Selwood and Baril 1981). Increased sales are evident in 1886 and 1889 but at a much lower level than in 1881. Although the number of town lots sold in the late 1880s and to 1891 was less than 100 p.a., the value of sales during this period was, nonetheless, greater than $10,000 p.a. (Figure 8.5). Figure 8.5 further reveals that the years exhibiting the largest number of sales were not necessarily the years in which the greatest returns were realized.

By contrast, the peak number of sales made by the CPR in 1881 and 1884 corresponds to the peak value of sales obtained, amounting to over $100,000 in each of these years. Peaks in the volume of lots sold by the CPR are evident in 1881 and 1891. This is likely a reflection of the building of the railway lines during this period, and the concomitant availability of urban land for sale in newly created townsites. Given the slump in land sales that is generally referred to in the literature as having followed the boom years of 1881 and 1882, the peak in 1884 is less expected. In that year the CPR sold 1460 lots, that is, 36 per cent of the company's total sales up to 1891, for $358,900. Of these, 1403 were in Brandon alone. Since Brandon had a population of only approximately 2000 at this date, it is probable that land was purchased by speculators anticipating the growth of this settlement which, in addition to being a divisional point on the CPR main line, was in a fertile agricultural area.

An analysis of the volume and value of town lots sold by the Canada North-West Land Company reveals a positive correlation, since the years in which the company disposed of the largest number of lots tend to coincide with the years of the greatest returns to the company. The largest number of lots disposed of in any one year by this company to 1891 was in 1882, the year in which the company's town lots first became available. This, once again, reflects the boom in land sales in Manitoba in the early 1880s. Sales dropped dramatically to 1883, however, in terms of both the number and value of sales. Subsequent smaller peaks tend to follow the general trend of low, but increasing, numbers of sales p.a. This trend is evident for all three companies and for the joint townsite (Figure 8.4). The transactions in Virden, the joint townsite, tend to reflect the trends exhibited by the

FIGURE 8.5.   Value of lots sold in the townsites of the HBC, the CPR
and the CN-WLC and in the joint townsite of Virden, Manitoba,
1872–1891

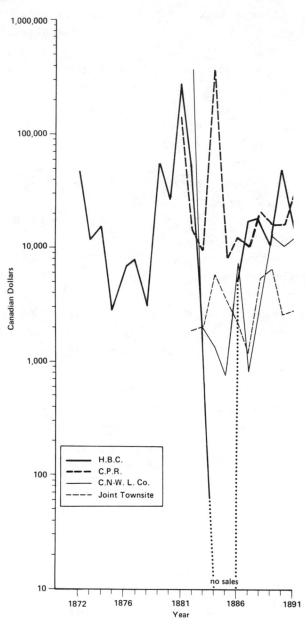

SOURCE: As for Figures 8.1, 8.2, 8.3.

TABLE 8.3.   Number and Value of Town Lots Disposed of by the
Two Highest-Ranking Townsites in Each Company, 1872 to 1892

Company	Rank	Townsite	As % of Company Number	As % of Total
HBC	1	Winnipeg	70.65	15.71
	2	Portage-la-Prairie	12.26	2.73
CPR	1	Brandon	57.72	32.09
	2	Carberry	12.26	6.81
CN-WLC	1	Brandon	58.17	8.38
	2	Oak Lake	13.37	1.93
			Value ($)	
HBC	1	Winnipeg	92.71	34.50
	2	Portage-la-Prairie	5.03	1.88
CPR	1	Brandon	78.62	28.70
	2	Carberry	7.50	2.74
CN-WLC	1	Brandon	95.62	23.09
	2	Elkhorn	1.61	0.39

SOURCE: See Figures 8.1, 8.2, 8.3.

CPR and the Canada North-West Land Company (Figure 8.4). This observation is expected, since Virden was under the joint control of these companies. The boom in urban land sales in the early 1880s reflects the influx of settlers to Manitoba. It is no coincidence that ten of the twelve centres incorporated as towns in Manitoba by 1891 were incorporated in 1882 and 1883 (Canada 1936). Two centres were incorporated as cities in these years, Brandon and Emerson, further reflecting the rapid growth.

Each company concentrated its sales in one townsite. For the HBC this was Winnipeg, while for both the CPR and the CN-WLC this was Brandon (Table 8.3). Both townsites are on the CPR main line and were the settlements with the largest populations in the province throughout the period to 1891. By that year Winnipeg was a well established centre on the prairies, having a population of 25,639, and Brandon was an important railway and agricultural centre of 3778 (Canada

TABLE 8.4.   Rates of Change in the Number and Value of Lots
Sold in the Townsite with the Greatest Number and Value of Sales by
Company

Company	Townsite	Periods ending in	% change in number	% change in value
HBC	Winnipeg	1876 and 1891	-2.80	18.72
CPR	Brandon	1881 and 1891	-97.91	-97.03
CN-WLC	Brandon	1886 and 1891	-68.75	-93.03
Joint	Virden	1886 and 1891	189.17	22.09

SOURCE: See Figures 8.1, 8.2, 8.3.

1893). Sales made in Brandon and Winnipeg together account for 86.35 percent of the total value and 56.18 percent of the total number of lots sold by the three companies and in the joint townsite between 1872 and 1891. An examination of the number and value of town lot sales in the two highest ranking townsites of each company reveals a marked difference between the townsites ranked first and second. Brandon, as a divisional point of the CPR, accounted for over 78 percent and 95 percent of the value of urban land sales of, respectively, the CPR and the CN-WLC. Sales in the second-ranked townsites of Carberry and Elkhorn, however, contributed only 7.51 percent and 1.61 percent to the value of total sales of these respective companies. While the difference in the proportion of the number of town lots sold in the townsites ranked first and second by each company is less than for the value of sales, it is still pronounced. There is a difference in the volume of sales of at least 45 percent between the townsites ranked first and second. this difference is greatest for the HBC townsites, where it accounts for over 58 percent.

The rates of change in the number and value of urban land sales provide another measure of the variation in land sale activity between townsites. Such rates of change are shown in Table 8.4 for the first and last five-year period of sales in the highest-ranking townsite of each company. The negative sign indicates that the number or value of sales was greater in the first five-year period of sales than in the last. Brandon exhibits a large decrease in terms of both the number and value of lots sold through time. The number of sales was greater, and of a greater value, in the early 1880s than in the late 1880s. This reflects the fact that town lots were purchased by intending settlers and speculators soon after they became available. Winnipeg, on the other hand, exhibits a small decrease in the number, but an increase in the value, of the lots sold over time. This provides further evidence of the Hudson's Bay Company's policy of withholding land from sale until its value had increased. By the 1880s, Winnipeg, as a well-established community, might also be expected to have real estate values higher than other townsites in Manitoba.

By determining the location of townsites, establishing them and selling town lots within them, the three companies had a direct impact on the development of the urban system in Manitoba. These companies created settlement nodes which came to organize trade and communication links between themselves, their trade areas and more distant markets within an urban system. Once these settlements were in place, together with those places not created by these three institutional land holders, the existing and expanding transport network provided the potential means for interaction.

ECONOMIC INTERACTION: AN ANALYSIS OF TRADE FLOWS

Once the framework of urban centres was in place, economic interaction could take place both between centres in Manitoba and with centres beyond the provincial boundaries. The movement of goods and commodities between settlements provides one measure of the interaction between those places. An analysis of trade flows operating at different geographical scales of interaction between urban settlements thus provides a measure that enables the nature and extent of an urban system to be defined. An analysis of import and export figures for the Winnipeg consular district, as defined by the United States

FIGURE 8.6.   Value of imports to and exports from the Winnipeg consular district, 1871–1887

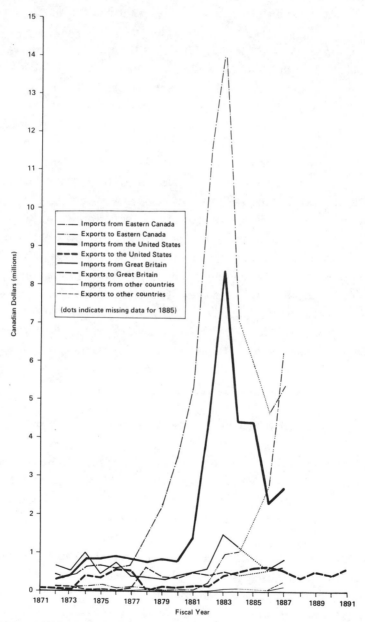

SOURCE: Public Archives of Canada, U.S. Dept. of State consular despatches from the Winnipeg Consular district.

Department of State for the years 1871 to 1891, provides both evidence and a measure of the urban system in the eastern prairies. Since trade was organized by towns and cities, these figures represent the aggregate external trade of the urban settlements in Manitoba and thereby reflect the growth and development of these places over time. An analysis of the origins of imports and destinations of exports, together with the volume of this trade, therefore reveals the changing degree and orientation of these places and, hence, of the rapidly emerging urban system. Data relating to these exports and imports are found in the U.S. consular despatches sent by the American consul in Winnipeg, James Taylor, to the Secretary of State in Washington. This source also provides some evidence of specific links between urban places. Additional information, providing evidence for the argument that the Manitoba settlements did not exist in isolation but were linked to other centres, is obtained from one Winnipeg merchant's invoices. These invoices, received by the merchant between 1879 and 1887, are examine to determine their place of origin and, hence, the specific and changing links within the urban system.

From a small beginning, the volume of trade increased significantly in the late 1870s (Kerr 1977). This is clearly exemplified in Figure 8.6, where the total imports are shown to peak in 1883, the year in which the CPR line was completed from Port Arthur, thereby facilitating the import of goods. In that year imports totalled $24,232,302.00, with over $14 million of goods being imported from eastern Canada, almost $8.5 million from the United States and over $1.5 million from Great Britain. This shows a remarkable change in orientation from the early 1870s, when Great Britain was the dominant source of imports, followed by the United States and, only in third place, by eastern Canada. As early as 1877, however, imports from eastern Canada began to increase at a greater rate than those from Great Britain and the United States. At no time during this period were imports from other countries of any significance, reaching a maximum of $130,672 only in 1887. The increase in imports from the United States from 1873 to 1874 was in anticipation of a change in tariff (U.S.A., Despatch 299, 20 April 1880). Early trade was by steamer along the Red River but, following the completion of a railway connection to Winnipeg from St. Paul and Chicago in 1878, goods could be transported by rail. After this date the number of goods travelling "in bond" from eastern Canada increased.

Apart from a small peak reflecting exports to the United States in the mid-1870s, exports were low to the late 1870s, hovering around $250,000 p.a. This was during the period of early migration to Manitoba, when settlers aimed to become established while preparing for entry into the export trade. In the early 1880s there was a general increase in exports to the United States and eastern Canada, reaching a peak of approximately $650,000 in 1886 for the former and an estimated $6 million for the latter in 1887. After reaching a peak in 1878, which, as already mentioned, likely reflected the recent completion of the railway line and the ability and ease of transportation by rail, exports to Great Britain declined to a relatively stable $500,000 p.a. According to contemporary accounts in the consular despatches, the increase in exports to eastern Canada in 1883 was due to the increased export of wheat from the Winnipeg consular district.

Winnipeg was already part of an international urban system in the early 1870s. Support for this argument is provided by a sheet from an invoice book of 1872 (U.S.A., Despatch 120, 4 January 1872). Of the twenty shipments of goods, consisting mainly of furs and buffalo robes, leaving Winnipeg during the last quarter of 1872, eight were destined for Montreal, two for Kingston, two for Toronto, four for St. Paul, and two for London, England. Two shipments specified no destination, other than Ontario and Canada. Another specific example of the interaction between settlement nodes in the system is provided by a consular despatch of 1888, reporting on the aggregate trade of the consular district for 1887. During this year fish was exported from the consular district destined for the following places in the United States: Buffalo, Chicago, Kansas City, Minneapolis, Omaha and St. Paul (U.S.A., Despatch 493, 5 January 1888).

An analysis of the places of origin of the invoices received by a Winnipeg merchant, E.L. Barber, provides another specific case study of economic interaction between settlement nodes. Barber, one of Winnipeg's first merchants, opened a general store near Fort Garry in

FIGURE 8.7.   Source of the invoices received by E.L. Barber,
1871–1887

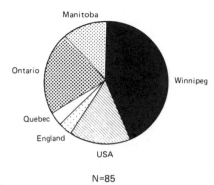

N=85

SOURCE: Provincial Archives of Manitoba, E.L. Barber Collection.

the early 1860s, having arrived from St. Paul. Eighty-five of his
invoices are available for analysis for a discontinuous period between
1870 and 1887. Information provided by the invoices reveals that Barber ordered a wide variety of goods for sale in Winnipeg. He ordered
goods, ranging from soap to pianos, directly from England and the
United States, as well as from places in eastern Canada and Manitoba.
The source of his invoices in shown in Figure 8.7. Approximately 43
percent of the invoices analyzed had originated in Winnipeg, 11 percent in Manitoba, 22 percent in Ontario, 15 percent in the United
States, and 3 percent in each of Quebec and England. There is a
change through time in the places of origin of the invoices (Figure
8.8). In the early 1870s they originated mainly outside Winnipeg and
came principally from places in Manitoba, Ontario and the United
States. Through time, however, the invoices tended to bear Winnipeg
addresses and those originating in Manitoba, Quebec, the United
States and England were absent after 1872. It is possible that evidence
of this trend is in part a reflection of the number of invoices that have
survived.

The 85 invoices in the study originated in 15 places, of which six
were in Manitoba, two in Ontario, one in Quebec, five in the United

FIGURE 8.8.   Number of the invoices received by E.L. Barber by place
of origin and by year, 1871–1887

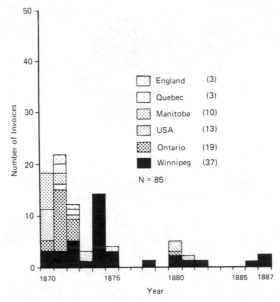

SOURCE: Provincial Archivse of Manitoba, E.L. Barber Collection.

States and one in England. The percentage of the number of invoices
received by Barber from the various centres is portrayed in Figure 8.9.
Almost three-quarters of all the invoices came from only four centres;
Winnipeg, Hamilton, Toronto and St. Paul. Economic interaction
between urban places was clearly of a local, national and international nature.

CONCLUSIONS

During the two decades following Manitoba's joining Confederation
in 1870, the province evolved from a relatively isolated, unsettled
region to one in which urban settlements were linked not only to each
other but also to urban centres nationally and internationally. The
results of this study create the argument for the existence of the early

FIGURE 8.9. Percentage of the number of invoices recieved by E.L. Barber between 1870 and 1887 by place of origin

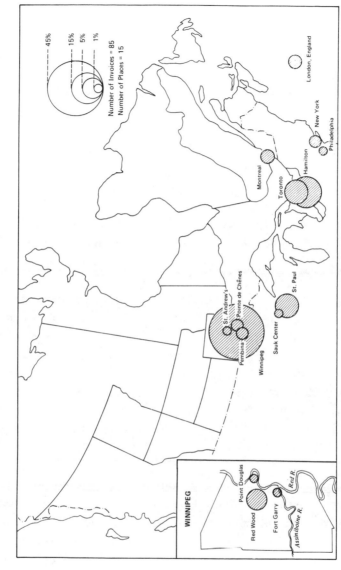

SOURCE: Hudson's Bay Co. Archives, Hudson's Bay Co. Townsite Land Sales Registers and Townsite Sales Registers.

stages of the evolution of an urban system in the eastern prairies and in Manitoba in particular.

The Hudson's Bay Company, the Canadian Pacific Railway Company and the Canada North-West Land Company selected, established and guided the development of 44 townsites in Manitoba to 1891. These townsites, together with those not created by these three companies, formed the nodes in the developing urban system. By 1891, seven of the townsites analyzed had emerged as incorporated centres: two as cities, four as towns and one as a village (Canada 1893, 1936). From an analysis of contemporary Henderson's Directories and Dun and Bradstreet Reference Books, it has been estimated that fewer than half of the unincorporated places had a population of less than one hundred, while the remainder ranged from one hundred to five hundred. Like their incorporated counterparts, these unincorporated places played an important role in the emerging urban system of Manitoba by providing essential services and performing trading functions. Once this framework of incorporated and unincorporated settlements had been established, trade links between and beyond these settlements could develop. An analysis of the companies' urban sales demonstrates the rapid growth within some of the nodes of the system in Manitoba, while the examination of trade flows to and from the province enables the extent and changing orientation of the urban system to be defined. The evidence indicates that the region experienced rapid change between 1870 and 1891, with the creation and development of an urban system during this time. Already in the early 1870s, when only just over four percent of Manitoba's population was classified as urban (Canada 1936), the existing townsites were part of an international urban system. They were linked to places in Great Britain and the United States, as well as to centres in eastern Canada. By 1891, almost 27 percent of the provincial population was urban. Towns and cities in Manitoba, while increasing in number, maintained their links within the eastern prairies and remained within an international urban system. The extent and orientation of this system expanded and changed over this short time, enabling Manitoba's urban places to take advantage of, and develop as part of, an international urban system.

ACKNOWLEDGMENTS

The financial support of the Royal Society, in the form of a Dudley Stamp Memorial Award, is gratefully acknowledged.

BIBLIOGRAPHY

Artibise, A.F.J. 1975. *Winnipeg: A Social History of Urban Growth, 1874–1974.* Montreal: McGill-Queen's University Press.

_____. 1977. *Winnipeg: An Illustrated History.* History of Canadian Cities Series, Vol. 1. Toronto: Lorimer and the National Museum of Man.

_____. 1979. "The Urban West: The Evolution of Prairie Towns and Cities to 1939," *Prairie Forum* 4, 237–62.

_____, ed., 1981. *Town and City: Aspects of Western Canadian Urban Development.* Regina: Canadian Plains Research Center.

Brennan, J.W. 1981. "Business-Government Cooperation in Townsite Promotion in Regina and Moose Jaw, 1882–1903," in A.F.J. Artibise, ed., *Town and City: Aspects of Western Canadian Urban Development.* Regina: Canadian Plains Research Center, pp. 93–120.

Canada 1893. *Census of Canada,* 1890–91. Vol. I. Ottawa: Queen's Printer.

_____. 1900. Order-in Council No. 2778 – 1900. Ref. 608181 on 69563 (No. 4). Report of the Commissioners in re Joint Townsites, 1900.

_____. 1936. *Seventh Census of Canada,* 1931. Vol. I. Ottawa: King's Printer, 1936.

Canadian Pacific Railway Company. 1889. *Annual Report for the Year 1888.* Montreal.

_____. *Land Sales Volumes, 1881–1891.* Calgary: Glenbow-Alberta Institute Archives.

Foran, Max. 1978. *Calgary: An Illustrated History.* Toronto: Lorimer.

_____. 1984. "The C.P.R. and the Urban West, 1881–1930," in H. Dempsey, ed., *The C.P.R. West: The Iron Road and the Making of a Nation.* Vancouver: Douglas and McIntyre, pp. 89–105.

Foster, J.E., ed. 1983. *The Developing West.* Edmonton: University of Alberta Press.

Friesen, G.A. 1984. *The Canadian Prairies: A History.* Toronto: University of Toronto Press.

Galbraith, J.S. 1951. "Land Sales Policies of the Hudson's Bay Company, 1870–1913," *Canadian Historical Review* 22, No. 1, pp. 1–21.

George, P.J. 1966. "Rates of Return to Railway Investment and Implications for Government Subsidization of the C.P.R.: Some Preliminary Remarks," *Canadian Journal of Economics* 1, pp. 740–62.

_____. 1975. "Rates of Return and Government Subsidization of the C.P.R.: Some Further Remarks," *Canadian Journal of Economics* 8, pp. 591–600.

Hedges, J.H. 1939. *Building the Canadian West: The Land and Colonization Policies of the Canadian Pacific Railway.* New York: Macmillan.

Hodge, G. 1965. "The Prediction of Trade Center Viability in the Great Plains," Papers, Regional Science Association, 15, pp. 87–115.

Hudson, J.C. 1985. *Plains Country Towns.* Minneapolis: University of Minnesota Press.

Hudson's Bay Company Archives, Winnipeg. A12/L 92/1 fo. 6, 26.

Kerr, D. 1977. "Wholesale Trade on the Canadian Plains in the Late Nineteenth Century: Winnipeg and its Competition," in H. Palmer, ed., *The Settlement of the West.* Calgary: Comprint Publishing, pp. 130–52.

Loveridge, D.M. 1986. "The Garden of Manitoba: The Settlement and Agricultural Development of the Rock Lake District and the Municipality of Louise, 1878–1902" (Ph.D. Thesis, University of Toronto).

Munroe, L. 1959. "Outline of History of the Company's Land Grants." Unpublished Document, Department of Natural Resources, Glenbow-Alberta Institute Archives.

Naylor, R.T. 1975. *The History of Canadian Business, 1867–1914*: Vol. II, Industrial Development. Toronto: James Lorimer and Company.

Norrie, K. 1979. "The National Policy and the Rate of Return on Prairie Settlement: A Review," *Journal of Canadian Studies* 14, pp. 63–76.

Selwood, H.J. and E. Baril. 1981. "The Hudson's Bay Company and Prairie Town Development, 1870–1888," in A.F.J. Artibise, ed., *Town and City: Aspects of Western Canadian Urban Development.* Regina: Canadian Plains Research Center, pp. 93–102.

United States of America, Department of State, Consular Despatches 1869–1891. National Archives of Canada. Microfilm reels M-691 - M-698.

Voisey, P. 1975. "The Urbanization of the Canadian Prairies, 1871–1916," *Histoire Sociale/Social History* 8, pp. 77–101.

Wiesinger, J.P. 1985. "Modelling the Agricultural Settlement Process of Southern Manitoba, 1872 to 1891: Some Implications for Settlement Theory," *Prairie Forum* 10, pp. 83–103.

II THE AGRICULTURAL EXPERIENCE IN WESTERN CANADA

DAVID E. SMITH

9 James G. Gardiner
Political Leadership in the Agrarian Community

JAMES G. GARDINER WAS elected to the Saskatche-
wan Legislative Assembly in a by-election three months before the
opening of the First World War; he lost his federal seat of Melville
thirteen years after the conclusion of the Second World War. His
career in elected office may not be the longest in Canadian history,
but it must rank among the most varied: provincial MLA, cabinet minister, Premier and leader of the Opposition, then federal cabinet minister and opposition MP. The one office denied him, leader of the Liberal Party of Canada, he sought unsuccessfully in 1948.

A teacher by training but involved in farming as a youth and later
as owner of a Saskatchewan farm for 45 years, Gardiner's political
responsibility for agriculture did not begin formally until he joined
the King government in 1935. In Saskatchewan politics he had been
identified either with the party organization, a responsibility publicly
recognized when he joined the Dunning government in 1922 as minister of Highways (the transportation portfolio by tradition being held
by the minister in charge of party matters), or with the multiple
duties discharged as premier, a position he assumed in 1926.

Thus it is to Gardiner's 22 years as a federal minister of Agriculture
that the discussion will turn, although even here the possibility of
imposing order on history in a few pages is impeded by the succession of complex events (drought, depression, war, and reconstruction)

with which he had to contend and by the breadth of his department's activities. As the new federal minister of Agriculture in 1935, Gardiner assumed responsibility for a department whose installations included three dozen experimental farms and stations from coast to coast, laboratories for the study of animal diseases on the same scale, and seed laboratories from New Brunswick to Alberta. The department in 1935–36 had exhibits at 64 fairs and shows. In the same year its inspectors carried out 94,377 on-the-spot examinations of fruits, vegetables and containers, and its publicity division answered 851,712 requests for information, while sending out several million releases which had not been asked for. Three hundred kits of educational lantern slides were prepared and sent out.[1]

The mass of departmental material and Gardiner's own papers, which number over 65,000 pages, chronicle Gardiner's lengthy career. For purposes of this paper Gardiner's career as politician, as leader and as agrarian advocate is focused on. The paper is divided into three parts: the first concentrates on Gardiner's career in ascendance, the next in decline, while the last evaluates the long-run changes, revealed through the earlier parts of the paper, which influence the ability of current political leaders to represent the agrarian community in Canada.

GARDINER THE POLITICIAN

Gardiner the politician is a phrase that might be thought redundant for a man who became synonymous with party, even machine, politics. Leaving aside for a moment the "machine" label, Gardiner himself heartily welcomed the partisan designation. His whole career was devoted to promoting the Liberal party as the authentic voice of westerners and Canadians in general. Despite his prowess as an electoral strategist (a reputation not consistently borne out by the returns), Gardiner repeatedly asserted the primacy of ideology in politics, which for him meant defending minorities and attacking privilege and special status. These were values he frequently invoked when speaking on behalf of agrarian and western interests. The Liberal party as the party of "the common man" was his ideal, and it was this belief that made him "the working democrat" his supporters admired.[2] In his mind there was no inconsistency between respect for majorities and the defence of minorities, although as he believed he had learned in Saskatchewan in 1929, majorities improperly informed might respond in an illiberal and restrictive manner toward minorities.

A party with a platform, argued and defended on the hustings, which was returned with a majority to Parliament became the crucial instrument of what he called "representative, responsible government."[3] Victory at the polls was possible, he argued, only where party members organized and worked together. Similarly, success as a government depended upon rank and file support of policies introduced by the leaders once they were in power. Thus, high policy and local organization were all part of an integrated pattern. He had little reverence for constituency opinion (what he called "the old Manitoba form of democracy"), if it operated to the detriment of the party as a whole. Conversely, it was the duty of the member of parliament to keep in touch with his constituency and to keep the constituency informed of government policy, a practice he tirelessly maintained by returning to Melville every summer and at regular intervals during the Session. According to his model of politics, general and by-elections constituted the supreme popular test of party and government policies; all the rest remained to Parliament as the supreme institution of accountability.

Gardiner's actions throughout his career remain inexplicable, indeed subject to interpretation as dictatorial or autocratic, unless his political creed is understood. It explains well his abhorrence of coalitions and third parties, for in his opinion, both diluted if they did not negate the principle of responsibility he cherished, since the first option imposed compromise on the carrying out of policy and the second condemned its followers to political impotence. Philosophically, Gardiner was a national politics man and saw himself in what he called the Laurier tradition of "national Liberalism;" an inheritance he believed Mackenzie King but not St. Laurent followed. But he was an advocate of national parties for practical reasons as well: the distribution of Canada's population made it a certainty that regions like the Prairies and the Maritimes could only make their voices heard from within the caucus of a major party; third party representation on the opposition benches was a recipe for being ignored.

The origins of this national perspective on the part of a man whose adult life was spent in a section of the country that gave birth to more third party and coalition experiments than elsewhere deserves explanation. At age 22, Gardiner arrived in Saskatchewan on the eve of provincial autonomy. He stayed to witness and participate in the founding of the province's new institutions. This experience exerted a powerful influence in forming attitudes which remained constant throughout his life; a belief in the efficacy of institutions, in pragmatic development, and in the capacity of the Canadian system to solve social, political and economic problems. Of most importance for this paper, the early Saskatchewan years established for him a model of government and interest group relations which he followed thereafter. In 1905 Saskatchewan provided an ideal environment for party building. Beginning with a clean slate, the Liberal party quickly established close ties with prominent nonparty groups, of whom the organized farmers were the most prominent and to whom the party looked for policy inspiration and approval. That agrarian relationship was to pass through many stages, each of which reaffirmed Gardiner in his decision to make the party the master organization. Most crucially, when the farmers flirted with direct electoral action, Gardiner set out to stop them. In the first of several crusades against third parties, he developed in Saskatchewan beliefs about politics that never changed.

Gardiner's views on leadership were of a piece with his conception of party politics. If responsible government meant that followers supported leaders who took initiatives, the leaders must be free to act unimpeded. Here lay the source of his antagonism to "high-class thinkers," "brain-trusters," and "men sitting in offices," who on the claim of expert knowledge sought to tell the politician what to do.[4] This was the basis of his quarrel with the Wartime Prices and Trade Board and with regulatory bodies generally, and of his criticism of the new administrative agencies created by the CCF in Saskatchewan after

1944. On principle, he rejected direction from bodies he labeled as nonresponsible, while in practice he viewed the federal government's administrators, whose numbers burgeoned during the war, as centralists and therefore ignorant of and unsympathetic to regional questions. Part of his problem with administrators lay in the little regard they held for agricultural matters, a grievous lapse in the opinion of one whose personal knowledge of farming and farmers informed almost every public statement he ever made.

Gardiner said he had come to Ottawa "to raise Agriculture from the rank of 'poor relation' to that of a 'basic industry' and to bring Agriculture to the front as one of the most important departments of government;"[5] in the first half of his federal career he succeeded in these objectives. Paradoxically, one explanation for his success lay in the very lack of interest others had for the subject. For ministers and bureaucrats preoccupied with the new and pressing demands of war, the complex and arcane world of agricultural policy over which Gardiner reigned insulated the department from scrutiny. The result of isolation, said Bruce Hutchinson some years later, helped make Gardiner "a kind of semi-sovereign power."[6] Possessed of indefatigable energy and strong opinions, and unburdened by membership in the war committee of cabinet (except for one year, 1940–41, when he was also minister of National War Services), Gardiner occupied an unusually influential position from which to champion agriculture's cause. As it turned out, that cause in the late 1930s and early 1940s proved exceptionally strong.

His first objective on coming to Ottawa, and the one he continued to promote until his defeat nearly a quarter of a century later, was to restore and secure prairie agriculture in the nation's economy. From 1935 to 1939 that meant eradicating the effects of drought and depression. The instrument he adapted to his personal use was the Prairie Farm Rehabilitation Act (PFRA), initially seen by its author, the Bennett Government, as a temporary cure. Gardiner's achievement was to enlarge its budget, convert it from a temporary to a permanent institution and expand its powers. In the process he made it an organization of his very own, untouched by other ministers or departments. Its value to him could hardly be over-estimated, for it allowed him to deliver needed services to desperate farmers, to elicit support for the department and the government and to create a band of dependable workers for the Liberal party. It was this last benefit, to the exclusion of the PFRA's professional soils and engineering work, which attracted criticism and fed the folklore of Gardiner the machine politician. It is worth remembering, however, that for those in opposition who knew the worst years of the drought, PFRA also won Gardiner and the King Government plaudits.[7]

PFRA brought water to the parched prairies; it did not necessarily bring income to cash-starved farmers. In 1939, as a result of Gardiner's labours in cabinet, the Prairie Farm Assistance Act (PFAA) introduced the principle of acreage payments to assist farmers whose crops had failed. In Gardiner's mind PFAA was to be part of a permanent wheat policy which would guarantee minimum income to those farmers who needed it regardless of the price of wheat but which, in the long run, he described as part of his "national policy for agriculture": rehabilitation and development (1935–40), guaranteed markets (1940–45), and assured and balanced prosperity (post-war).

This breadth of vision for agricultural change was part of what Gardiner later called "a reconstruction of ideas" made necessary by the disasters of depression, drought and war.[8] His immediate achievement with the PFAA (and the details are too complicated to describe here) was to secure from his cabinet colleagues acknowledgement, grudgingly given by all but King, that grain was an essential industry, farming an endangered way of life worth saving, and the West a region deserving equal partnership with central Canada.

As Hansard and the King Diary make clear, Gardiner's success in pressing the case of the ravaged West lay in his "hard pressure" and "tenacious(ness)" in Council and Parliament.[9] It lay as well in the multitude of ties he had established with the Pools, the newly resurrected Canadian Federation of Agriculture and with the farmers in every constituency in the West. But as the Diary significantly demonstrates, he would have failed in his campaign without the support of the prime minister. Although King sat for Prince Albert, it was no parochial consideration that informed his view. He accepted Gardiner's argument that aid to the West was necessary after all it had endured and because, he believed, if aid were withheld, two classes of citizens would be created: the favoured and the disadvantaged.[10] In this instance, with the prime minister and the agricultural constituency behind him, Gardiner was able to move all obstacles before him.

Gardiner's leadership of wartime agriculture tested not only his political resources but also his administrative skills. The war disrupted every aspect of agricultural policy, not just on the prairies. The dairy and fruit industries of eastern, western, and central Canada had to be restructured to take account of new demands and lost markets. But again the grain industry occupied an inordinate amount of his attention, both because of the loss of European markets and the shift in the British market away from wheat imports, and because these changes threatened, in Gardiner's mind, the initial rehabilitation of the prairie economy begun before 1939. For instance, the war helped to restore western prosperity but also aggravated the contrast between farming and nonfarming sectors of the economy. Cash farm income increased but not as fast as income in other sectors, with the result that the West continued to lag behind the rest of the country. By 1945 the value of agricultural exports stood at three-and-a-half times the 1939 figure but in every year of the war agriculture's proportion of national export earnings was less than before.[11]

A bare list of some of the innovations the war brought to grain farmers suggests the magnitude of the problems the minister faced: wheat acreage reduction in 1940 (so that by 1943 the acreage sown in wheat had declined over the 1940 figure by 42 per cent), delivery quotas in 1940, a two-price system for wheat in 1941, and an increase in feed grains of 72 per cent between 1940 and 1943, with the result that for the first time in the West's history more coarse grains were grown than wheat. And all of this had to be accomplished by voluntary compliance. Thus, to the primacy Gardiner normally attached to political education and consultation was added the imperative of securing as quickly as possible a broad base of support to ensure the success of wartime policies.

Outside of an exceptional organization like PFRA, the federal department did not have strong "field services," while the provinces did and it was this disparity in manpower and expertise, and the consequent lack of information that encouraged the federal department early in the war to summon the first of many federal-provincial agricultural conferences to help regulate production. By 1943 at least nine conferences had taken place. They were attended not only by officials from both levels of government but by CFA representatives and members of the farm press. Annual meetings continued after the war, providing Gardiner with a major platform from which to pronounce his department's accomplishments and from which to gauge agricultural opinion. Near the end of his federal career, he compared the conferences "more or less (to) a party caucus...behind closed doors...(so as to) get free expression of opinion" and he revealed that "I and my officials discuss every important matter (with the CFA) concerning agriculture before action is decided upon."[12] However described, the meetings became another part of the distinctive machinery Gardiner created to join farmers to the federal government, machinery whose reciprocating parts carried opinion to Ottawa and policy back to those on the land.

The third aspect of Gardiner's career, that is as an agrarian, has already been alluded to in several respects. He was a farmer, an occupation (not an avocation, as T.C. Douglas had once slightingly suggested and Gardiner had heatedly rejected) whose argot infused all his rhetoric. He belonged to a rural society he had first helped build and then come to represent to others. An athlete, a supporter of temperance, prominent in the Presbyterian church and then in church union, Gardiner was an activist in every field that interested him. He belonged to most of the major farm organizations of his day and many of the minor ones. His advice was always the same when it came to the question of the politician's right relationship to farm groups: join them, give them information, help them communicate with government. In light of his model of political leadership that was the only reasonable response a supporter of responsible government could give. As he more than once noted, "the American Block system" did not operate in Canada; if interest groups wanted to be heard they had to concentrate their energy on informing those who did make decisions. On occasion, he availed himself of this system and his close ties with agricultural organizations to bring pressure upon colleagues in Council whose response to his policies might be lukewarm or hostile.

Despite far-reaching changes in the methods and conditions of Canadian agriculture over which he presided for more than two decades, Gardiner's ideas about farming were rooted in the past. Or so it must seem to a modern observer. He thought of agriculture not so much in terms of the individual farmer as he did of groups of farmers and their families. There was a pronounced historical consciousness in his view of politics, with one constant being the importance of agriculture across space (between and within countries and regions) and over time (from one generation to the next). Repeatedly, he referred to the federal government's obligation to those farmers it had encouraged, while Ottawa still controlled the West's natural resources, to settle on quarter- and half-sections, particularly in the semi-arid Palliser Triangle. They had opened the West and made the nation, and the Empire, prosper. A malign conjunction of events following the transfer of resources in 1930 did not absolve Ottawa of its duty. Part of the prairies were overpopulated as a result of federal policies, so all farmers had a "claim of right" to assistance, even if it were only to help in moving to better land and their old farms returned to grass.[13] As well, he never tired of issuing warnings about the dismal consequences for the nation that would follow the refusal of young people to stay on the land, which he prophesied would happen without the kind of help PFAA provided.[14]

While always identified with the prairies, Gardiner never saw himself as a regional politician. The responsibilities of his department would have prevented him from adopting so limited a perspective in any case. Moreover, for him, politics was about more than representation, certainly about more than geographic representation. That being said and notwithstanding the national constituency of farmers who looked to the federal Department of Agriculture for assistance and direction, grain was the most important defining characteristic in his political region: those who grew grain fell within, indeed constituted, his political universe. The security of that universe, that community, became his passion; one which explained the direction of his principal activities from PFRA to PFAA to the wartime food contracts. It also made explicable his intense support for two other policies with which his name became indelibly associated: the Canada-United Kingdom Wheat Agreement, 1945–50, and the South Saskatchewan River Dam. The Dam will be discussed later because the long and inconclusive debate that surrounded it is evidence of Gardiner's waning political influence in the early 1950s.

Although few agricultural spokesmen but Gardiner ever defended the Agreement, its terms and history deserve mention, for they illustrate as clearly as any subject Gardiner's leadership in the agrarian community. With its fixed price and production schedule, the Agreement was modeled after the successful wartime contracts to supply foodstuffs to Great Britain; and, as with them Gardiner expected that he could mobilize Canadian grain farmers through a continuation of wartime collaborative machinery. In fact, because the price of grain on the open market moved higher than provided for in the Agreement, this last best contract proved a financial reverse for the farmers and a political rebuff for Gardiner.

Gardiner argued to his dying day that what the farmers might have lost due to the British Government's failure to honour the Agreement's spirit and thus renegotiate the contract price in the last two years was less important than what they got: a fair and stable return. The Agreement assured the producers that at least until the end of the decade there would be no return to the disaster of the 1930s or the short but sharp slump in wheat prices after the First World War. Whether or not one agreed with him (and almost no one did), the negotiation of the Agreement against widespread opposition was a measure of his persuasive power in government, of the deference his colleagues paid him, and of the tight control he still exercised over the agrarian community and its organizations, who depended upon a sympathetic hearing from the minister and his officials if they wished their interests transformed.

At the end of the war, Gardiner thought he saw (correctly, as it turned out) a shift in federal interest away from concern for righting regional imbalance in Canada and a return to central Canadian pursuits, particularly an influx of foreign investment into Ontario and Quebec. The Agreement proved to be a short-term and ultimately an unsuccessful attempt to stem that reversal in national policy which he believed was detrimental to the interests of agriculture generally and the West in particular.

GARDINER'S DECLINE

By 1950 the conditions that had accounted for Gardiner's leadership in the agrarian community had altered, or were about to alter, and each change depreciated his once commanding influence.

Gardiner's political strength had derived from his control of an integrated party organization that extended from constituency poll to Parliamentary caucus. At the war's end, the army of dedicated and energetic workers in Saskatchewan who could be mobilized to fight for the Liberal cause found their ranks depleted by the huge out-migration of the province's rural population due to economic dislocation, military enlistment, or the attraction of war industries located in central Canada. The impact of these changes on a party organization with essentially rural foundations disturbed electoral and party practices extending back to the days of autonomy. In the cities a comparable shake-up in settled routine occurred, for the federal government's local bureaucracy and regulatory agencies had quickly swelled to meet wartime needs, in the process paying slight heed to the partisan loyalties of those enroled. Gardiner's correspondence for these years is filled with references to the detrimental effects of the war on accepted party practices.

Paralleling the deterioration of the once dominant Liberals was the rapid and confident rise of the CCF. That party, who flattered the Liberals by emulating their intensive organization, posed an unprecedented threat to Gardiner. Western farmers, irritated at the many and complex wartime policies and regulations of the federal government, vented their anger at the Liberals by transferring their allegiance to the CCF. Gardiner refused to accept that the farmers had become socialist; rather, he argued, the explanation for this massive desertion lay in the Liberal party's wartime identification with big business and big unions.

Partisan tremors magnified as the post-war upheaval in federal-provincial relations progressed. In part due to the tax rental agreements, the provinces after 1945 enjoyed the first period of economic prosperity in a decade and a half. The return of provincial fiscal health and the end of emergency government in Ottawa set the provinces on course for an era of activism that only became fully apparent a decade later. Saskatchewan, however, was well in the lead in this development and became the first of the Canadian provinces to modernize its provincial institutions and processes. The explanation lay in the CCF's commitment to bureaucratic innovation: a departmentalized civil service, active use of crown corporations, program planning and budgeting, and consolidation of local authorities. Each of these reforms hit at political institutions and practices at the heart of Liberal organization; together they threw the provincial Liberals into disarray and thereby deprived Gardiner of his dependable political organization. In the 1945 federal general election, Saskatchewan returned only two Liberals from the province's 21 seats in Parliament, and thus, with no friendly provincial government in Regina, Gardiner found himself a leader of a prairie rump.

In 1949 the balance tilted toward the Liberals again, when they won 14 of 20 seats, but by then Saskatchewan and the West in general counted for less in federal politics than at any time since 1935. Because Canada after the war was less an agricultural nation than before 1939, Gardiner's political base began to shrink, a truth brought home by his unsuccessful bid for the Liberal leadership in 1948. Gardiner depended upon the loyalty of his agricultural constituents at the convention and, though generally loyal, their loyalty did not translate into a majority of delegate votes; he won 323 votes to St. Laurent's 848, while Chubby Power garnered 56. The determining factor, Gardiner concluded, was that "those who represented interests other than agricultural interests...preferred to have Mr. St. Laurent [who was] closely associated with their development over a long period of years."[15]

Whether or not, as one disappointed supporter said, the outcome constituted "a defeat for the West," it ended Gardiner's leadership ambitions and curtailed his role in national politics.[16] Although not a sore loser, Gardiner began to limit his political interests to fit his perceived regional or agrarian base. To advance the cause of agriculture, he continued to use the instruments he had honed since 1935; his department's administrative structure, House of Commons debate, cabinet discussion and established contacts with farm organizations. He used them so effectively that he still received accolades as "the real fighter for the farmer's cause" and "the West's most stalwart supporter at Ottawa," but increasingly the reputation was not matched by results.[17]

ISSUES

Two issues dominated his remaining years in office: a grain surplus that grew to alarming proportions and the interminable question of the Dam. In the 1950s surpluses replaced scarcity as the problem of western agriculture. The Canadian Wheat Board, to which Gardiner had become an enthusiastic convert, no longer won universal acclaim for its policies. The Board had assumed monopoly control of wheat in 1943, with the consequence that in the eyes of the farmers the federal government alone, and uniquely, became responsible for this crucial industry. Although Gardiner coveted the Board from the moment he arrived in Ottawa, its control eluded him, for it remained a responsibility of either the minister of Trade and Commerce, or during the war, of the wheat committee of cabinet on which Gardiner sat. Despite this formal allocation, Gardiner's long association with wheat matters identified him in the public mind with the Board and he reciprocated that assumption by playing a highly visible role in its defence. Thus, when the St. Laurent Government proved reluctant to respond to pressure to develop a new policy to deal with the grain glut and consequent cash shortage, Gardiner bore the burden of criticism for government inaction and Board ineffectiveness. When in response to protracted demands for interest-free loans on farm-stored wheat the government proposed a scheme of low-interest loans, the outcry was sharp and severe. The Liberals' apparent insensitivity to strongly-held western concerns seriously eroded Gardiner's claim to speak for the prairies; his powers of persuasion appeared exhausted.

The same unhappy judgement followed the St. Laurent Government's decision in 1952 not to proceed with building the South Saskatchewan River Dam. For twenty years Gardiner had advocated a dam to increase water resources and therefore broaden the base of prairie agriculture through irrigation and to provide hydroelectric power to attract industry which in turn would help diversify the region's single-crop economy. Some of the PFRA's early engineering reports were commissioned by him to explore these themes. By the early 1950s every provincial organization and party in Saskatchewan was committed to the project; Gardiner's task remained to convince his cabinet colleagues.

By then, however, the prime minister believed that unless the Dam could be defended as a work of national development, in the same category as the St. Lawrence Seaway or the Trans-Canada Highway, it would have to be delayed. Gardiner argued that its national significance lay in what it would do for the region.

Decentralized industry would diversify and strengthen the West's economy at the same time as it promoted a greater balance to Confederation, which had from the very first been tilted toward the central provinces. That readjustment would be assured, Gardiner thought, because the new West would be the magnet to attract hundreds of thousands of immigrants. The region would be restored to, even surpass, its former importance before the drought and depression of the 1930s. The economic benefits of a revitalized agriculture based on prosperous, independent farmers should have been added attractions for Liberals: it would undercut the movement to bigger farms but fewer owners, a condition Gardiner called corporate farming and scathingly equated to a new "Feudalism," and it would defuse the socialists' arguments that planning and public ownership were the only alternatives to check centralized political and economic control in Ontario and Quebec.[18]

At its root Gardiner's argument for the Dam carried the older argument for the PFRA and the PRAA to its conclusion. Regional in its terms but national in its effect, the Dam originated in Gardiner's concept of national Liberalism. Until his death he believed that "if King had survived three years longer," the Dam would have been built. There is no evidence that King ever gave assurances to this effect but his support for Gardiner's efforts to extend the PFRA earned him the undying appreciation of his minister, who believed that King at least understood the magnitude of the West's problems and accepted the federal government's duty to help. With St. Laurent it was a different matter; there was "not the same understanding of western needs...and the educational work required delayed actual construction for 10 years."[19]

Federal response to the wheat surpluses and to the demand for a Dam crippled Gardiner and the prairie Liberals. The era (1935–50) of rejuvenated federal policies for developing western agriculture had passed, while initiative in matters affecting the day-to-day life of farmers had moved to the provincial governments. Of greatest concern in the 1950s was the decline in farm population due to rural-urban migration, itself caused by farm consolidation and increased mechanization of agriculture. Combined, these forces posed a threat to the integrity of the rural community which the CCF met directly by a proliferation of policies to maintain the attractiveness of rural life. This activism confirmed in the public mind the greater immediacy and sensitivity of the provincial government. Thus, to the decline in Gardiner's personal political fortunes was added the decline in the prestige of the federal government as agriculture's advocate.

Evidence of the mounting disillusionment could be found in the Saskatchewan Wheat Pool's annual submission for 1957 to the federal government. That document pointedly observed "the harsh fact that...the great prolonged boom in the Canadian economy had passed the farmers by."[20] The conclusion drawn by more than one westerner was that "the federal government does not seriously pay much attention to the problems of any province except the ones who, by the power of their votes, can make or break a government."[21] Implicit here was a critical comment on Gardiner's waning influence. The Canadian electoral map had not substantially changed. There had always been more people in the St. Lawrence heartland than anywhere else in the country. What had disappeared was the federal commitment crystallized in the late 1930s to restore and maintain national standards through government policies. Through these policies Gardiner had brought the federal government closer to western farmers than at any time since the homestead period. The federal retreat marked the beginning of the end of Gardiner's influence in the agrarian community.

GARDINER'S INFLUENCE

Gardiner's leadership of the agrarian community is remarkable for its longevity but also for its easy obliteration by the Diefenbaker sweep that followed it. Saskatchewan Liberals generally resisted the swing to the Progressive Conservatives in 1957 but after only nine months in Opposition, Gardiner and the rest succumbed to the Tory tide in 1958. Liberals on the prairies became one more example of that Canadian phenomenon: long tenure in office followed by total collapse. Despite two decades in power and the perpetual repetition of one theme, the acceptance of agriculture and its primary producers as a basic industry in the Canadian economy, Gardiner left no disciples to carry this message to a new generation of leaders. Nor did he bequeath an organization, even the rudiments of one, that could be employed in this task. He did not live to see Ross Thatcher and the Saskatchewan Liberals come to power in 1964, although he saw enough of the Grit renaissance to doubt its credentials as a true inheritor of his "national Liberalism."[22] The growing separation of the federal and provincial wings of the party, a phenomenon he never understood, undermined the integrated view of partisan organization he promoted and the possibility of securing his goal of "representative, responsible government."

Gardiner's political leadership was rooted in an agrarian community fast disappearing by the late 1950s. He once boasted that during his tenure in office "agriculture (had) passed through the greatest and most costly revolution in methods ever experienced in this country at least."[23] Gardiner did not say, nor did he appear to recognize, that the same revolution helped destroy the political organization that had made the revolution possible. By the end of his career, the close personal ties he had established with farmers and farm organizations had become increasingly difficult to maintain. As agriculture began to diversify, the farmers' associational structure experienced fission. Even Gardiner's rhetorical skills, by which he held farm and party audiences alike "spellbound," could not restrain the disparate demands of agriculture as its interests grew more specialized.[24] The centrifugal force of the industry proved too strong to be dominated by one individual. And Gardiner's political model required single control from the top. At the same time, the growth in provincial marketing and subsidy schemes across the country challenged the leadership pretensions of the federal Department of Agriculture. A quarter century of direction and guidance from Ottawa began to give way to innovative and interventionist provincial policy.[25]

Without question, grain remained a federal responsibility but if the party organization suffered from sclerosis, so too did this staple industry. In the 1960s and 1970s Ottawa chose the route of modernization, first through rationalizing the transportation network and then by abolishing the farmers' Magna Carta, the Crowsnest Pass Rates. These incendiary reforms, which shared a functional perspective of the grain industry as a sector of the economy in need of major overhaul, elicited generally hostile opposition. Had Gardiner still been alive, he doubtless would have shared the opponent's concern, for neither policy granted the preservation of rural life the primacy he awarded it.

Indeed, the policy priorities of the Pearson and Trudeau governments scarcely referred to agriculture. What they did promote (along with social welfare and bilingualism) was regional economic expansion and equity through new agencies of the federal government such as the Department of Regional Economic Expansion. Significantly, the principle of redistribution, which this paper credits Gardiner with introducing into the policy of the King Government, was removed from an old line department like Agriculture. As a consequence, the administrative and political base of Gardiner's successors narrowed both in comparison to the resources he had possessed and to the resources some of their colleagues possessed in the 1960s and 1970s.

The regional (western Canadian agrarian) voice that spoke so audibly through Gardiner in cabinet grew fainter and less authentic, especially as Trudeau's ministers came to depend increasingly on patronage to influence federal party matters in their provinces and regions.[26]

Gardiner was a successful leader because he was an acute listener, much of his listening being vicarious through his army of workers. In later decades with the department constrained in its activities by the presence of new and high spending regional ministries, his successors had less opportunity to hear their constituents. Also they had less motive; their careers were shorter than his (six ministers of Agriculture in the 22 years after 1957) and their experience, at least with western agriculture, less extensive. Few ministers tried to reverse this trend away from a regional perspective; none succeeded. Their failure underlines once again Gardiner's singular accomplishment as leader of the agrarian community during a period of massive change.

NOTES

1. Canada, *Report of the Minister of Agriculture for the Dominion of Canada for the year ended March 31, 1936, passim*.

2. Papers of the Rt. Hon. James G. Gardiner (hereafter Gardiner Papers), Gardiner to A.C. Stewart, 19 October 1950, 61094–96; Gardiner to Karl Jaeger, 15 March 1947, 59570–72; Les Mutch, MP, to Gardiner, 4 January 1947, 48034.

3. Gardiner Papers, Address to the National Office Management Association on "The South Saskatchewan River Project," 15 September 1959, 27410–11.

4. Ibid., Gardiner to W.H. Heffernan, 3 August 1944, 42887–92; Radio address, "Social Planning, Liberalism and the War," 21 April 1943, 46536–42; Gardiner to T.C. Davis, 7 July 1943, 41598–415600.

5. Ibid., "Don" (McNiven) to Gardiner, 30 December 1955, 33425–27; W.R. Motherwell to Gardiner, 15 March 1943, 52827; Gardiner to H.R.L. Henry, 23 January 1947, 47979.

6. Bruce Hutchinson, *The Incredible Canadian* (Toronto, 1952), 431 in Reginald Whitaker, *The Government Party* (Toronto, 1977), 178.

7. *House of Commons Debates* (1941), 3426 (E.E. Parley), 3429 (A.M. Nicholson), 3441 (M.J. Coldwell); (1944), 5138 (J.G. Diefenbaker).

8. Gardiner Papers, no title (Address re. agriculture's contribution to the war effort), Ottawa, 10 November 1941.

9. King Diary, 5–7 March 1941, in Charles F. Wilson, *A Century of Canadian*

Grain (Saskatoon, 1978), 680; King Diary, 23 February 1942, 175; 18 December 1942, 1106; 21 February 1944, 184; and 8 June 1944, 570.

10. Ibid., 30 July 1940, 667 and 20 March 1941, 231.

11. G.E. Brintnell and V.C. Fowke, *Canadian Agriculture in War and Peace, 1935–1950* (Stanford, 1962), 74 and 391.

12 Gardiner Papers, Speech to the Sixteenth Annual Meeting of the Canadian Federation of Agriculture, 23 January 1952; Gardiner to J.C. Lewis, 17 December 1956, 48132–36.

13.. Ibid., Gardiner to Paul Martin, 4 July 1959, 66781; see also, Speech by Hon. James G. Gardiner, The Canadian Club, Regina, 16 September, 1936 and *Commons Debates*, 5 June 1941, 3586–87 and 20 July 1944, 5140–41.

14. Ibid., Address to Kiwanis Club of Montreal, 18 May 1944, and 30 September 1954; Address...to Annual Meeting of the Lethbridge Board of Trade, 15 January 1947; Speech to the Kansas State Board of Agriculture, Topeka, 13 January 1955; Address...to the Closing Session of the Eighteenth Federal-Provincial Agricultural Conference, 5 December 1956; Gardiner to Paul Martin, 4 July 1959, 66781.

15. Gardiner to P.M. Anderson, 10 August 1948, 60224–25; Gardiner to George G. Grant, 9 August 1948, 60213.

16. Ibid., P. Stapleton to Gardiner, 9 August 1948, 60209–10.

17. Ibid., John Decore to Gardiner, 20 November 1952, 62000; Thos. S. Farquharson to Gardiner, 30 June 1945, 36984–85; Max Stuart to Gardiner, 27 October 1953, 28695.

18. Ibid., Address to the Canadian Club, Montreal, 4 December 1939; Ontario Election Speeches, 1937 (Strathroy, 21 May 1937); Gardiner to W.H. Heffernan, 8 May 1943, 42834–35; Address to AOTS, Regina, 6 February 1939.

19. Ibid., Gardiner to J.O. Gour, 2 July 1958, 66615 and Address to National Office Management Association on "the South Saskatchewan River Project," 15 September 1959, 27410–11.

20. Ibid., Saskatchewan Wheat Pool, Memorandum for Submission to Members of the Government, 9 March 1957, 30514–27.

21. Ibid., Sam Ousdahl to Louis St. Laurent, 29 November 1955, 29887–88.

22. Ibid., Gardiner to Ken Mayhew, 4 September 1959, 64347 and Gardiner to Thatcher, 22 August 1959, 64323.

23. Ibid., Gardiner to Howard Winkler, 9 December 1958, 67498; Gardiner to Peter Newman, 11 February 1959, 67219.

24. Wilson, *op. cit.*, 732.

25. See Grace Skogstad, *The Politics of Agricultural Policy-Making in Canada* (Toronto, 1987).

26. See Herman Bakvis, "Regional Ministers, National Policy and the Administrative State," paper presented to the annual meeting of the Canadian Political Science Association, 1986.

J.E. REA

10 T.A. Crerar and the Progressive Challenge

BETWEEN EARLY DECEMBER 1921 and October 1922, the political drama of Progressivism in Canada was played out; after that, all was denouement. Thus the focus of this paper, both chronologically and thematically, is rather narrow. It examines three events in the political career of T.A. Crerar and the Progressive Movement which have been misunderstood, distorted, or misinterpreted in our historical literature. These events were of regional, to some extent national and, of course, personal importance to the prairie West, the Progressive Movement, and to Crerar. They are all well known to western Canadian historians: the negotiations between Liberals and Progressives which followed the election of 1921, the decision of the Progressives not to accept the role of official opposition in the House of Commons and Crerar's resignation of the party leadership in October 1922. It seems almost foolhardy to tackle these hoary old chestnuts again, but recent excursions into the massive Crerar Papers at Queen's University Archives have persuaded me that there may yet be more to be said.

The traditional, that is the Ontario story, since until very recently most of the textbooks for English Canada have been written there, can be sketched very quickly. The stunning result of the 1921 election was the arrival of 65 Progressives, mostly from the West, into the House of Commons, astonishing the rest of the country, ending forever our two-party system and condemning us to multi-party politics, minority governments and new, and very likely dangerous, ideas. But these western guns were spiked by Mackenzie King who, shrewd as he was, realized that the Progressives had little choice but to support him. They could hardly support Arthur Meighen and the Tories. The traditional story, being centralist, appears to have no room for other possible alternatives.

In any case, these bumptious Progressives were so inexperienced and so badly divided that they refused the responsibility of official opposition to which their numbers entitled them, thereby confirming that they posed little threat. Even the biographer of the movement and quintessential westerner for most of his career, W.L. Morton, was later to describe them as "a restless and unreliable band." The party soon collapsed into warring factions, dubbed Albertans and Manitobans (it was never made very clear where the 24 Ontario and 15 Saskatchewan Progressives, over half the total, lined up, or indeed, except for Agnes Macphail and one or two others, who they were). After only a few months their erstwhile leader, Tom Crerar, frustrated and disillusioned at the unruly lot who could not even conduct a civil caucus meeting, threw up his hands in despair and quit.

This is somewhat over-drawn, I concede, but is it really that different from the impression left by the average survey text? Another look at the story from a rather different perspective may help to redress such a caricature. That perspective is Crerar's.

If central Canada was surprised at the strong showing of the Progressives in the election, Crerar was rather disappointed. He had expected a minimum of 75 seats and believed that the United Farmers of Ontario (UFO) had let the side down. The reason, for Crerar, was very evident. "The narrow nature of the appeal...largely stamped our movement as a class movement in that Province," he wrote to J.B. Musselman in Saskatchewan, "with the result that...our candidates did not get more than ten per cent of the vote of the cities, towns and villages." Since the next electoral redistribution would reduce rural Ontario's political strength even further, the strategy of J.J. Morrison and the UFO was hopelessly self-defeating.[1] It is unlikely that Morrison really understood Crerar's concern; or, if he did, he did not believe or accept it. Even before the election, Crerar had told Morrison that when it was over, "it will probably be found that no party has a majority." This would result in a "general demand from all over Canada that a strong government be formed and we will be in a position where we will necessarily be an important factor in the reckoning."[2] This was the core of the misunderstanding and the split which followed between the two men.

To Crerar, an inconclusive election would create the opportunity for "getting the policies we have advocated made effective."[3] Throughout the entire election period and its aftermath, it was the policies of the movement that were vital to him and not the narrowly political aspects of the questions of Cabinet formation or the party's role in the House of Commons. As he put it later to W.C. Good, "I was not mainly concerned at all with the triumph of a party as a party...I was interested then, and still am, in sound policies of development for Canada."[4] He rejected, even before the election, Morrison's strategy of using a balance of power position to extort concessions. He considered such a policy as quite irresponsible, he recalled for Grant Dexter, "[It] was wholly impossible since it was contrary to our whole concept and theory of democratic Government."[5] Parliamentary cooperation must be founded on agreed policies and only secondarily on considerations of political advantage or personnel.

Long before the election of 1921, the possibility of a Liberal-Progressive alliance of some sort was being considered. On three separate occasions between late 1920 and early 1921, King had suggested to Crerar and E.C. Drury, the Progressive premier of Ontario, a coalition of the two groups before any election, since, presumably, King saw no insurmountable differences of policy.[6] Nothing came of these overtures, perhaps because of suspicion of King's sincerity. During the course of the 1921 campaign, Crerar met secretly in Montreal with W.S. Fielding at the latter's request. Fielding was seeking to keep open the lines of communication to reciprocity with the United States, whatever that implied.[7] Consequently, Crerar was stunned during the last three weeks before the election when King on several occasions denounced the Progressives, the idea of a coalition, and seemed even to reject the possibility of any post-election cooperation. To the editor of the *Globe*, Crerar acknowledged that "he was at a loss to understand [King's] attitude." The Liberal leader "was foregoing the opportunity," according to Crerar, of building "a real Liberal party in Canada."[8] But to A. Kirk Cameron, a well-placed Montreal businessman and Crerar's friend and correspondent for over 35 years, and to John Dafoe of the *Free Press*, Crerar's closest confidant, the political fix had already been arranged. In a letter to Clifford Sifton on the day after the election, Dafoe, using information from Cameron, speculated openly that the CPR and the Montreal faction of the Liberal Party led by Sir Lomer Gouin, had already gotten to King, thus explaining the latter's statements during the last days of the campaign. His willingness to negotiate after the fact was due simply to his minority position.[9]

Crerar, however, was still waiting to give King the benefit of any doubt; an attitude that gave some consternation to his friends. Dafoe believed that the Progressive leader "is of a boyish and trusting nature" and it would be up to his friends to save him "from putting his head in the noose."[10] There was certainly no shortage of advice forthcoming. Two days after his election, Sifton, who seems to have been congenitally incapable of resisting any temptation to meddle, however unwelcome his intentions, told Dafoe that Crerar should stay clear of King unless he was offered a fifty-fifty cabinet share and definite agreement on policy. Dafoe passed the message on to Crerar that same day but the latter was politely noncommittal.[11] Much more important was a letter written that day by Tommy Wayling, Crerar's secretary in Ottawa, who was in touch with the dominant Morrison faction of the Ontario Progressives. Wayling warned Crerar that they were "unanimously opposed to an alliance of any kind," but he would nevertheless try to keep them loyal to the ostensible leader.[12] In other words, Crerar was aware before any overtures were made that the Ontario group, driven by Morrison, would accept no deals with King and the Liberals.

The story of the not-so-secret negotiations between King's emissary, Senator Andrew Haydon, and Crerar is well known. But the question of motivation deserves to be explored further. It may also help to explain some of the confusion created by the players and observers who have left conflicting and often self-serving accounts of the delicate game that took place after the election. It does appear at the outset that King's anti-Progressive outbursts had been very much for effect, designed to quell any anxiety in Montreal, and that Crerar's confidence in him was not entirely misplaced.[13] Certainly King's first post-election instinct was to create as broadly-based a party as possible. On 8 December he told Haydon that he was willing to take both Crerar and Drury into the Cabinet and later informed Fielding that he would be able to meet their policy concerns to which he was generally sympathetic.[14] This was before any consultation with the Quebec Liberals.

Haydon had wired congratulations to Crerar on the day after the election. In his reply, Crerar emphasized King's opportunity to remodel the Liberal Party and warned against over-reliance on the Quebec bloc which, he argued, "was not good for Liberalism, nor Quebec nor the country. A solid Quebec now will inevitably mean a solid Ontario a few years from now."[15] But Quebec was not as solid as Crerar believed and would soon learn. After instructing Haydon to contact the Progressive leader, King summoned Ernest Lapointe from Quebec City, who stopped in to see Cameron in Montreal on his way through. According to Cameron, Lapointe was quite anxious for an arrangement with "the farmers" and spoke of "six to seven cabinet posts," but the government must be a "liberal Government."[16] This would, of course, eliminate the Montreal interests. Lapointe seems to have had his own agenda. Cameron's message made Crerar "a good deal more hopeful." He greatly feared that if "King forms a Government out of his present supporters...dominated by the Montreal end...he will bring on racial and sectional animosities fiercer than anything you or I have seen in this country. Ontario will be full of smouldering resentment." The only solution was a truly liberal party which included the Progressives. The crucial matter was policy. "While I cannot go further than I can take my supporters with me," he went on, "I feel certain that we can go a long way to meeting King on a thoroughly Liberal program. I am thinking of Canada before anything else at the present time."[17] This would all sound suspect and pretentious in a public statement; but he was always candid in his letters to

Cameron and almost never wrote for effect. Lapointe reported back to Cameron that King was trying to have it both ways and was considering a cabinet which included Crerar, Drury, Fielding, Gouin, and himself.[18] Haydon, meanwhile, was en route to Winnipeg to see Crerar; but his preoccupation with cabinet positions was quite inappropriate. It was never a matter of men but of measures.

Crerar, in fact, was being pressured from several quarters. Fielding was working through Cameron to induce Drury, A.B. Hudson of Winnipeg, and Crerar to join the government. J.J. Morrison, after learning Haydon was heading to Winnipeg, feared Sifton was now involved and excitedly wired Crerar to "remain steadfast to your principles. You are master of the situation. See that you maintain this position." Crerar tried to reassure him after his first meeting with Haydon who claimed King was proposing a low tariff policy and the elimination of the Montreal interests: "but I want satisfactory guarantees before taking the matter up with my support." The advice of the editorial board of the *Globe* was probably more to his liking. They were concerned primarily with protecting the infant national railway and feared the power of the CPR in Montreal. The *Globe* was convinced that if King were surrounded by "such a trinity as Fielding who can speak with authority for the Maritimes, Lapointe, who is the successor of Laurier in the affections of Quebec, and Crerar" with his mandate from the West, "Canada will enjoy good government."[19] Cameron, for his part, was pressuring King directly to take in the Progressives, arguing it would free the Prime Minister from the Bank of Montreal and CPR group led by Lord Atholstan of the *Star* who seemed determined to wreck the national railway.[20]

But King's attitude toward Cabinet positions was (and would remain) a severe obstacle. He saw them as means of control rather than instruments and symbols of policy; and he resented Crerar's insistence on prior agreements on a program. He complained to Drury, whom he considered more reasonable, by which he meant more malleable, that "Crerar was making a mistake and asking too much to suggest terms *re* tariff, railway rates, natural resources etc. that he should have faith in men proposed not exact conditions." Crerar and the others would "have to come in on the same conditions as other ministers."[21] This was precisely the sort of co-option that Crerar was determined to avoid.

The discussion in Winnipeg lasted for four days and telegrams flew back and forth between Haydon and King. Crerar took his counsel from a small group of intimates who were known, only partly facetiously, as the Sanhedrin and who, over the years, had a pronounced influence on Canadian affairs. The core of this tightly-knit group was comprised of Crerar, Dafoe, Hudson, and Frank Fowler, Secretary of the Grain Exchange Clearing House and soon to be Mayor of Winnipeg. For over thirty years they combined frequent lunches, first at a local restaurant and later at the more exclusive Manitoba Club, with solving the problems of the Liberal Party, Canada and the world. Associated with them at times, were James Coyne (known affectionately as "Bogus"), H.J. Symington, a brilliant transportation lawyer, E.J. Tarr of the Canadian Institute of International Affairs and Kirk Cameron of Montreal, a sort of visiting member and indefatigable correspondent of the inner four. While he was never dominated by his three friends, Crerar almost always consulted them and listened carefully to their advice. During the talks with Haydon they were never far away, especially Hudson, and Crerar's position began to harden.

Dafoe only thinly disguised his role when he wrote to Sifton that "I have no direct personal knowledge of these conferences but Crerar kept in touch with me and on Saturday night [after Haydon departed for Ottawa] there was a small gathering which I attended." The group knew that the UFO would spurn any deal with King and that the latter was very reluctant to make any guarantees in advance. They feared, and rightly, that if Crerar and Drury went into the Cabinet without firm commitments, "they would find themselves in a hopeless minority" and "the whole Progressive Movement could be headed off and destroyed." Their conclusion was that there could only be cooperation on the basis of a formal coalition with public guarantees. The Progressives, to protect themselves (and Crerar for that matter), must maintain their separate identity. This was the message which Crerar would take to a meeting of the western Progressives in Saskatoon on 20 December.[22]

By coincidence there was another gathering going on in Winnipeg that week. The executive of the Canadian Council of Agriculture was in town for its regular meeting, presided over by Henry Wise Wood of Alberta. He told the Secretary of the Council, Norman Lambert, that "the Alberta members met in Calgary last Saturday before proceeding to Saskatoon to meet Crerar, and that the Alberta representation was unanimously in favour of co-operating with Crerar and King on the coalition basis...feeling that they have more to gain by emphasizing issues than the personal equation." Lambert was quite aware that Hudson was being sent to Ottawa immediately to make clear to King that "the political traditions of Western Canada have always placed issues before men."[23]

Crerar went to Saskatoon with a firm plan of action, expecting an endorsement there given what Wood had indicated, and perhaps hoping that this would soften the attitude of the UFO members. He got what he wanted. "Resolved: If an invitation is extended to Progressive members to enter Hon. Mr. King's Cabinet as individuals *upon conditions they feel are satisfactory* we give our tacit approval...including the Hon. Mr. Crerar."[24] There have been many distortions since of this meeting. E.J. Garland, later a member of the Ginger Group, for example, claimed in his recollections some years later that Crerar "wanted us to endorse his acceptance of a Cabinet position...at once we began to draw away from him and that was the beginning of the later separation of the UFA group from the Progressive caucus."[25] This can only be regarded as *post hoc* puffery. Crerar wired the result to Hudson in Ottawa that night and set out for Toronto to meet the Ontario members.[26]

When Hudson passed the information on to King, the latter seemed to feel that a deal was still possible, even though he had been made aware that the Progressives would retain their separate identity. But he was not ready to cut his connection with Gouin and the Montreal Liberals.[27] Even before Crerar met with the Ontario Progressives, the new prime minister was coming under tremendous pressure from Montreal. Cameron made it clear that Gouin was now determinedly hostile to any arrangement with the Westerners and "had thrown in his lot with the others," who included Atholstan of the Star, Sir Herbert Holt, Sir Charles Gordon and the CPR.[28] While Crerar was closeted with the UFO in Toronto, King called Hudson in once more and tried to persuade him to convince Crerar "not to bargain for terms, but to come in on the basis of men in Govt to work out policies together."[29] The prospects of any agreement were already fading rapidly.

Crerar's hand was certainly not strengthened by his reception in Toronto. *The Farmers Advocate*, which spoke for Morrison, warned shrilly that Sifton and the *Free Press* were behind the whole nefarious scheme to deliver the Progressives into the hands of King.[30] Drury, who was Crerar's only real hope for Ontario support, had already taken himself out of the game.[31] So it was no great surprise to Crerar that the UFO flatly refused to consider cooperation of any kind, even on matters of legislation which the Progressives favoured. He regretted their "narrow and uncompromising spirit," since it would endanger any chance to forward their policies on the national railway and the tariff.[32] Norman Lambert, in a letter to J.D. Atkinson of the *Toronto Star*, claimed this was the clincher, since the Saskatoon resolution had to be approved by the Ontario group.[33] I have found no evidence to corroborate this assertion and Crerar certainly did not feel constrained by any strings on the Saskatoon resolution.

On Saturday 23 December, Crerar met with King and it was evident that any formal agreement was now impossible. According to Crerar, "a considerable change had taken place. The activities of the *Montreal Star* and *Gazette* had made anything in the nature of an understanding impossible."[34]

There were few recriminations; only some regret and self-delusion in the wake of failure. Crerar's view was that King, through a failure of will, had missed an opportunity to forge a truly liberal party based on a national railway, lower tariffs, reinstatement of the Crowsnest rates and more autonomy from Britain; all of which could be supported by King, Lapointe and the Progressives. There is considerable irony in King's immediate reflections on the events. Where the UFO believed Sifton was pushing Crerar into a deal with the Liberals, King was convinced that it was Sifton who was behind the refusal of Crerar to join the Cabinet. He never, of course, blamed himself. To his diary he confided, "I see Crerar's position. I admire him for considering his following's wishes, but it is real lack of leadership which prevents him from inspiring and dominating his following." His satisfaction came from the realization that Crerar was a lesser man than he. "I feel genuinely indignant at Sifton. What poor tools men are who will permit themselves to be the puppets of such a man. I was shocked at Drury, Crerar and the others."[35]

Kirk Cameron was depressed by the breakdown of the negotiations and he blamed King. "He should never have made the move unless he proposed to see the thing through...he has delivered himself into the hands of the Montreal crowd."[36] Norman Lambert was more hard-headed. "The fact that Mr. King was unable to give the assurances to the Western men...was offset by the fact that Mr. Crerar would not have been able to guarantee to Mr. King the solid support of 65 Progressive members."[37] Perhaps the most acute observer in Ottawa, J.K. Munro of *Maclean's Magazine*, argued that when Crerar came in to see King after the election, Gouin had already ensured there would be no alliance with the Farmers.[38] As for Crerar, the Cabinet question was secondary. He wrote to Cameron afterward that "I have been subjected to a good deal of criticism because I even considered any suggestion from King. It does not worry me in the slightest. If King had adhered to his original programme of policy I think I would have gone in anyway. As for the future, we shall have to wait on events."[39] The most immediate would be the role of the Progressives in the new Parliament.

With 65 members of the House of Commons, the Progressives could claim the position of Official Opposition. That they did not has usually been explained by their inexperience and their inability and unwillingness to act cohesively. While both these factors affected the situation, it was not nearly that simple, especially in Crerar's mind. There were other, more important, elements involved. Neither Crerar, nor King for that matter, had completely abandoned hope that some arrangement could yet be made in the future. Crerar's conception of the party system and Parliamentary stability influenced him greatly. And above all, there was the desirability of certain public policies that had brought the farmers into politics originally.

Despite his disagreement with Crerar, W.C. Wood was not far off the mark when he reflected that Crerar "honestly believed that the two-party set-up or system was the best, and that we would be well advised to get back to it as soon as we could...the Progressives should go into the Liberal Party, drive out the reactionary Liberals, and create a new Liberal Party."[40] Rather surprisingly, given the conventional interpretation, Henry Spencer, a member of the Ginger Group, blamed Crerar for not forcing the issue. "We had the right to be the official Opposition. Crerar at the time advised us not to be. I think now that that was a great mistake, that it would have been a great thing for us to be the official Opposition."[41] This, at least, rejects the balance of power strategy that many of the radical Progressives were said to favour and which Crerar explicitly condemned in a speech to the UFM convention after the election.[42] *The Canadian Forum* had endorsed such a policy, arguing, curiously, that it would have the effect of driving Grits and Tories together.[43] Paul Sharp, in *The Agrarian Revolt in Western Canada*, somehow persuaded himself that because Crerar could only think in terms of legislative objectives, the Progressives were "wedded to a balance of power concept."[44]

The historical record, however, is not so contradictory.

Early in 1922 Crerar was concerned primarily with the legislation to be advanced by the new government. King's program, drawn substantially from the Liberal convention of 1919, was encouraging. And there were signs of willingness to accede to some Progressive legislative wishes. Not only was King now making conciliatory speeches but a direct overture came from Fielding, the new Minister of Finance, who regretted "that you are not with us. But while officially I have no right to ask your assistance, I wish to say that I am still anxious to be favoured with your help...in matters to which western folk attach importance."[45] It may be that the Liberals feared the result if the Progressives became the Official Opposition, since that might necessarily limit cooperation, threaten King's minority position, and build in a structural rigidity thwarting any future union.

Crerar seems to have made up his mind by mid-January 1922. In a personal and private letter to an old friend and colleague in Neepawa, he pointed out that, "If we become the Official Opposition we are expected to oppose. If we fail to do that and support the government when it is right, Meighen, whether he occupied the position of Official Opposition or not, would come to be so regarded in the country." There was also the problem of inexperience. He continued "it is difficult for a man who is past middle life, and has had little or no public experience, to adapt himself effectively to the requirements of Parliament. I think, then, that the best place for our group is on the side lines."[46]

What remained, for Crerar, was the vital question of legislation and he expected the Liberals to move in his direction. When the new parliament opened, the Progressives had several meetings to consider their options. The most immediate concerns were the tariff, the Crowsnest Pass rates and Canada's relations with Great Britain. Crerar later summed up the situation for Grant Dexter.

> It was clear that if the new Liberal Government under King moved substantially in the direction of tariff reduction, we would not be opposing them but would be supporting them. Likewise, if they decided to let the Crows Nest Pass rates be restored when the statutory limitation of three years had expired, we would also be supporting them; and also if they moved to a really Liberal position in the matter of Canada's relations vis-à-vis Great Britain, we would be supporting them. We expected that in all these matters if the government took a forward position, the Conservatives would be opposing them. It can thus be seen that as an official Opposition the Progressives would have been in an impossible position.[47]

It was also very possible, of course, that the Progressives as a party would never have accepted the discipline of Opposition and disintegration would have been immediate. Crerar thought it necessary to nurture his forces. "While I think we have a few men who will develop good ability the great majority will be ordinary, some of them perhaps very ordinary, members. If we become the Official Opposition we are expected to oppose."[48] Opposition made little sense to Crerar in such a fragmented House.

When Crerar spoke in the Throne Speech debate in early March, King must have been pleased indeed to hear him say that the Progressives intended to further their own principles and not oppose the Government for the sake of opposing.[49] This disclaimer allowed his Progressive colleagues to plunge into the proceedings with much enthusiasm and few inhibitions. J.K. Munro reported that:

> ...every gap in the conversation finds a Farmer to fill it. The end of the first awful week showed that the sixty-five devoted followers of the Hired Man's Hero had furnished fifty per cent of the speakers while a score of others had scented the battle at close quarters and were displaying symptoms of a great desire to get in closer and garner a mouthful for themselves.[50]

Crerar's resignation as party leader was affected more by circumstances outside the House of Commons than it was by the course of the session. There was little to gratify him there. He now knew there would be no significant movement on the tariff with Gouin in the cabinet. The western agrarians were badly divided on the issue of a permanent Wheat Board. The only real accomplishment was the reinstatement of the Crowsnest rates.

Outside the House, the enthusiasm of the western farmers for political action was waning quickly. Membership in the grain growers associations was plummeting as they returned to economic solutions to their problems and, in great numbers, embraced the pooling technique and the gospel of Aaron Sapiro promoted by the United Farmers of Canada. Crerar was also under pressure from his colleagues on the Board of United Grain Growers, which had suffered badly in the sharp depression of the wheat market which began in 1920, and was surviving on its reserves.[51] He had continued as President of the company, and retained his salary, ever since his entry into the Union Cabinet in 1917. The board and the membership had supported him loyally but now the company desperately needed full time leadership to reverse its fortunes and face the challenge of the

pools. Crerar would have to choose. The prospect of trying to manage the fractious Progressives in the Commons on the salary of an ordinary member was not attractive. There remained the continuing possibility of entering King's cabinet.

When the Chanak crisis broke in September 1922, King summoned Crerar and Hudson. They and almost all of the Progressive members supported King's stand against any participation in European affairs. Indeed, all three considered the issue so important that it might be the occasion to bring the two parties together. But it would have to be on King's terms. He was more than willing to bring Crerar into the Cabinet but he refused to drop Gouin which Crerar made an absolute condition.[52] Discussions dragged on for two weeks, the emergency passed and the chance was lost. Crerar then set out for Winnipeg to attend a crucial meeting of the board of United Grain Growers. En route, he received the news that his younger daughter, Audrey, had died of diphtheria. It took the heart out of him. Still in shock, he wrote his friend Cameron that he had no will to go on in public life at present.[53] He resigned the leadership a week later.

Like most people of some talent and strong will, Crerar had his share of ambition. But his commitment to a conception of Canada which demanded regional cooperation and his attachment to principles of individual responsibility growing increasingly dated, made him a difficult, even stubborn, colleague. Indeed, they would later cost him his Cabinet seat and almost denied him his Senate appointment in 1945. But on the issues considered here one can make a fair case that Crerar's motives and actions were determined by his attempt to translate Progressive goals into legislative accomplishments. That he fell short of the mark in 1921–22 indicates as much about the political culture and personalities of the day as about Crerar.

NOTES

1. Queen's University Archives, Crerar Papers (CP), 79, Crerar to Musselman, 5 January 1922; CP, 107, Crerar to Stewart Lyon, Editor, Toronto *Globe*, 9 December 1921.
2. CP, 125, Crerar to Morrison, 29 November 1921.

3. Ibid.
4. CP, 110, Crerar to Good, 23 January 1954.
5. CP, 105, Memorandum for Dexter, 25 March 1955.
6. See Frederick W. Gibson, *Cabinet Formation and Bicultural Relations: Seven Case Studies* (Ottawa: Royal Commission on Bilingualism and Biculturalism, 1970).
7. CP, 137, Crerar to John Stevenson, a former journalistic ally.
8. CP, 107, Crerar to Lyon, 9 December 1921.
9. NAC, MG 30, John Wesley Dafoe Papers, Box 4, Dafoe to Sifton, 7 December 1921. CP, 97, Cameron to Crerar, 10 December 1921.
10. NAC, Dafoe Papers, Box 4, Dafoe to Sifton, 31 December 1921.
11. Ibid., Sifton to Dafoe, 8 December 1921.
12. CP, 152, Wayling to Crerar, 8 December 1921.
13. CP, 97, Cameron to Crerar, 10 December 1921.
14. King Diary, 8 and 13 December 1921.
15. CP, 113, Crerar to Haydon, 9 December 1921; see also Gibson, *Cabinet Formation*, p. 77.
16. CP, 97, Cameron to Crerar, coded telegram, 10 December 1921; copy also in NAC, A.K. Cameron Papers, vol. 33.
17. Cameron Papers, vol. 33, Crerar to Cameron, 10 December 1921.
18. Ibid., Cameron to Crerar, 12 December 1921.
19. Cameron Papers, vol. 33, Cameron to Crerar, 13 December 1921; CP, 78, Morrison to Crerar, 13 December 1921 and Crerar to Morrison, 14 December 1921; CP, 110, Harvey Anderson (*Globe*) to Crerar, 15 December 1921.
20. King Diary, 14 December 1921.
21. Ibid., 14 and 15 December 1921.
22. Dafoe Papers, Dafoe to Sifton, 19 December 1921.
23. QUA, Lambert Papers, Box 1, Lambert to J.A. Stevenson, 20 December 1921.
24. Copy in CP, 78.
25. Cited in Anthony M. Mardiros, *William Irvine: the Life of a Prairie Radical* (Toronto: Lorimer, 1979), p. 116.
26. CP, 78, telegram, Crerar to Hudson, 20 December 1921; see also King Diary, 20 December 1921.
27. King Diary, 21 December 1921; see also NAC, A.B. Hudson Papers which contain a memoir of events.
28. CP, 97, Cameron to Crerar, 23 December 1921. The letter was awaiting Crerar when he arrived in Ottawa from Toronto.
29. King Diary, 23 December 1921.
30. *The Farmers Advocate*, 21 December 1921.
31. CP, 78, Crerar to Drury, 21 December 1921.

32. CP, 96, Crerar to T.W. Caldwell, 6 January 1922.
33. Lambert Papers, Box 1, Lambert to Atkinson, 31 December 1921.
34. CP, 96, Crerar to Caldwell, 6 January 1922.
35. King Diary, 24 and 28 December 1921.
36. Cameron Papers, vol. 33, Cameron to Crerar, 28 December 1921.
37. Lambert Papers, Box 1, Lambert to Atkinson, 31 December 1921.
38. *Maclean's Magazine*, 1 February 1922.
39. Cameron Papers, vol. 33, Crerar to Cameron, 19 January 1922.
40. W.C. Wood, *Farmer Citizen*, p. 126.
41. Cited in Mardiros, *Irvine*, pp. 117–18.
42. *Grain Growers Guide*, 17 January 1922.
43. *Canadian Forum*, November 1923.
44. Paul F. Sharp, *The Agrarian Revolt in Western Canada: A Survey Showing American Parallels* (N.Y.: Octagon Books, 1948), p. 155.
45. *Canadian Annual Review*, 1922, p. 216; CP, 107, Fielding to Crerar, 11 January 1922.
46. CP, 104, Crerar to Fred Davis, 19 January 1922.
47. CP, 105, Memorandum for Dexter.
48. CP, 104, Crerar to Davis, 19 January 1922.
49. *Canadian Annual Review*, 1922, p. 227.
50. *Maclean's Magazine*, 1 April 1922.
51. U.G.G. Board Minutes, 12 October 1921.
52. King Diary, 22 and 23 September 1922; Cameron Papers, Vol. 7, Hudson to Cameron, 17 October 1922.
53. Cameron Papers, vol. 33, Crerar to Cameron, 21 October 1922.

GERHARD ENS

11   Métis Agriculture in Red River During the Transition from Peasant Society to Industrial Capitalism
The Example of St. François Xavier 1835 to 1870

UNTIL THE LAST FEW decades much of the history of the Canadian Métis[1] has been written from the perspective of the political history of Canada or that of the fur trade, with the underlying premise that the Métis were a primitive people unable to adjust to civilized society.[2] Consequently, Métis society was generally viewed as a nomadic frontier precursor to a more settled and agricultural society.

Recent historical work, much of it spurred by the interest in Métis land claims and the centenary of the Rebellion of 1885, has concentrated almost wholly on the period after Manitoba's entry into Confederation in 1870, and focused almost solely on the dispossession of the Métis and the politics of the Rebellion of 1885.[3] These political studies of the Métis dispossession make only passing reference to the origin and development of Métis culture and economy previous to 1870; this despite the fact that the changes in the economy of the Métis undoubtedly had a large influence on their retention of land in Manitoba.

While there is, in general, scholarly agreement that agriculture and the hunt were supplementary to each other in Red River, recourse is still made to the "attraction of the hunt" to explain the varying degrees of commitment to agriculture. Based on a detailed analysis of selected Red River censuses, land records, and concentrating on the parish of St. François Xavier, this paper argues that by 1835 the vari-

239

ous communities of Red River (excluding the Hudson's Bay Company) were characterized by a peasant economy relying on subsistence agriculture and hunting. Growing divergences in the cultivation practices of the various Red River communities in the 1840s and thereafter were not primarily related to some innate preference for the hunt, but rather a product of an economic transition occurring in the region. The opening of new fur and robe markets, the suspension of the HBC's monopoly, and the influx of merchant capital created an alternative to this peasant society. Thus the choice for the Red River Métis (at least before the 1870s) was not between a "progressive agriculture" and the "primitive hunt" but increasingly between a kin-based capitalist fur trade, wage labour, and peasant agriculture. The response of the various Métis communities to these choices had a good deal of significance for the persistence of the various communities in Manitoba.

While Métis agriculture in Red River will be discussed generally, more specific analysis will be made to the parish of St. François Xavier, a French-Métis community, with some comparison to St. Andrew's, an English-Métis community. The parish has been selected as the unit of analysis because the Red River parish was the focal point of the social life of the Métis, as it incorporated the educational, religious, and communal needs of the inhabitants. With the advent of Confederation in 1870 the parish, for a time, also became the basis of political representation and administration. Thus parish boundaries are the most appropriate geographic boundaries for including the essential networks that give a community its identity. The local or case study approach to historical analysis has the advantage of permitting a detailed enough investigation to reveal fundamental historical processes.

The parish of St. François Xavier was initially established as a mission in 1824 when the Métis of Pembina were relocated here on the insistence of the Hudson's Bay Company. Also known as the White Horse Plains, the site of this settlement lay on the Assiniboine River eighteen miles westward from the forks of the Red and Assiniboine.[4] Pembina had always been more populous than the Red River Settlement since it was the principal rendezvous point for freeman and

Métis hunters.[5] This large Métis population became a concern to the Hudson's Bay Company after the survey of the international boundary line laid down by the Convention of 1818 determined that Pembina lay in the territory of the United States. The Hudson's Bay Company, fearing that the Métis of Pembina would take advantage of their new citizenship to flout the Company's trade regulations, decided that no grant of land would be made there, and that they would move their trading post from Pembina. The Company also put pressure on the Catholic clergy of St. Boniface to move their Métis parishioners to the Red River Settlement.[6] The Company's attitude was reflected in the decision of Governor Simpson to give Cuthbert Grant a tract of land at White Horse Plains. Simpson hoped that Grant would be able to settle the Métis and freemen of Pembina there and keep them out of the fur trade. The tract of land conveyed to Cuthbert Grant lay on the banks of the Assiniboine and began at a point 12 miles west of Fort Garry extending 6 miles westward and 6 miles on either side of the river. Here Grant settled the Métis refugees from Pembina and the Northwest, giving each settler one of the river lots (12 chains wide) running two miles back from the river.

These Métis families not only settled and built houses, but began breaking land and farming. This move away from the wandering life of the voyageur, hunter, and fur trader was to a large extent a function of the limited economic opportunities in the 1820s and 1830s. Not only was the Hudson's Bay Company releasing superfluous men from their service, but there was also a limited market for furs and produce. The Métis had by no means given up the hunt for buffalo that had been the mainstay of their economy, but increasingly combined this with small scale farming. By 1827 the settlement consisted of 19 permanent families with a total of 111 inhabitants. Cuthbert Grant was by this time cultivating 34 acres, Angus McGillis 20, and Alexander Poitras 4.[7] By 1832 the settlement had grown to 57 families and 294 individuals, and by 1835, 97 families or 506 individuals were cultivating 594 acres.[8]

St. François Xavier and the other French and English Métis communities of Red River had by 1835 established a functioning way of life whose primary constituents were semi-autonomous village communities and cultures. Land tenure was based on grants and sales from Lord Selkirk and the Hudson's Bay Company, squatters' rights, and a tradition of communal jurisdiction. The economic basis of these communities was a household economy comprised of small scale agriculture, the buffalo hunt, and seasonal labour for the Hudson's Bay Company. It was, in effect, a "specialized" peasant society and economy whose primary aims were to secure the needs of the family rather than make a profit. This society would have conformed to A.V. Chayonov's concept of a peasant society, which posits a balance between subsistence needs and a substantive distaste for manual labour, determining the intensity of cultivation and size of net product.

> In a natural economy, human economic activity is dominated by the requirement of satisfying the needs of each single production unit, which is at the same time a consumer unit. Therefore, budgeting here is to a high degree qualitative....Therefore, the question of comparative profitability of various expenditures cannot arise....The degree of self-exploitation is determined by a peculiar equilibrium between family demand and the drudgery of labour itself....As soon as the equilibrium point is reached, however, continuing to work becomes pointless.[9]

While the Red River Settlement was connected to commercial capitalism through the Hudson's Bay Company, there existed at the household level a parallel and contradictory economic system. It was an economy which could best be described as peasant in that it was largely oriented to household consumption and not for market. This peasant economy, however, should not be considered "subsistence" in a strict sense of the word. As in most peasant economies there was a dual orientation to market and household. As Daniel Thorner has pointed out, "We are sure to go astray if we try to conceive of peasant economies as exclusively 'subsistence' oriented. It is much sounder to take it for granted, as a starting point, that for ages peasant economies have had a double orientation to both."[10] Produce from the buffalo hunt and farm were exchanged in Red River for other goods, and the

Métis were engaged in other activities such as occasional wage labour, but the family remained the main unit of production in an essentially noncapitalistic mode of production.[11] While the Hudson's Bay Company purchased pemmican, dried meat, and agricultural produce at an early date from the settlers of Red River, the annual demand was fairly constant by the 1820s, while the population of the Colony increased rapidly.[12] By the 1830s the increase in the Métis population, and the attendant increase in the production of pemmican and dried meat, had so saturated the limited market that the Hudson's Bay Company refused to buy much of the pemmican offered to them.[13] The Company was also not able to absorb very much of the agricultural produce of the settlement. The demand of the trading posts was small and could easily be satisfied. Grain purchases seldom amounted to more than 600 – 800 cwt. These purchases initially amounted to 16 bushels of grain per settler, but as the population grew this fell to 12 bushels, then 8 bushels and was even below this by 1845.[14]

Thus while the trade with the Hudson's Bay Company provided a means to purchase manufactured clothing and commodities, production from the hunt and farm remained largely oriented to household consumption in the 1830s. In 1823, when W.H. Keating travelled through the Settlement, he noted that there were no cash transactions in the Colony. Wheat along with other commodities was "traded in the way of exchange for some other commodity."[15] Given the level of technology at the time and the absence of any real market, this was a rational course of action. The *NorWester*, looking back on the agricultural history of the Colony commented in 1859:

> In one respect, however, the farmers appear to have been generally agreed. We refer to their determination to raise little more than enough of produce for home consumption; and so strictly did they carry out their resolve—so nicely did they gauge the needed home supplies—that last year the temporary presence in the settlement of a couple of exploring parties and a few batches of fortune hunters...almost created a famine.[16]

While it is true that the Métis were participating in an illicit fur trade, this trade was largely circumscribed until the 1840s by the efforts of the Hudson's Bay Company, the lack of viable alternative markets, and the lack of capital and entrepreneurial skills on the part of the Métis.

Without going into the intricacies of tenure in Red River suffice it to say that land holding in Red River followed, in the main, a pattern of peasant tenure. The inhabitants of Red River possessed the "means of production," particularly land, even if they did not own them. They managed their farms as they saw fit, individually or collectively in a village community, but were subject to some form of domain that deprived them of perfect ownership.[17] Comments of visitors to Red River stressed the organic nature of this community which resembled a medieval village. J. Wesley Bond, a companion of Governor Ramsey of Minnesota Territory visited the settlement in 1851 and described a lengthy serpentine village:

> farmhouses, with barns, stables, hay, wheat and barley stacks with small cultivated fields or lots, well fenced, are stretched along the meandering river, while the prairies far off to the horizon are covered with herds of cattle, horses, &c., the fields filled with a busy throng of whites, half-breeds, Indian-men, squaws, and children all reaping, binding and stalking the golden grain.

The whole, he continued, presented an appearance such as one would find exhibited in pictures of English country villages.[18]

These river lot villages combined elements of the French Canadian river lot survey and the Scottish system of infield-outfield agriculture. In this old Celtic mode of land management introduced by Lord Selkirk

> the cottage and byre of the farmstead stood by the infield, often at a stream edge in a valley. Behind stretched a large outfield often pasture and fallow...on the hillside behind the farmer had the right to pasturage and in summer sent his cattle back into the hills to graze.[19]

In Red River cottage and byre had arisen by the river side with the small fenced plots or "parks" cropped year after year recalling the infield of the Scottish system. The rear section of the two-mile deep lot was pastured as the outfield had been in Scotland, and the two miles beyond this became the hay privilege of the owners of the lot.[20]

Settling on these narrow river lots, the inhabitants of Red River slowly developed a hybrid peasant economy that combined small scale farming with an organized buffalo hunt.[21] While this was supplemented by seasonal labour for the HBC, duck hunting and fisheries in Lakes Winnipeg and Manitoba, the river lot farm and buffalo hunt remained the economic focus of most settlers up to the 1840s.

The establishment of farms on the banks of the Red and Assiniboine Rivers was, according to one observer, much less difficult than in many other places. At most locations all that was necessary to put a plough in the ground was to clear or burn off some brush. In many places it was only necessary to erect an enclosure around a field and plough it.[22] Due to the necessity of enclosing all cultivated fields to protect the crops from cattle roaming at large, and because of the increasing scarcity of wood needed to build these enclosures, fields had to be kept small. Five acres was considered to be a large plot in Red River.[23] Cultivated plots were also kept small by the level of farm technology[24] and the absence of a market for surplus production.[25] Settlement and cultivation were in turn tied to the river lot, in large part due to the marshy state of the back land at the time and the inability of the steel-tipped wooden plough to cut through the heavily soiled meadow lands. These early ploughs, however, were able to handle the loamy silts of well-drained river lots.[26]

While the Settlement's first good crops were harvested in 1824, it was not until 1827, the year after the disastrous flood, that agriculture became established in the Colony.[27] Between 1827 and 1835 a succession of good crops put the Colony on a stable footing. By 1830 the Settlement was almost completely rebuilt with 204 new houses constructed and new barns and enclosures erected.[28] Land under cultivation, in turn, rose from 2152 acres in 1831 to over 3500 in 1835.[29]

It is clear from census figures that by 1835 small scale peasant agriculture was the norm in most Red River parishes. Contrary to the historiography on the subject, which has long posited a greater commitment to agriculture by the English Métis and European communities, there appears to have been little differentiation on the basis of cultivation between the various parishes in the Red River Settlement in the 1830s.[30] What emerges is a pattern of subsistence agriculture with an average of 5 to 6 cultivated acres per family, working out to approximately one acre per person. The average cultivation per family and individual in the parishes of St. François Xavier and St. Andrew's is, in fact, almost identical. The number of larger farms in the two parishes is also very similar with 22 families cultivating 10 or more acres in St. Andrew's and 26 families in St. François Xavier. Within both parishes, however, there was a discrepancy in cultivation between families headed by Europeans and those families headed by Métis. While almost all family members (wives and children) were Métis, those families that were headed by European males generally cultivated about twice as much land as families headed by Métis.

The staple crop of the colony was an early maturing spring wheat which produced high yields.[32] According to H.Y. Hind, who travelled through the Settlement in 1857, yields of 40 bushels per acre were common on new ground.[33] Father Lafleche, arriving in St. François Xavier in 1844, noted that wheat fields were the height of a man, and that a farmer sowing 17 minots of wheat harvested 372 minots.[34] Because of the absence of any real market most of this wheat was ground into flour for Colony consumption at one of the 13 wind and water mills in the Settlement in the 1830s.[35] Other crops included barley, oats, corn, potatoes and turnips.[36]

Livestock, while common on most river lots by the 1830s, were raised mainly for motive power and for household consumption. Cattle were introduced with limited success in 1822–23 and pigs shortly thereafter. Before 1827, livestock met with limited success due to the severity of winters and attacks by wolves.[37] The real problem, however, was a shortage of winter fodder due to the settlers' inexperience in haying.[38] As settlers gained experience in harvesting hay from the plains, livestock gradually became integrated into the economy of Red River. Between 1831 and 1835 total livestock production increased from 3725 to 7617. (See Table 11.2.) By 1835 most settlers

TABLE 11.1.   Population and Cultivation in Red River in 1835

	St. Andrew's	*St. François Xavier*	*Red River*
Total Population	547 (15%)	506 (13.8%)	3646
Number of Single Adults	3	5	—
Number of Families	94 (14.3%)	97 (14.7%)	658
Average Family Size	5.78	5.16	5.55
Percentage of Métis Family Heads	53.60	74.50	—
Cultivated Acreage	566 (16.2%)	594 (17%)	350
Acres Cultivated per Family	6.02	6.12	5.33
Acres Cultivated per Person	1.03	1.17	0.96
Farms larger than Ten Acres	22	26	—
Cultivation per Métis Family Head	4.04	4.62	—
Cultivation per European Family Head	7.93	9.34	—

SOURCE: Census of Red River, 1835.[31]

TABLE 11.2.   Livestock Production in Red River, 1835

	St. Andrew's	*St. François Xavier*	*Red River*
Total Livestock	1223 (16%)	884 (11.6%)	7617
Average Number per Family	12.87	8.93	11.50
Total Horses	87 (12.1%)	131 (18.2%)	718
Average Number per Family	0.93	1.35	1.10
Total Cattle*	824 (16.9%)	555 (11.4%)	4874
Average Number per Family	8.76	5.72	7.40
Total Pigs	312 (15.4%)	198 (9.7%)	2025
Average Number per Family	3.28	2.00	3.07

SOURCE: Red River Census, 1835.
* Includes oxen and calves.

had a horse for riding, a pair of oxen for plowing, along with some cattle and pigs for meat.[39] The discrepancy between the St. Andrew's and St. François Xavier totals for cattle and pigs was in all likelihood due to the greater reliance of the St. François Xavier Métis on the buffalo for meat.

A good deal of the colony's provision each year were provided by the biannual buffalo hunt. Contrary to W.L. Morton's proposition that agriculture and the hunt acted as fatal checks on each other, the one depressing the price of the other's produce, the subsistence agriculture and the buffalo hunt of Red River were much more complementary than competitive.[40] In years when the hunt failed the produce of agriculture helped meet the needs of the Métis hunters, and vice-versa.[41] Census returns also indicate that most residents in the various parishes had some cultivated land in the 1830s, dispelling the notion that the hunting and farming economies originated in different sections of the Settlement.[42]

The Red River buffalo hunt as an organized expedition appears to have begun around 1820.[43] Previous to this the buffalo were found near enough to the settlement. According to Alexander Ross the number of carts going on the hunt increased rapidly up to the year 1840.[44] There were two hunts a year—one in summer and another in fall. The summer hunt generally departed in June and returned in August,[45] while the fall hunt, generally the smaller of the two,[46] began in early October with the hunters returning in November. Both hunts were important to the economy of Red River and all the Métis communities took part in them. In the fall of 1829 Bishop Provencher commented that women were doing all the men's work in the French parishes as the men were on the plains hunting buffalo.[47] Similarly William Cockran, the missionary stationed in what was to become the parish of St. Andrew's, complained in 1830 that since the middle of June his congregation consisted principally of women, children, and old men, the others having gone off on the hunt.[48] The degree to which the hunt was complementary to the agricultural economy is attested to by the same William Cockran. An avowed opponent of the hunt, Cockran was nevertheless obliged to send a cart with the hunt in 1837 to gather provisions for the Indian schools, as there was no prospect of getting a crop from the ground that year.[49]

Changes in the political economy of the Red River Métis in the 1840s, changes which integrated the Colony into the wider world, produced large upheavals among the Métis, and had a significant effect on Métis agriculture. These changes, involving as they did the resurgence of Métis involvement in the fur trade, did not signal a return to "primitivism" or "nomadism," but a proto-industrialization of the Métis family economy. In the European context this term or concept has been used to analyze the process of industrialization before the movement of large numbers of workers to factory employment.

In Europe the development of proto-industrialization varied by region or craft, but amidst all the differences it exhibited a common structural foundation. This consisted in the close association between household production based on the family economy and the capitalist organization of trade, putting out and marketing of products. The functional inter-relationships between the family economy and merchant capital gave this configuration the traits of a socioeconomic system.[50] On the macro-historical level proto-industrialization appeared as the combined outcome of the destabilization and decomposition of traditional peasant societies, and represented the primary social relation of production in the transition from traditional peasant society to industrial capitalism.[51]

In the context of Red River, proto-industrialization emerged with the economic rationalization and changing labour practices of the HBC, the breakup of the Company monopoly, and the establishment of a new market for furs in the 1840s. Increasing Métis involvement in this new capitalistic fur trade, especially the emerging buffalo robe trade, took place within the context of the Métis family economy. It will be argued that involvement in this new "rural industry"[52] led to an abandonment of agriculture by a segment of the Métis population, and was an important impetus to out-migration from Red River.

The establishment of a trading post at Pembina (70 miles south of Red River) in American territory in 1844 had the effect of bringing the

American market to the front door of the Red River Colony.[53] Not only did this post create an alternative market, but it also became a source of supplies and capital transforming the Métis economy of the region and precipitating an outburst of trading in furs throughout the Red River district.

An indication of the extent and expansion of this trade can be gleaned from the increase in the number of carts travelling annually to St. Paul. In 1844 only 6 carts are recorded as making the journey to St. Paul.[54] By 1855 400 carts,[55] by 1858 800 carts,[56] and by 1869 2500 carts were carrying fur and goods to St. Paul.[57] Fur sales in St. Paul rose from $1400 in 1844 to $40,000 in 1853, to $182,491 in 1857, and an average of over $215,000 annually in the following eight years.[58] By 1862 the Settlement newspaper, the *NorWester*, commented that, "the great business in this country is at present the trade in furs...Farming, shop-keeping, and all other vocations whatsoever, dwindle to the merest nothing when compared, in point of profits, with this vast business."[59]

Increasingly the Métis took advantage of these opportunities and became involved in commodity production for market (furs, particularly buffalo robes) rather than for home consumption. And their surplus production, rather than being appropriated by the Hudson's Bay Company, was increasingly appropriated by merchant traders, many of whom were Métis themselves. Participation in this new trade cut across communities and ethnic boundaries as both English and French Métis responded to the opportunities.

The most important component of this new fur trade, and greatest impetus to wintering on the plains and hence abandoning agriculture, was the growing Métis involvement in the buffalo robe trade. This trade, with its intensive labour demands and the imperative for hunters and their families to winter near the buffalo herds as they drew ever further away from the Red River settlement, significantly altered the geographic mobility of those Métis families who participated in the trade. The demands that this trade, or household industry, placed on Métis families would draw them away from Red River in increasing numbers. As the demand for robes increased and as the herds moved further from the Settlement, the practice of Métis families wintering near the herds became increasingly common. By 1856 Governor Simpson was reporting the phenomenon of wintering villages:

A large body of people last winter found their way to the neighbourhood of Carlton and Fort Pitt where they employed themselves hunting and trading and collecting large returns. they proceeded to their wintering grounds in the autumn to the number of 70 or 80 men with about 300 carts, well provided with goods by the Americans. These people congregated for convenience and safety in villages consisting of huts roughly constructed but sufficient to protect them from the weather and to afford storage room for their goods and furs.[60]

The point to be stressed here is that the buffalo robe trade became a household industry for those Métis families involved in it. In securing the buffalo robes and hides there grew up a considerable organization within hunting groups with a clearly defined division of labour. Some engaged only in riding and shooting, others in skinning, while still others followed up to stretch and stake out the skins and robes.[61] there was, in fact, a good deal of intensive labour involved in producing a buffalo robe for market which had a significant effect on Métis family formation. The Métis family became, in effect, a household factory in the production of buffalo robes, necessitating long absences from the colony, making it impossible to continue the cultivation of their family river lots.

Due to the intensive labour required to prepare a buffalo robe for market, Métis wives and women were integral parts of the business of the buffalo robe trade. The process the Métis used in tanning buffalo robes was the same process used by the Indians, and one woman could only dress one robe in 3 to 4 days. Wintering camps or communities thus became virtual factories for processing buffalo robes.

A further stimulus to the transformation of the Métis economy in the 1840s was the succession of bad crop years, which failed to produce even enough for subsistence. In the five year period 1844 to 1848, only 1845 produced a harvest sufficient to feed the colony. The wheat crop was a general failure in both 1846 and 1847,[62] producing widespread famine, and the hay crop was so poor in 1847 that most settlers were making arrangements to winter their cattle out.[63] By August of 1848 the Settlement was on the threshold of starvation.[64]

Faced with a limited market for grain and a succession of bad crop years, it is little wonder that a large number of Métis abandoned agriculture and concentrated on the fur trade for which there was now an expanding market. Even without bad crop years, Simpson commented, "the want of market (for wheat)...has prevented any agriculturalist from expanding their farms and increasing their livestock beyond the requisite quantity to meet the demands of the Company and their own absolute wants."[65] By the late 1840s even the greatest proponents of agriculture, the ministers of the Church Missionary Society, realized that the land had, "scarcely any value being so abundant, and the produce of the land, which is at times thirty fold, has no market, and therefore cannot be converted into money."[66]

By the time the 1849 census was taken it was clear that some Métis families were abandoning their farms completely. While the total area under cultivation increased in Red River from 3504 acres in 1835 to 6392 acres in 1849, some communities showed a decrease in cultivated areas despite the fact that their population had almost doubled.

In St. François Xavier the average cultivated acreage per family had dropped from 6.12 acres in 1835 to 3.19 acres in 1849. Cultivated acreage per person during this time dropped from 1.17 acres to 0.58 acres. This was in contrast to St. Andrew's which maintained its subsistence level of about 1 cultivated acre per individual.

Thus, if the decline in cultivation can be seen as an indication of increasing involvement in the new fur trade, it is clear that the response was much greater in St. François Xavier. While there are a number of reasons for this differential, not the least of them would be the fact that the cultural antecedents of the St. François Xavier Métis were the Great Lakes Métis who had once before acted as middlemen in the St. Lawrence-based fur trade.[67] This indubitably gave them an added advantage in responding to new trading opportunities when they appeared in the 1840s. Another reason why St. Andrew's Métis were less likely to adapt to the new trading opportunities may have

TABLE 11.3.   Population and Cultivation in Red River, 1849

	St. Andrew's	St. François Xavier	Red River
Total Population	1068 (19.8%)	911 (16.9%)	5391
Percentage Increase since 1835	95.00	81.00	48.00
Number of Single Adults	10	4.00	—
Number of Families	187 (17.8%)	165 15.7%)	1052
Average Family Size	5.66	5.49	5.13
Percentage of Métis Family Heads	68.00	82.00	—
Total Cultivated Acres	1366 (21.3%)	527 (8.2%)	6392
Percentage Increase since 1835	141.00	-11.00	82.00
Acres Cultivated per Family	7.30	3.19	6.10
Acres Cultivated per Person	1.28	0.58	1.19
Cultivation per European Family Head	10.62	5.10	—
Cultivation per Métis Family Head	5.20	2.60	—
Number Cultivating more than 10 Acres	58 (31%)	22 (13%)	—
Number Cultivating more than 20 Acres	14 (7%)	5 (3%)	—

source: Red River Census, 1849

been that St. Andrew's contained more families headed by a European male.[68] Those Métis families headed by a European male generally cultivated about double the amount of those families headed by a Métis male in both parishes (see Table 11.3), and would have been less likely to give up agriculture to enter the fur trade. The fact that British troops were stationed at Lower Fort Garry (near St. Andrew's) from 1846 to 1848 would also have inflated the 1849 cultivation figures of St. Andrew's because these troops would have created a short-lived artificial market for agricultural products

The decision about whether to follow the buffalo robe trade or agriculture in the Red River Settlement was made easier for many by the general failure of crops in the 1860s. After fairly successful farming years in the 1850s, years of drought in the 1860s brought declining crop yields, while the reappearance of almost annual grasshopper infestations after 1864 made agricultural prospects bleak.[69] The infestations of grasshoppers in 1867 and 1868, combined with the failure of the plains hunt from Red River created a crisis of provisions. A relief committee was appointed in 1868 to distribute aid solicited from the U.S. and Canada, and many people in dread of scarcity left with their families to winter on the plains.[70] Louis Goulet, returning with his father to Red River after wintering on the plains from 1865 to 1868, found the Settlement destitute and quickly made the decision to return to the plains.[71] These conditions combined with rising buffalo robe prices led to a continued abandonment of agriculture and eventually emigration from Red River.[72]

The connection between the new trading opportunities and the decline of agriculture was observed by the *NorWester* in discussing the decline of sheep farming in the Settlement. Introduced in 1830, the number of sheep in the colony rose to a peak in 1846 at 4222, declining to 3096 in 1849, to 2245 in 1856, and even less by 1860. The reason for this decline, the *NorWester* noted had to do with the increase of dogs in the Settlement, which in turn was related to the increase in plains trading.

> About the year 1848 parties commenced their excursion out of the settlement to trade with the Indian, and were of course accompanied by dogs. As the traffic and the dogs increased the sheep diminished. They were attacked and destroyed by the dogs.[73]

Between 1849 and 1870 cultivated acreage in St. François Xavier rose marginally to an average of 3.99 acres per family and 0.7 acres per individual, no doubt reflecting the improved farming prospects in the 1850s. Even this small increase, however, is deceiving since most of it can be attributed to a few families in the parish. There were still only 18 families (5%) who cultivated 20 or more acres, with 6% of the families accounting for 50% of the cultivation. Another reason for the increase in cultivated acreage was that many who had abandoned agriculture had left the parish by 1870.

TABLE 11.4.   Population and Cultivation in St. Andrew's and St. François Xavier, 1856 and 1870

| | St. Andrew's | | St. François Xavier | |
	1856	*1870*	*1856*	*1870*
Total Population	1207	1456	1101	1857
Number of Single Adults	—	44	—	2
Number of Families	214	287	178	334
Average Family Size	5.64	4.91	6.18	5.40
Percentage of Métis Family Head	—	75.10	—	91.2
Total Cultivated Acres	1646	2002	582	1335
Acres Cultivated per Family	7.70	6.97	3.26	3.99
Acres Cultivated per Person	1.40	1.37	0.53	0.72
Cultivation per European Family Head	—	10.35	—	18.82
Cultivation per Métis Family Head	—	8.80	—	3.80
Number Cultivating more than 10 Acres	—	74	—	35
Number Cultivating more than 20 Acres	—	49	—	18

SOURCE: Red River Nominal Census of 1870. Red River Tabulated Census of 1856.[74]

In St. Andrew's the cultivated acreage per family and person remained at the subsistence levels they had been in 1849. Unlike St. François Xavier, cultivation was a little more evenly distributed among the population. By 1870 there were 49 families (15%) cultivating more than twenty acres, however, 9% of the families in St. Andrew's still accounted for 50% of the cultivation.

From the foregoing analysis of Métis agriculture between 1835 and 1870, it is clear that by the 1830s the Métis communities in Red River combined subsistence agriculture and hunting to secure the needs of the family rather than make a profit. Differences in cultivation between communities began to become apparent in the late 1840s as some Métis abandoned agriculture to pursue new economic opportunities in the emerging capitalistic fur trade, especially the buffalo robe trade. This transition was more evident in St. François Xavier than in St. Andrew's which continued to rely on peasant agriculture to a much greater degree.

The implications of these trends for the persistence of the Red River Métis after 1870 should not be overlooked. St. François Xavier Métis who had adapted to the new economic opportunities after 1840 showed a much lower persistence rate between 1870 and 1881 (40%) than the St. Andrew's Métis (65%).[75] Participation in the buffalo robe trade after 1860 necessitated abandoning agriculture, wintering on the plains, and eventually permanent emigration for most Métis involved. This choice between agriculture and the new fur trade should, however, not be seen as a decision between the "primitive hunt" and a "progressive agriculture." It might more profitably be seen the other way around. Agriculture remained, for the most part, peasant in nature and oriented to household consumption into the early 1870s.

That the abandonment of peasant agriculture after 1840, and concentration on the fur trade and domestic buffalo robe industry would in the long term prove an unsuccessful strategy for adaptation to the new order in the west after 1870, could not have been foreseen at the time. For those Métis successfully adapting to the commercial circumstances of this period the transition was cut short by the rapid destruction of the buffalo herds after 1870, and the sudden collapse of the buffalo robe market in 1875. This transition was also made more difficult by the retention of the family economy by most Métis. As a result they remained tied to the norms and rules of behaviour of the traditional family subsistence economy. This structural condition became a large obstacle in the transition to industrial capitalism.

Proto-industrialization historically has either led beyond itself to industrial capitalism, or retreated backward into de-industrialization or re-pastoralization. These contradictory possibilities arose from the regulating system of the family mode of production, the "labour-consumer balance," which governed productivity and surplus. In those situations of potential growth in which the capitalist putter-out would have obtained maximum profits, the family mode of production would have affected the replacement of productive labour effort through consumption and leisure, through feasting, playing and drinking. It was this contradiction which, in the long run, could not be squared with the dynamic of reproduction and expansion inherent in the proto-industrial system.[76]

For those Métis who maintained their reliance on peasant agriculture into the 1870s in such parishes as St. Andrew's, the transition to the new industrial capitalist order was not much easier. While they retained their river lots much longer, many into the 1890s, they found the transition to commercial farming difficult. By the late 1880s there was the clear perception of the inability to farm on their small subdivided parish lots.[77]

NOTES

1. The term Métis, for the purposes of this study, is used in a generic sense to designate all communities associated with niches in the fur trade to which neither indigenous Indian households nor European households had responded. As such it includes both the French-speaking Métis and the English "Half-breeds." This broad categorization facilitates analytical conceptualization, while at the same time allowing for differentiation of separate communities within it.

2. These works include: G.F.G. Stanley, *The Birth of Western Canada: A History of the Riel Rebellions* (London: Longmans Green and Company, 1936); Marcel Giraud, *Le Métis Canadien: Son role dans l'histoire des provinces de l'Ouest*, 2 Vols. (Paris: Institut d'Ethnologie, 1945). This work has recently been translated into English as Marcel Giraud, *The Métis in the Canadian West*, translated by George Woodcock (Edmonton: University of Alberta Press, 1986); A.S. Morton, *A History of the Canadian West to 1870–71* (London: Nelson, 1939).

3. D.N. Sprague, "Government Lawlessness in the Administration of Manitoba Land Claims 1870–1887," *Manitoba Law Journal* 10, no. 4 (1980); "The Manitoba Land Question 1870–1882," *Journal of Canadian Studies* 15, no. 3 (1980); Gerhard Ens, "Métis Lands in Manitoba," *Manitoba History* 5, Spring (1983); Nicole J.M. St.-Onge, "The Dissolution of a Métis Community: Pointe à Grouette 1860–1885," *Studies in Political Economy* 18, Autumn (1985); P.R. Mailhot and D.N. Sprague, "Persistent Settlers: the Dispersal and Resettlement of the Red River Métis, 1870–1885," *Canadian Ethnic Studies* XVIII (1985); Don McLean, *1885: Métis Rebellion or Government Conspiracy?* (Regina: Gabriel Dumont Institute, 1985); Thomas Flanagan, *Riel and the Rebellion: 1885 Reconsidered* (Saskatoon: Western Producer Prairie Books, 1983).

4. The name White Horse Plains derives from the Indian Legend of the

White Horse involving the Cree, Assiniboine and Sioux. See Margaret Macleod and W.L. Morton, *Cuthbert Grant of Grantown* (Toronto: McClelland and Stewart, 1974), pp. 90–92.

5. Archives of the Archdiocese of St. Boniface [henceforth referred to as AASB], Letter of Father Dumoulin to Bishop Plessis (Quebec) 5 January 1819. Father Dumoulin estimated that there were 40 families and 300 persons settled at Pembina in 1819.

6. PAM, Selkirk Papers, Simpson to Colville, 20 May 1822; Halkett to Bishop Provencher, 20 July 1822 in Grace Lee Nute, ed., *Documents Relating to Northwest Missions 1815–1824* (Saint Paul: Minnesota Historical Society, 1942), p. 354. The Company was also worried that the Americans who had repeatedly threatened to seize their post might do so now that it was determined to be in American territory. Report of George Simpson, 1 September 1822 in Minutes of Council Northern Department of Rupert's Land, 1821–31 (London: Hudson's Bay Record Society, 1940), p. 382.

7. HBCA E5/1, Statistical Statement of the Red River Settlement, 31 May 1827. These population figures are notably lower than George Simpson's estimates of 80 to 100 families at White Horse Plains in 1824. See PAM, Selkirk Papers (8,221), Simpson to A. Colville, 31 May 1824. These higher figures probably reflect a large nomadic element in the settlement in the early years.

8. PAM, Census of Red River 1832, 1835.

9. A.V. Chayonov, *The Theory of Peasant Economy*, edited by Daniel Thorner, Basile Kerblay and R.E.F. Smith (Homewood, Illinois: R.D. Irwin, 1966), pp. 4–6. This study was first published in 1925.

10. Daniel Thorner, "Peasant Economy as a Category in Economic History," in Teodor Shanin, ed., *Peasants and Peasant Societies* (Harmondsworth: Penguin Books, 1971), pp. 206–207.

11. The Métis participated to a limited degree in the wage labour system of the HBC, hiring on for a specific period (boat run, cart brigade) for which they were paid a credit in the Company's account books that would be spent for provisions or goods in the following months. As Gerald Friesen has noted, "...this labour system might be described as typical in a non-industrial society, and in its informal work discipline and rough measures of time, not far removed from that of the casual laborer or cottage artisan in 17th century England." Gerald Friesen, *The Canadian Prairies: A History* (Toronto: University of Toronto Press, 1984), p. 92.

12. John Foster, "The Country-Born in the Red River Settlement 1820–1850," Ph.D. dissertation, University of Alberta, 1973, p. 219.

13. Alexander Begg, *History of the North West*, Vol. I (Toronto: Hunter, Rose and Co., 1894), p. 232.

14. Giraud, *Le Métis Canadien*, p. 787.

15. William H. Keating, *Narrative of an Expedition to the Source of St. Peter's River, Lake Winnipeck, Lake of the Woods, as performed in the year 1823*, Vol. II (London: Geo. B. Whitaker, 1825), p. 42.

16. *NorWester*, 28 December 1859.

17. See Allan Greer, *Peasant, Lord and Merchant: Rural Society in Three Quebec Parishes, 1740–1840* (Toronto: University of Toronto Press, 1985), p. xi.

18. Quoted in W.L. Morton, "Introduction" to *Eden Colvile's Letters* (London: Hudson's Bay Record Society, 1956), pp. xxiii-xiv.

19. Ibid., p. xxv.

20. Ibid., p. xxv.

21. W.L. Morton, "Agriculture in the Red River Colony," in A.B. McKillop, ed., *Contexts of Canada's Past: Selected Essays of W.L. Morton* (Toronto: Macmillan, 1980), p. 70.

22. AASB, Letter of Louis Lafleche, St. François Xavier, 1 Juin 1845, P0908–09.

23. Morton, "Agriculture," p. 80. Barbed wire was not introduced to the area until the 1880s.

24. Cultivation techniques before 1850 included broadcast sowing on roughly ploughed and harrowed land, while the harvest was carried out with sickle, scythe, and flail. Ibid., pp. 79–80.

25. Henry Youle Hind, "Papers Relative to the Exploration of the Country between Lake Superior and the Red River Settlement" (London: HMSO), p. 554.

26. Morton, "Agriculture" pp. 79–80.

27. Alexander Ross, *The Red River Settlement: Its Rise, Progress and Present State with Some Account of the Native Races, and its General History to the Present Day* (London: 1856), p. 78.

28. Ibid., p. 110.

29. PAM, Censuses of the Red River Settlement.

30. This interpretation runs from Alexander Ross's *The Red River Settlement*, through G.F.G. Stanley's *The Birth of Western Canada*, Marcel Giraud's *Le Métis Canadien*, W.L. Morton's various works to more recent studies such as W. Leland Clark, "The Place of the Métis within the Agricultural Economy of Red River during the 1840s and 1850s," *The Canadian Journal of Native Studies* III (1983). The basis of this interpretation is the census of Red River in the mid to late 1840s, ignoring the earlier census and the 1830s, and thus missing the crucial economic transition that occurred in the 1840s.

31. While the 1835 census did not break down the population by parish, this was accomplished using parish registers, the HBC land register and other censuses.

32. The standard strain of wheat before 1850 was the Prairie du Chien variety. Morton, "Agriculture..." p. 74.

33. Hind, "Papers Relative to the Exploration of the Country...," p. 544; according to Hind, the wheat was ready for harvesting three months after sowing. A more careful calculation by W.L. Morton put the growing season at about 110 days, W.L. Morton, "Agriculture..." pp. 71–73.

34. AASB, Letter of Father Lafleche, 1 Juin 1845, P0909–09099. 1 minot = 1.107 bushels.

35. Ross, *The Red River Settlement*, p. 121.

36. Hind, "Papers Relative to the Exploration of the Country...," p. 555; Morton, "Agriculture..." p. 70.

37. Morton, "Agriculture...," p. 70.

38. Barry Kaye, "'The Settlers' Grand Difficulty': Haying in the Economy of the Red River Settlement," *Prairie Forum* 9, no. 1 (1984), p. 3.

39. Using the technique of multiple regression on the various census variables, it was discovered that the most important variable in predicting the number of cattle was cultivated acreage. Horses according to the same statistical test had a low correlation to cultivated acreage and apparently were not widely used for plowing.

40. Morton, "Agriculture..."

41. Barry Kaye, "Some Aspects of the Historical Geography of the Red River Settlement from 1812 to 1870" (M.A. thesis, University of Manitoba, 1967); G. Herman Sprenger, "The Métis Nation: Buffalo Hunting vs Agriculture in the Red River Settlement (circa 1810–1870)," *The Western Canadian Journal of Anthropology* 3, no. 1 (1972), pp. 158–78.

42. In the 1835 census 80 of 97 families (82.5%) in the Parish of St. Andrew's cultivated at least one acre. In St. François Xavier, 76 of 102 families (74.5%) cultivated at least one acre.

43. F.G. Roe, *The North American Buffalo* (Toronto: University of Toronto Press, 1951), p. 368.

44. 1820: 540 carts; 1825: 680 carts; 1830: 820 carts; 1835: 970 carts; 1840: 1210 carts. Ross, *The Red River Settlement*, p. 402.

45. Ross, *The Red River Settlement*, pp. 144–169.

46. The reason Belcourt gave for the smaller size of the fall hunt was that some hunters had already left the settlement to winter on the plains. Other reasons could have been the need to harvest late crops, to prepare winter forage, and the opportunity of working on the HBC boats.

47. AASB, Bishop Provencher to Bishop Panet, 1 July 1829.

48. Church Missionary Society (CMS) Records, Reel 3, Incoming Correspondence, Letter Book I, pp. 399–400, Wm. Cockran to Sec., 29 July 1830.

49. CMS Records, Reel 3, I.C., L.B. II, Cockran Journal, 12 June, 1837.

50. Hans Medick,"The Proto-Industrial Family Economy: the Structural Function of Household and Family during the Transition from Peasant Society to Industrial Capitalism," *Social History* 3 (October 1976), p. 296.

51. Ibid., pp. 297–304. This transition had identifiable demographic implications. Because of its heavy dependence on family labour household size increased, and with new economic opportunities for young people men and women married sooner than they would have done under the old system. this in turn led to higher fertility.

52. As Irene Spry has written, the buffalo hunt "was, in fact, the basis of the first great industry in Western Canada." Irene Spry, "The 'Private Adventurers' of Rupert's Land" in John E. Foster, ed., *The Developing West: Essays on Canadian History in Honor of Lewis H. Thomas* (Edmonton: University of Albert Press, 1983), p. 54.

53. Alvin Charles Gluek, "The Struggle for the British Northwest: A Study in Canadian-American Relations," Ph.D. Dissertation, University of Minnesota, 1953, p. 27.

54. Hattie Listenfeldt, "The Hudson's Bay Company and the Red River Trade," *Collection of the State Historical Society of North Dakota*, Vol. IV, 1903.

55. HBCA, D4/75, George Simpson to Governor and Committee, 29 June 1855.

56. CMS Records, Incoming Correspondence, Letter Book VI (Reel 6), Rev. Kirkby to the Secretaries, 2 August 1858, p. 368.

57. G.F.G. Stanley, *Louis Riel* (Toronto: McGraw-Hill Ryerson, 1963), p. 37.

58. *Norwester*, 31 January 1866; "To Red River and Beyond," *Harper's* (February 1861), pp. 309–10.

59. *Norwester*, 1 September 1862.

60. HBCA, D4.76A, Simpson to Governors and Committee, 26 June 1856.

61. Merrill G. Burlingame, "The Buffalo in Trade and Commerce," *North Dakota Historical Quarterly* 4 (1928–9), p. 287.

62. CMS Records, Incoming Correspondence, Letter Book IV, Letter of Smithurst to Sec., 18 November 1846 and Wm. Cockran to Sec., 5 August 1847, pp. 196–97 and p. 213.

63. PAM, MG1 D20 Donald Ross Papers, File 161, Alexander Ross to Donald, 9 August 1847.

64. CMS Records, Incoming Correspondence, Letter Book IV (Reel 5), Rev. James to Sec. 2 August 1848.

65. HBCA, D4/68, Report of 1847, p. 264.

66. CMS Records, Incoming Correspondence, Letter Book IV (Reel 5), Bishop of Rupert's Land to Sec., 22 November 1846, p. 582.

67. Jacqueline Peterson, "Prelude to Red River: A Social Portrait of the Great Lakes Métis," *Ethnohistory* 25, No. 1 (Winter 1978). The connection between the Great Lakes Métis and St. François Xavier is based on a cursory comparison of the family names in the St. François Xavier parish registers with those of the Mackinac Registers 1629–1821. These latter registers are found in Reuben Gold Thwaites, ed., *Collections of the State*

Historical Society of Wisconsin, Vol. XIV (Madison: Democrat Printing Company, 1898).

68. While almost all families in both parishes were Métis, a number of the families in both St. François Xavier and St. Andrew's were headed by European or Euro-Canadian males. Throughout the period studied there were 16% more of these European male headed families in St. Andrew's than in St. François Xavier.

69. HBCA, A12/44 London Correspondence Inward, John McTavish to London, 27 August 1864; Joseph James Hargrave, Red River, pp. 219, 246–47, 336, 419; PAM, Lane Papers, McTavish to Lane, 26 April 1862, and McTavish to Clark, 1 July 1864; Stanley, *Louis Riel*, p. 49.

70. HBCA, B239 C18, fo. 190–92, William Cowan to York Factory, 10 December 1868; A12/45 London Correspondence Inward, fo. 88d-89, McTavish to Wm. Smith, 11 August 1868.

71. Guillaume Charette, *Vanishing Spaces: Memoirs of a Prairie Métis* (Winnipeg: Éditions Bois Brûlés, 1980), pp. 62–65.

72. These prices were abstracted from the HBC ledgers for sales of buffalo robes in Montreal. See HBCA, A14, Grand Ledger, "Consignments to Canada."

73. "Sheep Farming in Red River," *NorWester*, 14 May 1860.

74. Since the 1870 census did not give cultivation figures these were abstracted from the surveyors' returns of 1871–73. This census, unlike the earlier Red River censuses, also listed each individual rather than adults and family groups. Family groupings, however, were easy to discern from the census returns. Since a complete copy of the nominal census for 1856 no longer exists, many of the calculations made for the other census were not possible.

75. These figures were obtained by a comparison of the 1870 and 1881 nominal census returns.

76. Hans Medick, "The Proto-Industrial Family Economy: The Structural Function of Household and Family during the Transition from Peasant Society to Industrial Capitalism," *Social History* 3 (October 1976), p. 301.

77. PAM, St. Andrew's Parish lot files.